A Fine Place to Daydream

A Fine

Place to Daydream

RACEHORSES, ROMANCE, AND THE IRISH

Bill Barich

ALFRED A. KNOPF   NEW YORK   2006

Originally published in slightly different form by Collins Willow, an
imprint of HarperCollins Publishers, London, 2005

Title page photograph by Healy Racing Photos

Library of Congress Cataloging-in-Publication Data
Barich, Bill.
   A fine place to daydream : racehorses, romance, and the Irish / Bill
Barich.—1st ed.
      p. cm.
   Includes bibliographical references and index.
   ISBN 1-4000-4279-8 (alk. paper)
      1. Horse racing—Ireland. 2. National characteristics, Irish. I. Title.
SF335.I8B37 2006
798.4009417—dc22   2005044545

For Imelda
bright star

I can also truly say that of all races, that which comes nearest to Paddy's heart is a rattling steeplechase. It is so essentially Irish. There is incomparably more excitement—a chance of a broken limb, therefore more "fun" to be expected. It is regarded with far greater interest than any other diversion. . . . The reckless daring of the bold peasantry endears a spectacle which shows so much intrepidity, and there is a sympathy between the rush of the racing hunter and their own impetuous natures.

—"Life and Adventures of Bryan O'Regan"
The Dublin Saturday Magazine, 1865

The Irish obsession with racing, matched only in fervour of religion and alcoholic refreshment, can with justification be accused of diverting the national intellect from more gainful pursuits.

—Flann O'Brien
The Hard Life

The sport of kings is our passion, the dogs too . . . Nothing human is foreign to us, once we have digested the racing news.

—Samuel Beckett
Texts for Nothing

A Fine Place to Daydream

The Crossing

Now through the night come the horses. They come from obscure little villages like Lisaleen and Closutton, Coolagh and Moone, dozing and possibly dreaming on the long, dark ferry ride from Dun Laoghaire across the Irish Sea to Wales. They are Ireland's pride, the finest jumpers in a country obsessed with jumping, with grand historical leaps over daunting obstacles, so they've been prepared for the trip with the utmost care. Some have IV drips to balance their electrolytes, others have been fed exotic Chinese herbs for an energy boost, and almost all have had their lungs checked for infections, their blood tested, and their weight recorded precisely, down to the last ounce, to be sure they have reached a peak of fitness for their annual tilt against the British at the Cheltenham Festival in England.

They've heard the word *Cheltenham* countless times, of course, uttered by their trainers in both delighted anticipation and utter despair, so it has some resonance for them. It might even have some meaning. Horses know more than they let on; after all, they're in touch with elemental things. In the old days, farmers in rural Ireland believed their horses could see ghosts. Whenever one stopped dead and refused to budge, they reckoned a shade was nearby. If you looked between the horse's

3

ears, you could catch a glimpse of it, the farmers claimed. To prevent the fairies from stealing a good horse, they tied a red ribbon to it, or a hazel twig, or they spat on it. Folklore had it that a wild horse could be tamed by reciting the Creed in its right ear on Friday, and its left on Wednesday, until it came to hand.

So the legends go. In truth, horses do live by their instincts, and those on the ferry understand that because they're traveling, they'll probably be racing soon. Perhaps they can sense a few ghosts on the horizon, too, since the Cheltenham Festival has been around for a long while. Originally designed as a showcase for the National Hunt Steeplechase in 1904, it evolved into a three-day extravaganza that features twenty highly competitive races over fences and hurdles, ten of them Grade One championships. (The Festival expanded to four days in 2005.) More than fifty thousand people turn up each day, many of them ripe with drink and increasingly empty of pocket, and they would raise a mighty roar when Best Mate, the current wonder horse, shot for his third straight Gold Cup, hoping to equal a mark that Arkle, the greatest chaser ever, set in 1966.

There was a time when you couldn't walk into an Irish pub without hearing Arkle's name. The horse was an institution, a national treasure. Glasses were raised in his honor, and children around the world wrote letters addressed to "Arkle, Ireland" that were actually delivered by the grace of God. Trained in north County Dublin by Tom Dreaper, a self-styled "humble farmer," he won twenty-seven of his thirty-five starts, often carrying twice the weight of his rivals. His fans cruised by the farm on weekends, eager for a snapshot or just a peek at him. They were loyal and devoted and could describe his favorite meal in detail—mash, dry oats, six raw eggs, and two bottles of Guinness stout mixed in a bucket. They even forgave his owner,

Anne, Duchess of Westminster, for being British and holding a title.

Some experts thought Arkle's feat would never be duplicated again, but now Best Mate was on the scene, and every newspaper on the ferry carried a story about his quest. The stories always mentioned his superb physical condition—the very picture of a racehorse in the full of his health, as impressive as any champion George Stubbs ever painted—and told how the bookies favored him odds-on in 2004, and how Henrietta Knight, his sweetly eccentric English trainer, had recently lost thirty pounds on the Atkins diet and couldn't bear to watch her darling run for fear she'd see him fall. Her husband, Terry Biddlecombe, a former jump jockey, also provided excellent copy with his jokes about Viagra and his gruff but emotional manner. He'd wept in public when Matey won the Gold Cup a second time.

A victory in the Gold Cup, where a horse must jump twenty-one fences over a distance of three and a quarter miles, requires speed, stamina, and faultless execution, but those qualities are worthless without some racing luck. Even a wonder horse can make a mistake, time a jump badly, hit a fence, and fall. Knight knew this, naturally, and so did the Irish trainers dreaming of an upset, such as the canny Michael Hourigan from County Limerick, who was sending Beef Or Salmon, his stable star, to the Festival again. A talented but awkward eight-year-old, Beef Or Salmon had run in the race last year and had fallen at the third fence, his challenge over before it began. But maybe the horse had improved. It could happen, couldn't it? Fantasies have been built on less. The same might be true of Harbour Pilot from Noel Meade's yard in County Meath, third to Best Mate in 2003, albeit by a whopping thirteen lengths.

Fortunately, the sea is calm tonight, so the horses can rest easy. In stormy weather, they get spooked at times and need constant attention, but now the grooms and van drivers can take a catnap, consult their dog-eared copies of the *Racing Post*, or stretch their legs on deck, looking up at a sprinkling of stars and studying the inky water for omens. They duck into the café for tea or coffee or a quick pint of beer, comparing notes and hot tips and gossiping about their employers, airing the dirty laundry while also sharing the lessons they've learned on the job. Some know more about horses than the boss, and many know less, but they still voice their opinions, regardless of their relative expertise.

They talk about the Festival, too, and how important it is, and how that translates into pressure, stress, and anxiety, all complicated by the hardships of travel and the brain-numbing effect of a three-day booze-up. Cheltenham always produces its fair share of basket cases, but every owner, trainer, and jockey longs to be there in March, if only once in a lifetime. The jumps season lasts virtually year-round in both the U.K. and Ireland, but no other event has the same cachet as the Festival, not even the Grand National, that brutal steeplechase featured in *National Velvet*, where little Mickey Rooney booted home a winner. The prize money is excellent, as well, with the Gold Cup worth close to four hundred thousand dollars, a sizable purse by the hunt's lowly standards, plus the whole affair comes wrapped in bells-and-whistles—prime-time TV coverage, hype on the grand scale, and instant celebrity for the lucky few.

For the Irish the Festival has an extra dimension, though, a metaphoric value. In their familiar role as underdogs, they accept the disadvantage of shipping their horses to Cheltenham, glad for an opportunity to take on their colonizers on hallowed English ground. The contest is friendly and no blood has yet been shed except by accident, but every patriot in Ireland prays that the Hourigans and Meades will stick it to the Brits. The Irish have an extraordinary way with horses, after all. The earliest invaders from England remarked on how a rider and his mount appeared to be inseparable, a single creature with nothing between them, skin-to-skin. Often the rider lacked a saddle and used a mere snaffle for control, the lightest of bits. Respect for a horse, empathy with it, those were elemental concepts for the Celts, who believed that the Otherworld, a place beyond death, was bright and happy. In their myths, horses transport souls across the divide.

Around dawn, the ferry arrives at the Welsh port of Holy-head, north of Caernarfon Bay. The grooms and drivers may be grumpy and a little bedraggled after their hours at sea, but they click right into action and make certain each animal is comfortable, quiet, and suffering no ill-effects from the trip. In general, horses manage well on the ferry. They can stand upright and clear their lungs of mucus, something that's more difficult to do on a plane. They don't usually kick up a fuss, either, when the overland part of their journey resumes, with the vans following a route through Anglesey that crosses the border into England near Chirk, then cuts through the Severn Vale and skirts Bir-mingham's suburban sprawl before dropping south toward Cheltenham and the western edge of the great limestone escarpment of the Cotswolds.

Eventually, the vans reach Cheltenham Racecourse, a huge complex at the foot of Cleve Hill. The dutiful grooms, even wea-rier now, lead their charges to the stable yard, where an official checks the horses' passports to confirm their identities, and then to the barns. The horses are given some water (they don't drink much on the ferry) and sniff out their new surroundings before they take a walk over the course. Today—a Monday—the weather is fairly warm and springlike, although the sky is overcast, and gradually they relax and lose any trace of stiffness. They look contented, returned to a world they know. They're alert and enjoying the fresh air and the feel of the grass beneath them, all agreeably familiar sensations, and they recognize from the cameras and the buzz along the rail that what lies ahead is far more significant than a simple weekday meeting at home.

With the Festival scheduled to begin on Tuesday, the racecourse is besieged. Delivery trucks come and go, e-mails zip through hyperspace, and callers begging for last-minute tickets (at better than $150 a pop) jam the phone lines. Letheby & Christopher, caterers to the event since the 1920s, are laying in around eleven thousand pounds of beef, sixteen thousand pounds of potatoes, thirty-nine thousand chocolate bars, and forty-seven thousand sandwiches. Champagne is stacked in cases, the beer kegs are ready to be tapped. Groundsmen replace divots on the track and inspect the fences and hurdles for flaws. In the Tented Village, a bazaar of sorts, merchants are setting up the stalls where they'll hawk their wares. Security guards patrol the entire five-hundred-acre site—no threat, however weird, can be discounted—while the police prepare for the traditional clash of merrymakers and pickpockets.

While the horses walk the course and get their bearings, fans all over Ireland are packing their bags and departing for the Cotswolds. The Irish crowd will be large, vocal, informed, and dying for a bet, their wallets stuffed with cash. Many are repeat visitors, among them diehards who've been staying at the dowager Queens Hotel downtown since Arkle's last run, and they can remember rowdier times when fortunes changed hands at the all-night card games. But there are also plenty of newcomers pouring into Birmingham Airport, lawyers and plumbers, teachers and CEOs, all crazy about horses and often at the mercy of travel agents who broker package tours and must dispatch their clients to lodgings in faraway towns—to Stratford-upon-Avon, say, or Twigworth in the middle-of-nowhere.

There, in a single room at the Twigworth Hotel, you'll find a gambler who doesn't quite fit the mold, being an American—a Californian, to be precise—although he lives in Dublin now and is just as obsessed with the jumps as the lads from Kilkenny and Waterford in the rooms around him. He has a bag filled with form books and notebooks and a corkscrew should he manage to locate a palatable bottle of wine at the hotel—there are no stores nearby and no village, and he doesn't have a car—and he is looking forward to the Festival in a major way since it marks the high point of his own journey, one that began back in October, when he joined the caravan of Irish horses, trainers, and jockeys to record its progress on the bumpy road to Cheltenham.

Or you could say that the journey really started when he sold his house near San Francisco and rented a flat in London to freshen himself, fully expecting to go home in a few months and buy a fishing cabin in the Sierra Nevada, where he'd rusticate from middle into old age. That was three years ago, but instead he had the good luck to fall in love with an Irish woman and the surprising bravery (given his usual shyness in these matters) to fly to Dublin and pursue her, and now he has a brand-new life. The move required a leap of faith, but no doubt love in any form, at any time or any age, demands such a gamble, and at odd moments he feels a sharp kinship with the horses who, when they take flight and leave the earth, hang for a half-second in a cloud of uncertainty before they know what the future will bring.

Stirrings

I t was early autumn when I settled in Dublin to be closer to Imelda Healy, my new love. Apartments were scarce in the city, so I took what I could get, a tiny one-bedroom in a fancy gated complex, where the other tenants were all baby stockbrokers and Chinese students of English. The building was a tribute to Ireland's booming economy and dwarfed the little Victorian cottages on the Dodder River nearby. Our porter was a fierce-eyed, black-haired rogue, and when he saw me parsing the *Racing Post* one afternoon, he gave me a tip on a horse running at Punchestown in County Kildare. That caused an odd stirring in me. I felt I belonged.

The horse lost, of course, but that was all right. I wasn't in it for the money, not yet. In a way, the porter *had* opened a gate, and I saw how uninformed I was about Irish racing compared to the English scene. In London, I'd fallen into the habit of playing the televised races every Saturday, rising early and poring over the *Post* as diligently as a convict ransacking law books for a loophole to set him free. I liked the dense columns of statistics, the paper's oddly poetic jargon, and the underlying assumption that the puzzle could be solved, and the brambly nature of existence untangled, if only for an instant.

While the English are fond of their racing, I discovered the Irish can't live without it. Their embrace of the sport is passionate, a streak of lightning in the blood. Nothing grips them as powerfully as the sight of horses jumping over hurdles and steeplechase fences, maybe because it carries an echo of the country's rural, agricultural heritage and has the power to touch people, and even move them. Whatever the case, this was new territory for me, and I took to it so readily that the flat races began to bore me. Devoted to speed, they were over in a flash, while a good chase unfolded as leisurely as a Hardy novel. The jump races were rich in subplots and dramatic reversals of fate, too, plus they had a pastoral aspect that was transcendent, and entirely beautiful.

A year later, I moved in with Imelda, into her house in a quiet neighborhood. I was hooked on the National Hunt by then and often strolled down the block to our neighborhood bookmakers. We have two nearby, Paddy Power and Boylesports, both Irish-owned chains. The shops are so neat, clean, and wholesome they make gambling a normal, even welcome part of everyday life. Their motto might be, "Stop in and bring your grannie," rather than Boylesports' urgent injunction, "Bet here!" as if you wouldn't have a chance to be a loser again for many a mile. Indeed, I did see a grannie in the shops on occasion, filling out a betting slip (the ticket you give to a clerk, specifying your wager) with her poor wrinkled fingers.

Soon I was a devoted customer and drifted between the shops on the tides of fortune, good or ill, loyalty in gamblers being linked to the flow of luck. My fellow punters, as the Brits and the Irish say, were a diverse crew. The regulars were retired, or unemployed and on the government dole, and they were joined at intervals by working people taking a break—a barman, say, or a grocer—all glued to the shop's TVs and betting on races in Ireland, England, South Africa, and even Dubai, along with computer-generated virtual races and, possibly sinking lower, the greyhounds. They were quiet for the most part, rarely raising their voices to cheer or object, but at times I heard a muted cry of "Go on, my son!" to boost a faltering horse, and also the words *fookin'* and *feckin'* used frequently, often applied to certain jockeys.

The more I watched the jumps, the more I understood the Irish passion. There would be no National Hunt without Ireland, in fact. Even in England, the best horses are Irish-bred, and the best riders are also imported. Tony McCoy, who's broken every record, is a stable jockey for an English trainer, and so, too, are Mick Fitzgerald, Ruby Walsh, and Jim Culloty, while Barry Geraghty rides in England's big races on a freelance basis. The British actually looked down their noses at the steeplechase during the colonial period, dismissing it as a "bastard amusement" inferior to flat racing. Yet chases have long been a feature of Irish country life, born of the landscape and a profound love of the hunt. To recycle a hoary legend, the first chase supposedly occurred in County Cork in 1752, a match race between Edmund Blake and Cornelius O'Callaghan from Buttevant Church to St. Mary's Church in Doneraile, its steeple visible about five miles away. The prize was a hogshead of wine.

By the nineteenth century, the steeplechase was firmly established as an Irish sport. The courses, noted one observer, "were laid out over perfectly natural country; not a single sod or stone would be removed nor a fence trimmed, and there was no leveling of places where the going was bad." A rider picked his own line to follow and jumped whatever he met along the way. The races could be terrifying, but the public loved it. Every horse fell at least once, and it wasn't uncommon for a winner to fall three or four times. Heroes emerged, among them Black Jack Dennis, a daredevil of renown, who once jumped a five-foot-high fence and the donkey cart parked in front of it. To cash a bet, Dennis rode the awesome course at Rahasane (ten stone walls, twenty-five fences) without a saddle or a bridle, relying on a cabbage stalk for a whip.

I read about those amazing feats at the National Library in Dublin, a timeless old building as sleepy and dusty as any scholar could wish for. On my walk into town, I'd buy a few pencils at our newsagent's (pens are banned from the library to prevent some creep from imitating Joyce's marginalia), then cross over to Baggot Street and pass the birthplace of Francis Bacon, whose father trained racehorses while Bacon screwed around with the stable lads. The temptation to stop for a jar of the black stuff at Doheny & Nesbit's was always strong, but I resisted and rounded a corner by the Shelbourne Hotel, host in 1842 to William Thackeray, who complained that his room hadn't been "scoured" for months, although he praised the kind and gentle staff. For Elizabeth Bowen, the hotel—so solid and prosperous—wasn't typically Irish. "We have a reputation for distress, miscarried projects, evanescent dreams, and romantic gloom," she wrote, "and the Shelbourne is the antithesis of those things."

Up the library's central staircase I climbed, into the deep silence of the reading room with my reader's ticket and its ghoulish passport photo (I'd closed my eyes by accident, so the picture resembled a post-mortem shot) on a chain around my neck. I blended comfortably into the mix of genealogy buffs digging up their ancestors, students doing research for term papers, budding writers courting inspiration, and the predictable quotient of evanescent dreamers. Soft-spoken, well-mannered clerks disappeared into the tomblike stacks to unearth the books I requested, and I sat and studied and got the lay of the land.

Sometimes when I tired of reading I'd lift my head, stare at the ring of cherubs on the ceiling, and realize with a profound sense of wonder that I was truly living in Ireland—in Dublin, a city I had visited only once before as an impressionable young tourist in search of literary landmarks. Out to Howth and Dalkey I rode the train, recalling Flann O'Brien and his curious archive, and I went to Sandymount Strand, as well, where I had an icy hike along the water and battled a fierce winter wind that removed a layer of skin from my cheeks. Near Mountjoy Square, in an act that now smacks of foreshadowing, I put a small wager on a horse running at Leopardstown, who shocked me by winning and caused a nightlong celebration and an awful morning-after.

Now those landmarks were an aspect of home to me. The transition was miraculous, but also completely ordinary. Imelda and I often talked about chance—fate, destiny, call it what you will—and how the tiniest missed signal could have kept us apart. We'd met by accident at a gallery opening in London where Dorothy Cross, an artist friend of Imelda's from Dublin, had a show. As Imelda and I chatted over the lukewarm glasses of white wine that seem to appear globally at such openings, I learned that she was an artist, too—a figurative painter, her subject matter a cross-referencing of her personal life with classical and Renaissance imagery—and that she had two teenage sons and had been separated from her husband for many years. To my surprise, I also learned that divorce has only been fully legal in Ireland since February 1997. I'd been divorced myself for almost a decade.

The gallery was so crowded and noisy, and so heavy with the torpor of art being appreciated, that I asked Imelda to join me at a quieter place where we could chat in peace, but she declined. That would be disloyal to Dorothy, she felt. She was there to support her friend, and I was so wounded by her failure to perceive me as I wanted to be perceived—as the man she'd been waiting for, that is, although in fact she hadn't been waiting at all—I stalked off in an arrogant huff and wound up in a wretched, noisier, absolute hellhole of a pub down the block in Soho. Worse, when I went to the gents, the fellow next to me peed inaccurately and splashed my shoes.

What if I hadn't swallowed my pride and returned to the gallery? What if Imelda hadn't called me on her next trip to London? What if I'd complained about the overpriced restaurant where I took her for dinner, instead of keeping my big mouth shut for once? And so on.

Though I have always believed in chance, fate, destiny, et cetera, Imelda frankly surpasses me. She has a mystical side and a sincere faith in the power of coincidence, being Irish to the core.

Certainly, I have never lived anywhere on earth where the citizens latch on to racing tips with such enthusiasm, as a drowning man might cling to a piece of flotsam. So-called inside information circulates with abandon, extracted from the most dubious possible sources—a barber, say, who cuts the hair of a man whose son goes to school in Tipperary with a nephew of Edward O'Grady, the trainer. Yet even though I recognized the sorry provenance of those tips, I wasn't immune to their allure—not at first—so when I was getting *my* hair cut one day and heard the barber whispering to another customer about Caishill, a "sure thing" running at Listowel in County Kerry— this was in September 2003—I dashed to Boylesports and threw a fiver on the horse.

The race was a steeplechase over two miles and six furlongs. On the face of it, Caishill was up against it, being younger and less experienced than others in the field, but he had a talented jockey in Shay Barry. The race was a handicap, too, meaning that each horse carried more or less weight depending on its level of success, so Caishill was among the lightest, but Caishill banged into the ninth fence and fell, despite his advantage. Horses hit the ground so hard, with their delicate legs flailing, I am always shocked by how swiftly most of them recover, upright again in seconds and often none the worse for wear, except for the potential psychological damage. Some jumpers shake off a fall as Caishill did, later winning a chase in November, but others become scarred and inhibited and shy from fences as they would from any source of pain.

But it's the jump jockeys who take the greatest risk, really, since they're more fragile and vulnerable than their horses. I once read a list of the injuries Carl Llewellyn, a veteran rider in his late thirties, has suffered in his career, and it made the hair on my head stand up: a broken cheekbone, two broken collarbones, nine concussions, eight broken noses, two broken jaws, two broken ribs, a broken wrist, a broken elbow, and a broken pinkie, along with soft tissue bruising and ligament, tendon, and muscle damage too extensive to mention. The catalog would be familiar to many jockeys, a fact that stands in testimony to their courage and love of the game. Though Llewellyn has endured a battering, I knew he counted himself lucky to still be riding at his age because most men (women jump jockeys are rare, except in the amateur ranks) don't last so long.

That same September, I saw some hard evidence of how abruptly a jockey's riding life can end when Norman Williamson, a gifted jock with over 1,200 wins to his credit, took an awful spill at Downpatrick, in Northern Ireland. He lay so still on the ground, not moving a muscle, that it scared everyone. The fans were hushed, afraid he was dead. He swore that he felt okay and even winked at Paul Carberry, another rider, to show it, but he did ask the paramedics to put a brace on his neck for safety's sake, and that meant he had to undergo a physical exam before he'd be permitted to ride again. After a subsequent MRI in London, the doctors informed him that his next fall might lead to paralysis—he had vertebrae in his neck that wouldn't settle—so Williamson, only thirty-four and in his prime, chose to hang up his boots.

Yet he, too, had to count himself lucky, aware of what had happened to others. Only a month before, Kieran Kelly, a popular and promising young Irish jockey, fell in a race and landed on his head. Though he wore a helmet, he broke his neck and lasted just a week on life support before he died. Others have survived such horrible accidents and stayed in the sport, as Shane Broderick did after injuring his spinal cord in a fall in 1997. It was as if Broderick had been in a motorcycle crash, tossed over the handlebars and smashed into the pavement headfirst, but he fought back, went through extensive rehabilitation, and now trains horses despite being a paraplegic.

Jump jockeys don't dwell on the negatives, obviously. They can't afford to, so they stay in perpetual motion, busy all the time. And that autumn—the autumn of Best Mate's quest for a third Gold Cup— they were more concerned about the weather, anyway, and how it was affecting their finances. The month of September was the driest on record in England, and Ireland was almost as dry. Without the soft, safe ground that jumpers need as a cushion, most horses were behind schedule, not yet wholly fit. Trainers were careful with their best stock, unwilling to take a risk, so the fields in many races were small, sometimes just three or four entries. Punters sniffed at the short prices available, and the bookies were reported to be bleeding.

Racing fans are optimists, though, so I had no doubt the weather would ultimately oblige. As a third-year Dubliner, I put the chance of a drought at 10,000–1 based on past experience. I knew how wet, cold, and sometimes miserable I'd be as I indulged my new passion and traveled around the country to investigate the Irish obsession with the jumpers. I wanted a proper education before I tackled the Cheltenham Festival and tried to prove my mettle as a gambler. Walking home from the library on an evening in early October, beneath the island's everchanging sky, I made a mental note to buy some waterproof shoes and fill my little silver flask, a gift from Imelda, with some good Jameson's whiskey against the trials to come.

SO I BEGAN MY JOURNEY the next morning and boarded a train for Kilkenny at Heuston Station, hard by the Liffey and the Guinness brewery, where the smell of roasted hops fills the air. I was bound for Gowran Park Racecourse to meet Jessica Harrington, always among Ireland's most successful trainers and one of the only women. As we traveled southeast past Kildare, Athy, and Carlow, there were more farms with each passing mile. The landscape had an earthy coherence, even a sense of rightness, and the new cookie-cutter suburbs looked out of place to me—too American, I thought, wishing I could stop the train and warn the Irish before it was too late. Sad to say, they were becoming victims of "progress."

From Kilkenny with its bright air of prosperity, I took a taxi to the track. We drove by more rich farmland, through woods where the trees were touched with autumn color. I'd noticed this before in Ireland, a sudden transition from the urban to the rural, as if time itself were switching gears, forced to slow down and adjust to the more measured beat of country life. Over a distance of eight miles, we'd left behind a bustling city and entered a different century. It could have been 1914 at Gowran Park, the year the racecourse opened. The fans were in no hurry for the action to start. They were happy to gather in small groups and talk, friends and neighbors at a fair. Old men in flat caps were everywhere. I counted twenty-two sitting on a long bench by the racing secretary's office, their heads bobbing as they shared the latest gossip. There were merchants selling candy and ice cream, and kids quizzing the bookies as they set up their pitches—their chosen spots, for which they paid a price to the track.

Gowran Park was so intimate and informal I felt I was less a spectator than a participant, inside rather than outside the racing. At the parade ring, or paddock, before the first race, I could have reached out and touched the circling horses. I could see the down on the upper lips of the youngest jockeys, lads still in their late teens. When the jockeys finished a ride, they had to walk right through the crowd to get to the weighing room, where they changed their silks and kept their tack. The passage would be unimaginable at most U.S. tracks, where disgruntled fans, probably armed, might shoot them for their failure. Here they were treated to sympathy and a little soft-core heckling.

"You picked the wrong one again!" somebody teased a skinny youth, who'd been on a loser.

"But I don't get a choice!" the lad complained. With his accent, *choice* became *chice* and sounded chewed upon.

I met Harrington after the race. Known to everyone as Jessie, she emerged from the weighing room with a purposeful stride, cutting a path through the scurrying jockeys, who were already stripping off their clothes. Tall and lean, she has the attractive, outdoorsy look of someone who has logged countless hours on horseback. Her idea of a great holiday is a riding safari in Kenya. In her late fifties, with lively blue eyes, she keeps her blondish hair cut short for a minimum of fuss. I had the impression she resisted fussiness at every turn, unwilling to waste a minute on anything frivolous. Her voice had a hint of Anglo-Irish stiffness, but her manner was cordial and helpful.

I thought Jessie's no-nonsense attitude might come from Brigadier B. J. "Frizz" Fowler, her father, who moved his family from England, where she was born, to Ireland in 1949, settling a few years later on a farm in County Meath he'd inherited from an uncle. The brigadier hunted, played polo, and raced in an occasional point-to-point, so Jessie grew up around horses and other animals. She can't remember learning how to ride—being on a horse was second nature. As a girl, she belonged to a pony club and became one of the country's top eventers, traveling to Los Angeles as a member of Ireland's Olympic team in 1984. Her background has granted her what military types call "command presence." If she had issued an order, I would have followed it without question.

The race card was mixed that afternoon, with three flat races, two hurdles, and a steeplechase. That's often the case in Ireland in early autumn, when the flat and jumps seasons dovetail. (There are no dirt or all-weather tracks in the country, so flat racing ends in November because the turf's too sodden.) Jessie trains a handful of flat horses, and she had You Need Luck entered in the second race, a mile handicap for three-year-olds. Though Jessie had won five races with such horses lately, the stats in the *Post* showed that she was one for thirty-three on the flat at Gowran Park, while she won with her jumpers about twenty percent of the time.

On our walk to the parade ring, she explained that she'd started training by chance. She and her husband, Johnny, a retired bloodstock agent, had some decent homebreds they couldn't sell on their farm in County Kildare, so she began working with them and did well enough to catch the eye of some owners. By 1990 she had a public license and an excellent reputation. At present, she has about ninety horses on the farm's 115 acres—Irish and English trainers operate at such lush private enclaves, generally referred to as "yards," rather than from the scrappy barns at a public racetrack, an injustice that once had a California trainer I know literally crying in his beer—and she is always among the leaders in terms of prize money earned.

You Need Luck did not inspire confidence. In his three outings to date, the colt had produced no wins, or any indication that he ever would. After Jessie issued some instructions to Timmy O'Shea, her jockey, she seemed to forget about me and made a beeline for an open stand with a few rows of concrete steps. The stand was so basic I'd have wagered it had been there since 1914. It didn't offer the best vantage point, being several lengths from the finish, so I guessed Jessie favored it as a lucky spot, and she admitted it. As jittery as I am about such things, still capable of being undone by the sight of a black cat about to cross my path, most jump trainers are far worse.

The legendary Englishman Martin Pipe provides a stellar example. Admired for his intelligence and his innovative methods, and interested enough in hard science to enroll in an equine studies course at Worcestershire College of Agriculture to further his understanding of horses, Pipe believes the color green is such a terrible omen that he once sent an owner home from the races to change her green dress. Seeing a chimney sweep on a race day is a frightening sign for him, as is the delivery of a load of straw to his yard. (Henrietta Knight shares that superstition, but a load of hay is okay with her.) He would never wear a red shirt or red socks to the track, or drive over a bridge while a train is going by underneath it.

Jessie visited Pipe's yard in Nicholashayne once, and she was struck by his attention to detail. He even bothered to make the wood chips for his gallops, the training strips where horses exercise at home, so he'd be certain of the quality. As an outsider, the son of a wealthy bookie rather than a member of the hunt-club set, Pipe had to go it his own way and rewrote the manual for handling jumpers. First and foremost, he insists on relating to horses as if they are human beings, granting them a psychological complexity they're often denied. He is a close observer and listener, as well, especially after a horse's workout when he concentrates on its breathing to judge its level of fitness. The faster a horse stops blowing, he says, the closer that horse is to "doing the business."

In his autobiography, *The Champion Trainer's Story*, Pipe revealed a few of his secrets. He doesn't let his horses trot at home, because he thinks the gait is unnatural. It puts too much pressure on the joints and can damage the cannon bone. His horses don't come off the bridle on the gallops, but they do sprint over a short distance. Horses who've spent the summer away, fat and lazy after their vacation, walk for six weeks on their return before they exert themselves again. Pipe monitors their feed carefully to be sure they lose weight and shed their lethargy. When he can see a horse's last two ribs, the horse is ready for a race.

Unfortunately, You Need Luck lived up to his name and dragged in next to last. Jessie was briefly depressed, but her mood improved when Imazulutoo, her best novice hurdler—novices are in their first season over hurdles or fences—and maybe the best in Ireland, beat a good field later on. It was a sweet race to watch over the green and undulating course. Here was racing at its most organic, without the nuisance of a starting gate, only a tape to restrain the riders. Again I had a sense of traveling back in time. The race caller's voice was a murmur, comforting rather than full of punch. He even added a nice, writerly touch by saying, "The jumping of the trailing group leaves something to be desired."

Under Barry Geraghty, Imazulutoo's performance was sharp enough for Jessie to imagine her horse might be a candidate for the Cheltenham Festival, yet she didn't want to count on it. She was aware of how many things could still go wrong before next March. "All I can do at this point is peddle along and keep dreaming," she sighed. Her only banker was Moscow Flyer, a quirky but supremely talented horse I developed a strange affection for when I was introduced to him at the Harringtons' yard in Moone a few days later.

MOONE IS A TINY VILLAGE, just a blip on any map. Tourists do leave the N9 expressway to explore Moone Abbey with its ruined Franciscan friary and ancient high cross, but not very often. I never saw another soul while I wandered around there. Like Gowran Park, the friary belongs to a different century, the fourteenth. Any horse who happened on the ruins would surely spot a ghost. There are crumbly old gravestones I dared not touch and a vaulted chapel open to the sky. Birds own the abbey now—birds and the long grass.

At its central crossroads, Moone has only a small grocery store that doubles as a post office. A rosy-cheeked gent well into his seventh decade stood by the front counter, dressed for work in a suit and tie, an accepted country tradition. When I asked for directions to Jessie's, he said, "First farm on the right. I mean, on the left. Anyway, you can't miss it." The farm *was* on the left, and I followed a paved drive lined with beech and lime trees to a sprawling pink house set against a back-drop of the Wicklow Mountains. Cottages were scattered around the property, along with some old stone buildings used as stables.

I walked past the stables and up a slight incline to open fields divided by fences, where I found Jessie on horseback. She was watching intently as a string of horses, a dozen or so known as a "lot," galloped around a circular four-furlong strip that cut through the fields and dipped with the hilly terrain. Each time the horses passed by, I heard the thump of their hooves and listened to the sound of them breathing, as Martin Pipe might do—an athletic, chest-expanding sound. The air rippled with animal energy.

For the riders, this was the best part of the day. They got to pretend that they were jockeys, but most were really only grooms, a job not everyone would covet. Several came from eastern Europe, five from Poland alone. They lived like college students in the farm's cottages, both men and women, and just as messily, too. Good stable help is dif-ficult to find these days, so trainers often rely on immigrant labor. The local lads who used to beg for a chance to muck out a stall, despite the poor pay and punishing hours, now look for work in Ireland's boom-ing cities. Jessie's team didn't have it easy. They were on duty from eight to five every day and responsible for five horses apiece. I couldn't imagine what they did for fun. Moone doesn't even have a pub, and grooms can't afford a car. You'd have to be devoted to horses, captive to jockey fantasies, or maybe a little desperate to sign on.

As the horses left the field to cool down, Jessie invited me to her house for a cup of tea. Her stride was brisk and efficient, and we were trailed by a number of dogs. In all my visits, I was never certain how many she has—eight, ten, possibly twelve?—in a variety of breeds. Hers is a peaceable kingdom, where the dogs and horses share equal rights with the human beings. We went through a back door and into an alcove piled high with muddy boots, where silks hung on a rod, ready to be grabbed on the way to the races. The line between work and the rest of life doesn't seem to exist for Jessie. Work *is* life, and she loves it. Driven and ambitious, that's how she comes across.

She doesn't stand on ceremony, either. Her kitchen serves as the gathering point for the staff, so Eamonn Leigh, her head groom and assistant trainer, was already at the stove and firing up the kettle. He's from Dunlavin, another small village nearby, and told me he began with Johnny Harrington more than thirty years ago, when Johnny still had the bloodstock business. (Johnny was golfing in Portugal that day, as the privileged retired are inclined to do.) Eamonn is practically family to the Harringtons, so he'd recently built a house for his own family on the farm. The only horse he cares for is Moscow Flyer, another indication of the trust he inspires.

At the kitchen table sat Robert Power. He'd been riding with the grooms even though he's a real jockey, an apprentice with fifteen wins under his belt already that season. Only twenty-two, Power appeared to have a bright future, but he still had a long, hard climb to reach the top. He had no trouble making weight now—jump jockeys are much bigger than their flat counterparts, taller and heavier—but that would change with age as his metabolism slowed down. Older jockeys don't bounce back as quickly from injuries, either, as Norman Williamson had just demonstrated. Regular riding used to be enough to keep a jockey fit, but the demands are harsher now—no turning up half-smashed, as some did in the old days—and they need more stamina, too, so they jog, hit the gym, and stick to a strict diet, although I did notice Power nibble on a cookie.

On the kitchen walls, I saw photos of horses, naturally, among them Space Trucker, a homebred and Jessie's first winner at the Festival in 1999. There were also some framed newspaper clips and pictures of her four children (three daughters and a son), two with her first husband and two with Johnny. They were all grown up except for Kate, the youngest at fourteen, who was at a Dublin boarding school. One jokey sign stood out. DULL WOMEN—HAVE IMMACULATE HOMES, it read, a sentiment that summed up Jessie's attitude. She could never be content in a traditional role, not when the pull of the horses was so strong.

While we talked, Jessie sorted through her mail. "Junk, most of it," she said, casting it aside, but one envelope held a check from an owner. It costs about $1,500 a month to keep a horse in training with her, exclusive of such extras as vets' bills, transport, and entry fees. In general, she gets on well with her owners ("particularly those who pay on time"), but a few drive her crazy. Just that morning, an owner had called to inquire about his gelding, asking, "How's she doing?" and glossing over a distinction Jessie felt he ought to be able to make. The dizziest owners blame her for every failure, and they're all dying to go to Cheltenham and freely offer plans A, B, and C for accomplishing the miracle, even when their horses are still maidens.

A trainer's headaches are infinite, I thought, and we soon witnessed an unexpected one when a Polish groom burst into the kitchen in a foul mood. His English was limited, so he had to rack his brain for the right vulgarities to express his outrage. "No money!" he shouted. "No phone! No Katrina money!" It took a few minutes to decipher, but we finally realized he'd been robbed. In Moone, no less. Someone had broken into his cottage and stolen his savings, and also his wife's savings and both their cell phones. Jessie called the police in Ballintore down the road and reported the crime, but that did little to soothe the overagitated groom, who continued to moan and pace and curse despite our efforts to comfort him.

AFTER TEA, I MET MOSCOW FLYER for the first time. He was going to the Curragh, which means "racecourse" in ancient Gaelic, for a gallop on a real track to prevent him from getting bored or lazy. He has his own paddock as befits a celebrity, arguably the best two-mile chaser when he concentrates as he did when he won the Queen Mother Champion Chase at the Festival last spring. (The Queen Mother is almost as valuable and prestigious as the Gold Cup.) He's fond of rolling around in his paddock after a workout, but he's more inclined to stand by a fence and watch the traffic zipping by on the N9 down below. The flash of distant metal specks entrances him, and he won't move a muscle for twenty minutes or so. He could be meditating, lost in his own airy thoughts. He's an intelligent, cerebral horse—maybe too cerebral, because he can go all dreamy during a race and forget his purpose, sliding by on the grease of his talent.

He whinnied when he saw Eamonn, eager to board the horse van with three of his stablemates. Eamonn drove the van, while I rode with Jessie in a high-end Mercedes that she treats like a Jeep, speeding around the yard over bumps and potholes and ignoring the rattle of the undercarriage.

On our bracing trip over Kildare's back roads, she told how she bought Moscow Flyer as a four-year-old at a Tattersalls Ireland sale in June 1998, acting as an agent for Brian Kearney, whose son, a racing-mad attorney, had convinced him he needed a hobby. She had a budget of 20,000 guineas, or roughly $35,000, to spend on a chaser, the preference of most owners. Moscow came up late in the auction, and though his breeding didn't amount to much—it seldom does with jumpers—she liked the look of him and paid 17,500 guineas, guessing he'd be a nice horse and nothing more.

When we reached the Curragh, I felt I could see for miles. It's among the flattest places in Ireland, a broad limestone plain where the Irish have raced horses for centuries. Bold winds whip across it, and one was blowing that afternoon, lending an arctic chill to an otherwise bright day. Eamonn and the other riders were already there, checking their tack. Moscow's first race, the Fortria Chase at Navan, was three weeks away, so Jessie asked Eamonn not to push the horse. She was concerned about the ground, too, still firm due to the lack of rain.

"Look at that!" She pointed to some withered clumps of grass that were only marginally green. "That's *dry* for Ireland."

While the horses hacked up on their way to the track, Jessie began shivering, so we got back into the Mercedes to escape the bitter wind. "Training from a car," she joked. "What a business!" I'd been wondering if it was easy for her to break into a male-dominated game, and whether her independent character was a help or a hindrance, so I asked her about it. Predictably, the begrudgers resisted the idea of a woman joining their ranks, she said, and assumed she couldn't be serious. They took her for a dabbler funded by an indulgent husband, someone who'd pack up and quit in a year or two when the strenuous demands of the job became clear.

"Nobody said anything directly," she went on, "because that isn't the Irish way. I could feel it, though." She spoke calmly at first, not wanting to complain, but her tone grew more heated, and I could see I'd touched a nerve. "It's still a man's world, isn't it? We don't have any female stewards. Women are rarely on the boards of racecourses, and all the beat writers for the papers are men." That bias wasn't confined to racing, Jessie felt. Instead, it reflected Irish society at large. She mentioned how she'd once applied for a bank loan, only to be ordered to bring in Johnny to cosign for it.

She drove closer to the track, over rocks and turf, and glued a big pair of binoculars to her eyes. Moscow Flyer looked so vital and natural as he began to gallop I could hardly believe he'd been slow to develop, but it was true. He started out in bumpers, or National Hunt flat races designed to test a horse's stamina and discover if it's adaptable to the rigors of jumping. There's a two-mile bumper on every

Irish card, usually the last race, and they're for amateur riders only, who aren't as skillful as pros and "bump" around in the saddle.

In his first four bumpers, Moscow Flyer never finished better than third, and when Jessie switched him to hurdles in a training race at Punchestown Racecourse, not far from the Curragh, in 1999, he screwed up completely and dumped Barry Geraghty. "He ran into a dolled-off [out-of-use] hurdle," she recalled. "He went left, and Barry went right. I was so cross with the horse!" Since jumping is Moscow's sore point, and Geraghty has the bruises to prove it, I once asked him for his thoughts. "The thing is, Moscow's very brave," he said. "He doesn't worry about it. He's like, 'If I get it wrong, fuck it.' His style isn't careless—it's care*free.*"

After the Punchestown fiasco, Moscow Flyer won a maiden hurdle at last, in October, defeating the highly regarded Young Buck from Noel Meade's yard. Jessie dropped him into a more difficult handicap hurdle at Down Royal a week later, where he faced another fancied horse of Meade's. "I don't know why we're odds on," Meade confided in the parade ring. "This horse isn't as good as the last one he beat." Those were prophetic words—Moscow romped home by fifteen lengths. Later that month, he scored another win in a Grade One at Fairyhouse in County Meath and might have gone straight to Cheltenham if he hadn't suffered a hairline fracture of the pelvis.

By next autumn, Moscow Flyer was a rising star, the young pretender ready to challenge Istabraq, a beloved though aging Irish immortal, whose record as a hurdler was extraordinary. They knocked heads in three curiously disappointing races at Leopardstown, Dublin's premier track. Moscow won the first race in late December, but the result was tainted because Istabraq had fallen. In January 2001, Istabraq countered with a win, but this time Moscow fell. Their rubber match provided no resolution, either, because Istabraq fell again. The races left everyone unsatisfied. They were reminiscent of the famous heavyweight title fight in Lewiston, Maine, where Cassius Clay decked Sonny Liston with a phantom blow.

For Istabraq, the end was near. He ran just twice more, but Moscow Flyer got bigger and stronger, more battle-hardened and mature, so Jessie let him go chasing, Brian Kearney's wish from the outset. (Chasers are the sport's home-run hitters. They earn more money and glory, because fences are a more intimidating obstacle—higher, stiffer—than hurdles.) Again Moscow was slow to catch on, falling in his first beginners' chase in October 2001, but then he won three in a row before he fell at Leopardstown in January. This established the disturbing pattern that has dogged him ever since—a mishap, three wins, and another mishap. As a chaser, he's never been beaten, except when he beats himself.

At the Curragh, Moscow Flyer was a vision of power in motion, his head carried low and his neck curled. He was tugging so vigorously Eamonn had to keep the tightest possible hold. "He's very well," Jessie said. She was very pleased with what she saw. "Eamonn's arms will be six inches longer. The horse has so much ability! He doesn't need to do very much to win a race. He'll look around here, look around there, and he's only in second gear. That's why the Queen Mother suits him. The pace is so fast, and the competition's so intense, he has to pay attention."

We collected the horses. Moscow was scarcely blowing. Jessie was concerned about Start From Scratch, though, who had a habit of hanging left in his races and had pulled left again today. She hazarded a guess that his teeth might be hurting him, and also suggested a ring bit or a cross-nose band as potential remedies for his tendency to hang, but she was scraping the bottom of the barrel. She couldn't find the key to him, really. Start From Scratch had a few more runs for her before his owner transferred him to a new yard, proving Jessie's earlier claim. Owners are fickle, and every trainer, however shrewd, is subject to their whims.

BY LATE OCTOBER, my bold prediction that Ireland would never experience a drought looked shaky. The weather continued to be bone-dry. Teasing clouds drifted over Dublin, but they only delivered showers and squalls. The Brits fared no better. In a race that summed up everybody's discontent, the English trainer Paul Nicholls collected a ten-thousand-dollar purse by sending his horse Satenay to Kempton Park Racecourse outside London for an unopposed walk over the track. Most trainers were still playing it safe with their best horses, too. Jessie wouldn't run Moscow Flyer in the Fortria Chase if the going stayed firm, for instance, so I was glad to see that Henrietta Knight was willing to trot out her old warrior Edredon Bleu, now eleven, for the Desert Orchid Chase at Wincanton, in Somerset, toward the end of the month.

The Desert Orchid was on a Sunday. I planned to watch it on TV at O'Herlihy's, our local pub. My weekends were a happy shambles now that I'd accepted I was hooked and had to wrap my life around the races. Like Moscow Flyer, I needed to concentrate and focus. The process was akin to runic divination, an attempt to break a secret code and reap the reward of untold riches. I began with the *Racing Post*'s form charts and circled recent winners who'd done it "impressively" or "comfortably"—an evident plus, yet one it's easy to miss if you skip the fine print. Next I turned to the Selection Box to check on the experts' views, and then read the trainers' comments about their horses, an exercise in filtering out the half-truths from the bald-faced lies.

Around noon I left for O'Herlihy's. Irish pubs can be divided into two categories: the striving-to-be-hip Euromodern and the devoutly traditional, a style that a visitor from the States once defined as "still having those little wooden stools." I disliked the Euromodern places, put off by the shrill pop music and the blinding décor, all mirrors and shiny surfaces that imitated California at its most trendy, so O'Her-lihy's, with its little wooden stools, was ideal for me. During the day the light is soft (and softer at night), and the upholstery is frayed. There are some antique balsa fishing lures in a display case and framed prints of horses, of course, as well as a pair of bronzed baby shoes behind the bar that someone forgot once, in the distant past, and never reclaimed. Instead of pop music, we have the gentle murmur of a radio pitched several decibels below the level at which the program (whatever it is) might be heard.

As usual, my friend T. P. Reilly was already at the pub. Our friend-ship is an odd one, I suppose, because we never meet except at O'Her-lihy's or a bookie joint. A self-employed carpenter, Reilly is a talkative, sweet-natured behemoth, with a full head of curly gray hair and an expansive belly that tends to sink his trousers ever so slightly. First drawn to me out of curiosity, charmed to see an American studying (and muttering over) the *Post*, he took it upon himself to educate me, being an amateur racing historian and a collector of memorabilia. There was considerable pride in the endeavor for Reilly, who didn't go to college and puts an unwarranted premium on learning of any kind, and at times he seems to regard me as his own creation, a punter he's molded from plain unpromising clay.

Like so many of the Irish, Reilly fell in love with horses as a child when a farmer uncle let him ride an old plow mare around the fields in Carlow. He hasn't been in the saddle since then, but he believes the experience makes him a superior judge of horse flesh and banks on it, in fact, gearing his bets to a horse's looks. As a system, it's probably no worse than any other, and it doesn't appear to cost him any money. He's always good for his round, dines at our pricey Chinese restaurant (cheap eats don't exist in Dublin, except at greasy spoons for folks whose trousers ride even lower than Reilly's), and owns a terraced house he shares with two cats and Oliver, a raggedy old spaniel. A wife has been alluded to, but I've never seen her.

Reilly has one other idiosyncrasy as a gambler. He prefers to bet on British races because they're more honest—"less bent," as he puts it. Though immensely fond of his native land, he gives the Irish poor marks for strict obedience to either the rules or the law.

The day of the Desert Orchid Chase, Reilly had finished his deliberations and moved on to a crossword puzzle. I ordered my usual pint of stout and prepared to be transported. Only over a beer can I pick the winner of a televised race, or so I've come to believe. The Guinness lifts me into a state I'd describe as "fuzzy clarity." I'm relaxed and yet able to address the *Post* with a more critical eye. Reading the paper again, I saw tiny filaments of meaning that my completely sober, less perceptive self had missed. Attractive horses revealed their limitations, while others I'd glided over gained new resonance. Thus enlightened, I thought Edredon Bleu couldn't lose, even though he carried twenty-eight pounds more than the other four entries.

No pub in the city is more than a block or two from a betting shop, so I reached Boylesports in under three minutes. Besides Wincanton, there were races at Aintree and Towcester in England, and also some good Irish racing at Galway and Wexford, affording the fans a wonderful opportunity for confusion. The twenty-seven TV screens in the shop showed the odds, the live action, and redundant ads coaxing us to have a "flutter," or bet. With so much going on, the overwhelmed clerks were gasping for breath. Edredon Bleu was a disagreeable 6–5, but you have to take short prices on small fields, so I swallowed hard and put fifty bucks on the nose, elbowing through the crowd to do it.

In the old days, the Irish wouldn't be caught dead at a bookie's office on the Sabbath, of course, but the church isn't the power it used to be. There's even a shortage of young men in Ireland willing to be priests. I was reminded of a story about Richard "Boss" Croker, a Catholic from Cork, who got rich as a corrupt Tammany Hall kingpin in New York and later set himself up as a trainer outside Dublin. When Croker entered Orby in the Epsom Derby in 1907, the British hacks blasted his presumption—"The turf in Ireland has no spring in it, and the climate is too depressing," one wrote—but the loyalists at home backed Orby, anyway, and lit bonfires around Trinity College after his victory, where an old woman cried, "Thank God, we have lived to see a Catholic horse win the English Derby!"

THAT AFTERNOON, Edward O'Grady had a fine time at Galway. He saddled Golden Row, who won a novice chase, and Windsor Boy, who took a handicap hurdle, both with Barry Geraghty riding. Rumor had it that Geraghty might replace Norman Williamson as O'Grady's stable jockey, a job to be envied. O'Grady is bright and sophisticated, with a dry wit, and has trained seventeen Festival winners, more than anyone currently active in Ireland. He also has the dubious distinction of being the only Irish trainer ever to be arrested at Cheltenham, charged with conspiracy to cheat and defraud the British bookmakers.

The scandal centered on a betting coup, later known as the Gay Future Affair. Tony Murphy, a crafty Cork builder, was its ringleader and borrowed his scam from greyhound racing. It involved a double or treble wager (two or three "win" bets) that coupled Gay Future with Opera Cloak or Ankerwyke, or both, who would be scratched on the day—August 24, 1974—thereby turning the treble into a single on Gay Future, as per the bookmakers' rules. All three horses were supposedly at the yard of Tony Collins in Troon, Scotland, although the Gay Future there was a decoy. The real Gay Future was with O'Grady in Tipperary, in serious and secretive training, being honed to a fine edge over hurdles.

Collins entered Gay Future in a race at Cartmel, an out-of-the-way track in the Lake District with the longest stretch in England. The phony horse departed from Collins's yard in a van, but it was switched for O'Grady's horse at a phone booth near the racecourse. Before sending Gay Future into the parade ring, the conspirators further covered their scheme by rubbing the horse with soapsuds, so he'd look nervous and washed out. They also arranged for Collins's top jockey to be on another horse, Racionizer, and plunged on Racionizer at the course to throw off the scent. Gay Future, priced at 10–1, soared home by fifteen lengths under Timmy Jones, an Irish rider flown in for the day—a perfect coup, it seemed, except that Collins had messed up.

Instead of dispatching Opera Cloak and Ankerwyke to their respective engagements at Plumpton and Southwell, and then inventing an excuse for their failure to arrive—a traffic jam, say, or an accident—he left them at his yard. A reporter uncovered the ruse with a simple phone call, speaking to a stable lass who told him she could see both horses from her window. The authorities were alerted and began an investigation, and the coppers arrested Murphy and O'Grady at Cheltenham the following March, on the Festival's first day, while Collins was detained in Troon. The case dragged on for a year or so, with the accused out on bail. When it came to trial, the prosecutor failed to present any evidence against O'Grady, who was cleared.

The judge, though sympathetic to the others—the fraud was "very minor," he said—still felt compelled to fine them because a jury had found them guilty. For the rest of his life, Tony Murphy denied that he'd done anything illegal. In essence, there was no fix. The right horse had run at the right track, as advertised. But the bookies didn't agree and only paid out on a fraction of the bets Murphy's Cork cronies had spread around London, investing about sixty thousand dollars as they dashed from shop to shop. Aside from the notoriety, the Gay Future Affair brought Edward O'Grady an unexpected bonus—a movie deal, with Pierce Brosnan playing him in *Murphy's Stroke*.

At Wincanton, the horses were milling around before the start of the Desert Orchid. As hopeful as I was, I suffered a nervous spell because Edredon Bleu is a front-runner, a style of racing I distrust. Often front-runners are like those celebrated novelists who publish a brilliant book at twenty-two, then burn out over the long haul and wind up reviewing novels by a new crop of brilliant twenty-two-year-olds. I shouldn't have worried, though, because Edredon Bleu had class to spare and won by a Gay Futuresque margin of fifteen lengths, setting a track record in the bargain, eleven seconds faster than the former one. Henrietta Knight, very gratified, thought she might try her horse at a longer distance next time and threatened to write his biography, as she'd done for Best Mate.

A winning bet confirms a man's genius and elevates his spirits. I never told Imelda about my losses, only about my scores, of course, and if I needed another reason to feel affection for her, which I didn't, it would be that she never asks how I'm doing at the track. Besides, her interest in racing is confined to the elegance of the horses and the beautiful places where they run, a scene that hasn't changed much since Degas painted it at Longchamp. We talked about such things on an evening walk to town, down Grafton Street with its giddy crowd of shoppers, to the Liffey. The river, though low and murky because of the long dry spell, its thrust curtailed by dams, still had the regal presence of all great streams that flow through cities, and we walked along it to the sea, delighted to be where we were, together.

And how did it happen? I had asked myself that question more than once. The initial attraction, the sheer bliss of a romance, the falling *into* love, those parts were easy, but there were difficulties, as well. Being older, we were both wary, on guard for each other's fatal flaw, desperate not to repeat our past mistakes, and cautious about her children's reaction to the newly minted fact of us. I had friends who thought I was rash or just plain foolish, while some in Imelda's circle wrung their hands over her choice of a partner, this gent from abroad traveling without portfolio—and a writer to boot. But trust and conviction grow if real love is in the mix, and with them comes the courage to say, *I* want this to work, an admission that centers you in the midst of swirling waters.

We splurged on a good bottle of Burgundy such as a winner deserves and a standing rib roast for our Sunday dinner. There would be roast potatoes, too, sprinkled with sprigs of rosemary from the garden at the younger boy's request, and a salad and some buttered carrots from the root-crop heaven of Ireland. We had a new CD to listen to, a coal fire blazing, the *Observer* for penetrating commentary, and a scandal sheet for the gossip—life in all its embraceable simplicity. The transition still seemed miraculous to me. I could have been on the porch of my hermit's fishing cabin instead, gray-bearded and alone, staring at those swirling waters. Amazing grace, indeed.

THE RAIN CAME AT LAST. October ended with a bristly, stinging storm that had a harsh foretaste of winter at its core. It struck while I was on a train to Thurles, a large but plain market town in County Tipperary, for a Thursday meeting. I sat across from a quartet of neatly dressed men in jackets and ties, who were toting old-fashioned leather satchels. If I hadn't known better, I'd have taken them for senior citizens on a holiday trip to Limerick, but they were just bookies on their way to the racecourse with a rough afternoon ahead of them, the weather the least of their concerns.

In the pecking order of Irish tracks, Thurles ranks toward the bottom, so the bookies could not expect any windfalls. Their costs were still fixed, though, whether or not the betting ring was active. They paid an annual fee for their pitch at the course, with the choice spots being the most expensive, along with a daily fee (five times the price of a ticket) and half of one percent of their turnover. Corporate bookmakers offer Internet betting now, so that cut into their profits, as did the high-street shops where punters can plunge on sports other than racing. (Going a step further, Paddy Power features novelty bets—10–1 that Bono will become a Buddhist, say.) They also had travel expenses and the cost of hiring a helper to chalk up the wagers. Only twenty percent of on-course bookies in Ireland earn a substantial living. In effect, they're an endangered species, although the public doesn't believe it.

I once arranged to visit a retired bookie to learn more about the trade. Kindly and arthritic, in his late eighties, the Old Bookie was a tenth-generation Dubliner from the tougher north side of the Liffey. "Can't you hear it in my accent?" he asked, as he greeted me. In his powder blue cardigan, sharply creased tan slacks, matching socks, and shiny loafers, he resembled a fringe member of the Rat Pack. His living room, furnished in the 1950s in a single decorative swoop, hadn't been touched since and presented a museum-quality tableau. He told me he'd made book for about sixty years, following in his father's footsteps. "I was brainless at the start," he said modestly, but he added that a bookie doesn't have to be super-intelligent, just good at math. "I knew three fellas who belonged to Mensa, and they were so hooked on theory, they were lousy at the job."

"Is it difficult to get a license?" I asked.

"Nah, the police will license anybody." He waved a hand dismissively. "Unless you have a criminal record, or serious enemies."

"Serious enemies," I repeated, picturing a row of shallow graves.

He nodded again, rather sadly, as if he knew where the bodies were buried. At any rate, he'd done all right in the business, flush at times and just scraping by at others. He went broke once, but that was par for the course. It was silly to worry about the setbacks, he thought. "I put it behind me with a stop at the pub, or at the Gresham Hotel if I was feeling good," the Old Bookie said, although he warned that the work was stressful and took its toll on family life. "The things I did wrong, they haunt me," he confessed, and again my head filled with colorful images of mayhem. The only way for a bookie to get rich was to invest his money wisely—in real estate, or a share in a betting shop—rather than pissing it away on a flashy lifestyle, with too many stops at the Gresham.

A lack of courage had inhibited his own success as a turf account- ant. "I didn't have the nerve to ride out a hot streak or take a big gam- ble when I had the touch," he explained. "And if somebody wanted me to lay a really huge bet—five grand, ten grand—I ran for cover. Care for a drink?" he asked. I watched in awe as he poured a generous shot of Bushmills from a tray layered with generations of dust, and when I didn't add any water, he gave me a look of mock horror. "Whoa, that'll kill you! Drinking that stuff straight!" He grinned and hitched up his trousers. "I'm going to be eighty-nine soon. Think I'll make it?" I had the good grace not to ask, "What are the odds?"

A line of taxis waited at the train station in Thurles. The racecourse was only about a mile away, but the rain was coming down hard now, whipped into a fury by a nasty wind, so I joined the bookies in a cab. At the track, I searched for a warm corner to hide out, a snug little bar or a cozy restaurant, only to discover they don't exist at Thurles. There *are* two bars, but they're unheated, as is the dour café, where the dull fluorescent lighting created a penitential gloom. Someone had put wilted carnations on the tables in tumblers and cream pitchers, a sight so pitiful it almost brought tears to my eyes. For all their gentleness, politeness, and conviviality, the Irish can be awfully good at punishing themselves.

I chose the smaller bar as my sanctuary, assuming it would generate more body heat. The track draws about two thousand stouthearted folks on an average Thursday, and I prayed they'd all show up at once.

I tried reading the program, but I was distracted by an ad for the bookies that played on a flickering TV. A jingle suggested how easy, and how much fun, it would be to bet with them. That would motivate anybody, I thought wryly, as I surveyed the regulars around me, whose ruddy cheeks and broken capillaries were the result of braving the elements, or maybe avoiding them at any handy pub. This was desolate territory. I started on the hot whiskeys myself—Jameson, sugar, hot water, and a lemon slice stuck with cloves.

To be fair, there are people who love Thurles. Built on rich farmland, the track is naturally free-draining and permits racing when other courses are waterlogged. Willie Mullins, among the game's best trainers, told me once how much he enjoys Thurles for the good galloping ground and the dedicated, informed patrons. Possibly Jessie Harrington felt the same way. She was in high spirits before the first race. "Don't complain about the weather," she scolded a grumbler in the parade ring, soaked to the skin like the rest of us. "We need this rain!" The race was for maidens on the flat, and Jessie had two horses in it, but she was up against Shangri La, a classy filly from Aidan O'Brien's yard, and had no real chance. It's unusual for O'Brien to lose a maiden race in Ireland, so classy are his colts and fillies.

"Things can only digress from here," said a man at the bar after the race, tearing up his losing ticket. "I mean, *regress*." Strangely, I understood him. The program had alerted me to what we had in store. Among the dicey performers competing in the Munster Handicap, for instance, were A C Azure (no wins in twenty-seven starts), Callas (zero for twenty-five), Camillas Estate (zero for thirty-one), and the comparatively gifted Hamlyn (one for thirty-eight). The fifteen horses, a full field, ranged in age from four to ten. They had a combined total of 409 starts and had won just fourteen of them, or 3.4 percent. In every flat race that day, there were fifteen runners plus reserves—the *average* field in an Irish race of any kind is fourteen—and that led to the inescapable conclusion that Ireland produces a lot of racehorses, and not all of them useful ones.

Whenever I asked about the boom, I was directed to the imposing figure of Charles Haughey, a former prime minister. (Haughey is *Eachaidhe* in Gaelic, meaning "horseman.") Like Richard Croker, he was called the Boss, carried himself with the swashbuckling authority of a high chieftain, and shared Croker's ability to reap questionable benefits from his position—a rogue, in other words, despised in some quarters and admired in others. But politics aside, Haughey's affection for horses was undoubtedly genuine. He bought his first in 1962 while he served as minister of justice, and gradually built up his stable by sending his mares to a stud farm in County Dublin presided over by Captain Tim Rogers, once an aide to Winston Churchill.

In 1968, Haughey acquired his own stud in County Meath, often a perk among the newly affluent Irish. A year later, as minister of finance, he introduced a tax exemption for the breeding industry at an opportune moment, just as similar exemptions were being scrapped in Britain. (In this case, "tax exemption" translated as no taxes whatsoever on a stud farm's profits from breeding.) Haughey's finest hour as an owner came in 1985, when his Flashing Steel won the Irish Grand National under top weight.

Toward the end of his political life, in 1999, the Boss spelled out his views on the breeding industry in a message to *The Irish Thoroughbred.*

"Natural advantages in climate and soil and favorable taxation treatment have contributed to our excellent reputation for horse breeding," he wrote. "However, it is the skill and innate love of horses in our breeders that have been the decisive factors. . . . In more recent times we have seen the development of large specialized stud farms. I consider this a positive development and complementary to the work of the small breeder."

Though Haughey survived many scandals, his tendency to confuse the national interest with his own caught up with him at last. Dragged into court, he was accused of accepting lavish gifts from businessmen, and he also owed the government millions in back taxes and undeclared income, although this hardly made him bankrupt—he still owns one of the Blasket Islands off the Kerry coast, for example. In some respects, his support for big-time breeders smacked of the same cronyism that brought him down. The tax loophole he opened allowed the "large specialized" stud farms to dominate the market, a nuisance rather than a complement to the little guys struggling to get by.

The famous Coolmore Stud in Tipperary, a global power with branches in Australia and Kentucky, has benefited most from Haughey's gambit. Coolmore owns many of the world's most desirable stallions, and its racing arm at Ballydoyle, where Aidan O'Brien presides, is intended to showcase the elegantly bred colts who'll stand at stud someday. The business is so profitable that John Magnier, its managing director, lives abroad to avoid paying taxes on his compensation and investments, although he has a home in Ireland and spends as much time there as the law permits. Nobody blames Magnier and his associates for taking advantage of the loophole, but Coolmore has been criticized for overbooking its stallions. Sadler's Wells, who is always in demand, covers up to two hundred mares a year, doing double duty in Australia and earning a reported $70 million or so.

It's fair to say that Haughey's legacy has been a double-edged sword. If it has allowed operations such as Coolmore to improve the breed and put Irish racehorses on the international map, it has also fostered a glut of inferior stock. The number of horses in training continues to rise, as does the number of owners, even though the "hobby" (that's what it is for most people) isn't cheap. Syndicates of six, ten, or even twenty owners are gaining in popularity, too, with 1,141 on record at present. Almost all male chasers and hurdlers are geldings and worthless at stud, while broodmares are only a little more valuable, so an owner's initial fantasies revolve around the prize money to be won and, more distantly and less reliably, on the glittery pleasure dome of Cheltenham.

That's not so foolish, really, because the average purse in Ireland is the highest in Europe—about $25,000 compared to $18,000 for the U.K. Although it's true that almost half the horses in training do win a purse (or a piece of one) sooner or later, the payday usually isn't big enough to fuel any more fantasies. As the bills mount up, many owners become hard-nosed, and they sell or retire their horses, a pet for the kids to ride, or they hang on to it for the *craic*—the fun, the good times—if they can afford to, enjoying drinks and a day out at a humble, homey track like Thurles. The overall attendance at 303 fixtures was up by eight and a half percent in 2004, another mark of how much the Irish love racing and are willing to embrace a horse of any kind.

THE RAIN HAD LET UP by the fifth race. I was very grateful for that, but my comrades seemed not to notice. They were determined to savor their fabled *craic* regardless of the weather. Why let a deluge dampen your pleasure? In fact, I never saw anyone with an umbrella all afternoon. (Dublin tough guys consider umbrellas unmanly; they'd rather catch pneumonia.) When the clouds parted, I could see Devil's Bit Mountain, the track's logo, on the horizon, a humped shape missing its tip—the bit torn off by the devil in "a fit of anger." It was still quite cold, but the hot whiskeys helped, three and counting, and I felt ready for the card's big race, a steeplechase with a fat pot of more than twenty thousand dollars.

Originally, fourteen trainers had entered horses, but because the going was still firm on Wednesday before the storm, all but two of them had dropped out, so we had a match race on our hands. The contestants were Splendour, a winner on good ground earlier in the month, and Risk Accessor, who'd last run (and lost) at Galway in July. After such a long absence, Risk Accessor's level of fitness was in question, but I still couldn't rule him out, not when he belonged to John P. McManus, Ireland's largest owner of jumpers. Enormously wealthy and influential, McManus acquired the nickname Sundance Kid for his brave raids on the betting ring in his younger days, when he "robbed" the bookies repeatedly.

Even at my neighborhood betting shops, the locals knew the tale of McManus's rise to the top, and I'd heard it many times myself. Born in County Limerick, J.P. began gambling as a child, although he was small for his age and had to rely on indulgent adults to place his bets. When he was nine, he cashed a dandy one on Merryman II in the 1960 Grand National at odds of 13–2. After leaving school, he worked on his father's dairy farm, but he quit to be a bookmaker on the greyhounds and went broke twice. The second time, his mother slipped him some money on the sly, vowing not to tell her husband, who disapproved of his son's occupation. "I suppose I had more respect for it than any money I've had before or since," McManus once said, perhaps because it carried a mother's blessing, no small thing in Ireland.

As it happened, he would never be *skint*, or broke, again. Instead, his fortunes improved dramatically. He had an agile brain for higher math and playing the percentages, and it paid off when he diversified into currency trading, the initial source of his fortune. Ahead of the game, he bought property, leisure assets in the Caribbean and elsewhere, and racehorses, of course, often pricey ones, with an eye toward winning the Gold Cup at Cheltenham, maybe the only goal he's yet to achieve. His legitimate ventures did not stop him from gambling, though. He fell into high-stakes backgammon for a while, but the bookies bore the brunt of his assaults. In 1982, he beat them out of nearly a half million dollars at the Festival by backing Mr. Donovan, a hurdler he owned, who won a major race. Edward O'Grady was the trainer.

McManus wasn't always a consummate pro. He shed some blood in the betting ring, particularly as a young man, when he scratched his itch too feverishly. Lacking the discipline to hold off when his luck ran cold, he once advised some English bookmaking firms that if they extended any more credit, they did so "at their peril." But as the years passed he gained an icy control over himself, never chasing his losses or trying to get even on the last race. He developed a complex set of guiding principles and could lay them out as precisely as any textbook. *The going is the most important thing. Set out to make a point or two over the odds and go in with two fists.* And above all, *Beware of certainties.*

When McManus's offshore corporation Cubic Expression sailed into the financial stratosphere, he moved to Switzerland as a tax exile in the 1990s. His office in Geneva is rumored to have a stunning view of Mont Blanc and a bank of TVs tuned alternately to the currency markets and the races. An avid golfer, he sponsors a charity tournament in Limerick on occasion and has a locker next to Tiger Woods's at the exclusive Islesworth Club in Orlando. With John Magnier, his fellow exile, he owns a large share of Manchester United, the most valuable English football franchise. His collection of jumpers, more than a hundred, is parceled out among several trainers in Ireland, England, and France.

In the manner of folk heroes, McManus likes to drop out of the sky and land at a racecourse in his green-and-gold helicopter, the colors of Limerick's South Liberties hurling club. (Hurling is Ireland's oldest sport, played with sticks and a ball at warp speed.) As the two horses went to post, I scanned the heavens for a sign of him, but he didn't show up that afternoon. Avoiding Thurles in stormy weather was another tribute to his cleverness, I thought. Still, he missed the match race (unless he watched it in his Geneva office), a much more intricate affair than I anticipated. It began as a tactical stalemate, with neither Conor O'Dwyer on Risk Accessor nor Barry Geraghty on

Splendour eager to make the running. About halfway through the two-plus miles, the rain-soaked turf worked against Splendour, who prefers good ground—the going is the most important thing!—and when O'Dwyer let Risk Accessor go, the horse never looked back.

RIDING HOME ON THE TRAIN, with my clothes drying out in the warm compartment, I set aside the *Racing Post* for Patrick Kavanagh's *The Green Fool,* an autobiographical account of the poet's formative years in County Monaghan on a farm not unlike those around Thurles. I had come across Kavanagh in anthologies before, back in California, but I didn't know his writing well and felt a marvelous sense of discovery when I began reading his poems closely, so different in tone and subject matter from those of Yeats, who had laid claim to Irish poetry in America in his time, just as Joyce had done with fiction.

Kavanagh had a farmer's directness, along with a raw and ribald wit. He loved horses and racing, of course, a logical consequence of growing up in rural Ireland and possibly of *being* Irish, and he was often observed in Dublin pubs raptly attending to the sports page. But as a youth, while practicing his craft more or less in secret—poets were rare in the hamlet of Mucker—he was a servant of the land, of his crops and cattle. He painted a fascinating portrait of his "clay-heavy mind" bursting into flames after he read the modernists, especially Gertrude Stein. In his work, he was truthful to his roots, painfully so, writing about pinched country lives and the travail of trapped and aging bachelors, counting himself among them.

Those ties to the land held back Kavanagh when *Ploughman and Other Poems,* his first book, came out in England in 1936, but only for a while. He was ambitious and so hungry for culture that he once walked fifty miles from Mucker to Dublin just for a taste of it. Still, he had to wrestle with his predicament, torn between moving on and staying behind. "The land is jealous of literature," he said, "and in its final effort to hold a poet offers him, like a despairing lover, everything, everything." Yet after much soul-searching, and almost thirty-five years on the farm, he chose to break with the land and pursue his literary future in London, where he was commissioned to write *The Green Fool*. He left home with about ten dollars in his pocket.

Kavanagh's book echoed in me as I walked to our home from Hueston Station, along the Liffey in the early dark and through the city center, then up Baggot Street until it turned into Pembroke Road, where the poet had rented an apartment for many years. The night air was cool but rain-freshened, and as I followed the Grand Canal, an old commercial waterway that linked the River Barrow to the Irish Sea, I sat for a few minutes on a bench next to a statue of Kavanagh, who wanted no "hero-Courageous tomb—just a canal-bank seat for the passer-by." I let the peace of the moment wash over me, recalling another sentence from *The Green Fool*. "Ireland is a fine place to day-dream," the author wrote, and that's how it seemed to me just then, a realm apart from ordinary cares, where the horses would be running again tomorrow.

The Great Unveiling

That blustery afternoon at Thurles, stored forever in my bank of soggy memories, proved to be a cheat. It didn't signal a change in the weather. Instead, the dull dry days returned, and the English courses were in such jeopardy they had to water the turf almost daily in order to hold their meetings. There was even talk that the Open Meeting at Cheltenham in mid-November, the early season's high point, might have to be scrapped. Trainers were more frazzled than ever. With the important National Hunt races soon to come in bunches, they had to decide what they were willing to risk. The tracks, ever watchful of the bottom line, would be hungry to make those races happen, regardless of the going.

According to Jessie, Moscow Flyer was still penciled in for the Fortria Chase, but I hadn't heard anything about Beef Or Salmon's plans, so I went looking for Michael Hourigan to see what he had in mind. I caught up with him at the Tattersalls National Hunt Sale on the company's lavish auction grounds in County Meath. Hourigan had driven over from Limerick to check out and maybe bid on some of the eight hundred or so lots for sale—unbroken stock, yearlings, and horses in training. At a desk outside the auction ring, I picked up a fat doorstop of a catalog, free to anyone. On the front cover was a painting of a red fox, and on the back photos of Best Mate, Moscow Flyer, and Monty's Pass, a Grand National winner, each purchased at Tattersalls.

Horses were everywhere on the grounds, in all shapes and sizes, constantly on the move. Grooms were busy combing and buffing them, polishing them up for their moment in the spotlight. They led the horses from a row of barns to a holding ring outside the auction building, where buyers gathered to inspect them, and when a horse's number was called, it went through an archway and into the sales ring, a little oval surrounded by theater seats in tiers. An electronic screen flashed the bids in sterling, dollars, and euros. The bidding seldom lasted more than two or three minutes, and the selling price rarely exceeded ten grand. Even I could afford an Irish racehorse, so large was the supply.

From an upper tier, I watched the auction for a while. The horses each reacted differently in the sales ring, revealing aspects of their character. Some appeared to be oblivious of the noise, the badgering auctioneer, and the crowd, an attitude you could interpret as a plus (superior, above it all) or a minus (plain ignorant)—your choice, and buyer beware. Others blinked and nickered in distress, shocked to be on the market and glaring at their grooms as the very source of their betrayal. Here came a furry little yearling so stunned and needy his entire being shouted, "I want to go back to the farm!" followed by a gangly, head-bobbing gelding who so resembled a cartoon animal I half-expected him to open his mouth and cough up a one-liner. The comedian was returned to his breeder unsold.

I bumped into Hourigan by the holding ring. A short, sturdy, energetic ball of man, he looked the trainer's part in a tweed cap, a shirt and a sweater, and corduroy trousers. He has a boxer's nose, flattened as if by a solid right hook, and small bright eyes that don't miss a trick. *The Irish Field,* a racing paper, once said of him that he "provides a great deal of entertainment to those who listen to him," and I would agree, although with a caveat. Hourigan likes a joke and often pokes fun at himself, but his self-deprecatory style masks a keen intelligence, and he uses the mask to his advantage against any fool who underestimates him. He has risen from nothing, liberated from the poverty of old Limerick to create a yard that wins more prize money than almost any other in Ireland.

Hourigan had a foot up on a fence rail, chatting with some pals, apparently relaxed. At the same time, though, he was assessing the horses minutely with those small bright eyes. I thought he could do it all day long and never be bored. His son Paul was with him, a jump jockey as Michael had been—and a good one, too, who'd won about two hundred races. But Paul would soon be too big to ride anymore, and he was taking it hard.

"The love for it doesn't go," Hourigan whispered when Paul was out of earshot, but he was also relieved. That very morning Sean Cleary, a flat jockey, was being laid to rest in the town of Athlone, having died in a freak accident on the flat at Galway. "First Kieran Kelly, then Sean," Hourigan said quietly. "Two dead in three months. You wouldn't believe it."

The horses kept emerging from the barns in a ceaseless stream. Lot 287 was a chestnut filly by Good Thyne (USA) out of Financial Asset (IRE). When I studied the filly's family tree, going back five generations, I found a dam called Sark, who'd given birth to Roll-A-Joint and Sarcastic. The Tattersalls catalog was a document worthy of structural analysis, a treasure for the postmodernists. As I thumbed through the information-dense pages, each thick with type, I suspected I could become as addicted to the science of bloodlines as I once was to baseball statistics, able to recite Roll-A-Joint's achievements (ten wins, nine over fences, including the Scottish National) as quickly, say, as Duke Snider's lifetime batting average (.295).

But a pedigree can only tell you so much, particularly about jumpers. To rely solely on a horse's breeding as the guide to its potential is a big mistake. It robs the process of intuition, magic, even poetry. Whenever I talked to trainers about buying a horse, they used the same phrase repeatedly, "Something about him [or her] I liked," as Jessie had said about Moscow. The attraction bore a close kinship to falling in love, starting with a glance across the room (or sales ring), an exchange of meaningful looks, and some flirting that led to an emotional connection. The horse telegraphs its readiness to surrender, and the trainer senses that pliability and translates it into a desire to be trained.

The art of judging a horse, of seeing into its heart, is mysterious, and Hourigan told me that nobody in Ireland is better at it than Tom Costello, his old friend. I'd heard the name before, of course. In the pantheon of Irish racing's folk heroes, Costello is on a par with John P. McManus, although he is more private and secretive. With his five sons, he runs a horse-trading empire in the tiny village of Newmarket-on-Fergus in County Clare and sells to such top clients as Hourigan and Willie Mullins, as well as to the English, but Costello can be so picky he rejects any would-be buyers who fall below his unstated yet impeccable standards. I had no doubt he'd be as celebrated someday as James Sullivan, a famous Irish horse whisperer of the early 1800s who—with a single command—taught a horse to lie on its back and remain so still that a glass of beer could be balanced on each hoof.

Costello's exalted status derives from the fact that he discovered and later sold six winners of the Cheltenham Gold Cup—Midnight Court, The Thinker, Cool Ground, Cool Dawn, Imperial Call, and Best Mate. There are positives in all their pedigrees, but not enough to justify that much success. As for Beef Or Salmon, he was another story altogether, with the lowly ancestry of a street urchin. Cajetano, his U.S.-bred sire, was such a lackluster stallion he was shipped to the minors in Italy, where he serviced scruffy mares until his demise. Beef

Or Salmon's first owner acquired him for a mere $9,000 or so at Tattersalls in 1999 and unloaded him a year later in another auction, where Hourigan snapped him up for about $11,000 because he "liked the look of him." The horse had repaid his faith, winning the Irish Hennessy Gold Cup and four other chases last season, before his fall at the Festival.

"I brought four horses to Cheltenham last year, and three of them fell," Hourigan said wistfully. "Hi Cloy ran on Wednesday, and he fell. Beef Or Salmon fell on Thursday, and so did Dorans Pride, who died. It's terrible to lose a horse like that! Terrible! But that's how it goes, doesn't it? Can't do feck-all about it."

"Will you be running Beef Or Salmon soon?"

"We might go to Down Royal for the Nicholson Chase," he told me. "But only if the ground comes right." Hourigan stopped talking abruptly, his eyes on a yearling in the holding ring. With a sign so subtle I missed it, he conveyed his interest to the groom, who brought out the yearling and walked it over a path, up and down, like a model on a runway. Satisfied with what he saw, Hourigan brushed a hand over its coat, knelt to feel its legs, and then, without a word, dismissed the groom.

"No good? What was wrong?" I asked him. He didn't answer, so I tried another tack. "Think you'll be buying anything, Michael?"

"I already have," he said smugly. He'd bought Lot 276 from Carraiganog Stud, a bay gelding by Saddlers' Hall (by Sadler's Wells) out of Lunalae. Further back, the yearling had some links to Northern Dancer and Bold Lad, and was also distantly related to Beef Or Salmon. Hourigan paid almost eighty thousand dollars in cash, on behalf of an unnamed owner.

That was the highest price of the sale so far, but it was later eclipsed in a bidding war over a Supreme Leader yearling. (Be My Native and Supreme Leader are the top two National Hunt sires, based on the amount of money their offspring have earned.) The yearling, bred at Spratstown Stud in County Clare, was out of a half sister to two or three Festival winners. Alastair Pim, the flamboyant auctioneer, asked for an opening bid of about $100,000. He got just $20,000, but the price escalated rapidly. Only two bidders were still game at $90,000, and only one was left when Pim banged down his hammer at $120,000, a new record for an Irish yearling. The buyer in absentia was J. P. McManus.

THROUGH THE FIRST WEEK of November, Cheltenham continued to parch. Rain fell in nearby Tewkesbury and Cirencester, but the racecourse might have been a desert. I wanted to go to the Open as a warm-up for the Festival, so I called John Nicholson, the head groundsman, for the latest update. He is a typical horse-loving vagabond, who'd served time as a rancher in Brazil, a works rider in Australia, and a stud-farm hand in England. His ties to Cheltenham run deep. His great-great-grandfather was clerk of the course in the 1860s, and his father, a champion trainer, had a yard around the corner at Jackdaws Castle, now part of the overstuffed McManus portfolio.

Nicholson was doing his best to salvage the meeting. For the past two months, he'd been watering the turf steadily for ten or twelve hours a day to ease the going. (Cheltenham has two courses, called the Old and the New for obvious reasons.) In a normal year, he goes through about seven million gallons of water, drawing on a reservoir that fills from a brook on the grounds, but he had used most of that already and had to buy five million extra gallons from the local water authority. To add to his worries, there were vigilant fishermen about. An anglers' club stocks the reservoir with such coarse species as roach and pike, and if the water level kept dropping, the fish might die and spark a rebellion.

Logistics form the core of Nicholson's job. He manages a large staff, even though Cheltenham hosts only sixteen meetings a year, all for jumpers. Ten staffers care for the turf and two for the twenty-five fences. The fences, made of birch packed in an oak frame, cost about twelve thousand dollars apiece and must be rebuilt every couple of years when the birch becomes brittle and rots. Nicholson buys it in bundles from commercial foresters, because it won't grow in the clay soil around the course. The sixteen sticks in each bundle are graded and trimmed, then jammed into the frame, pulled tight with a wire rope, and trimmed again to a proper height—a minimum of four feet six inches, by the rulebook—with a hedge cutter. Hurdles cost less at about two thousand dollars apiece, but they need more attention. Horses bash right through them at times—they give a little, while the fences don't—so they're repaired frequently. Eight to ten are in tatters after an average racing day.

At the end of a meeting, Nicholson hires a special team to mend the turf. The team walks the track and replaces any divots by treading on them. When the season is over in April, the chewed-up course undergoes a major reconstruction. It must be harrowed through the late spring and summer, and spiked in early autumn. The grass cover gets ripped out, and the soil is subjected to direct-drill reseeding, a painstaking procedure common at golf courses, too. Coordinating the effort can be complicated, but Nicholson takes pride in the results and hopes, given his historical ties to Cheltenham, that what he and his crew accomplish will still be around in the next century.

He must have a sunny disposition, I thought, because he was also hopeful about the Open Meeting. "We're doing all we can," he said, and even in faraway Dublin, I could almost hear him knocking on wood.

EVER CAUTIOUS with his precious goods, Michael Hourigan decided against sending Beef Or Salmon to Down Royal for the Nicholson Chase, the track's centerpiece for its two-day Northern Festival of Racing, a smaller-scale event than Cheltenham's grand ball. The ground was still too firm, he said, as it was at Leopardstown, where he'd recently walked the course—"soft on top but like flint underneath"— so his big horse would also skip the important November Handicap there a week later. Disappointed as I was, I still planned to visit Down Royal, then double back to watch Moscow Flyer's debut at Navan. It would be an enjoyable trip, I thought, because for the Irish any festival suggests a raucous party, and people who don't give a damn about the horses turn up just for the fun.

My drive to the north went smoothly at first. Traffic thinned out past the Dublin Airport, with only a few cars on the highway, and again I was aware of how underpopulated Ireland is, the broad fields and broader skies a kind of comfort. But my reverie clattered to a halt in Dundalk when I hit the morning rush hour and got trapped in the shadow of some gigantic chain stores—another sign of progress, alas. I felt relieved to break free and climb toward Newry and Armagh, where a zealot's billboard cried out, THE WAGES OF SIN IS DEATH. Soon I was skirting the Mourne Mountains and hearing the words *mourn* and *moan* as I looked out at the pretty but melancholy scenery, a series of gorse-choked hills brown and even slightly purple in the thundery light.

The landscape beyond the Mournes reminded me of the English countryside. Technically, I *was* in the U.K., and that must have contributed to it, but so did the farms, very tidy compared to Ireland's, where a wild raggedness often prevails. The Irish seem reluctant to interfere too much with nature, maybe out of a Celtic respect for the gods who preside over it, while the English are quick to provide order where none existed before. As attractive as the farms around Banbridge were, their fields divided by hedgerows and drystone walls in perfect repair, I responded to the rough edges in Ireland and that mystical sense of bowing to invisible yet potent forces.

Hillsborough was my destination. Situated on a strategic spot above the Dublin to Belfast road, it had grown up around an artillery fort built in 1650 by Colonel Arthur Hills. The fort is a park now and has a lake, where men were casting flies to trout. I had a fleeting desire to join them, but I checked into my hotel instead and got a taste of the mild paranoia of the north. My room, booked as a single, had twin beds, but the pillows were gone from one. The bathroom, too, had been edited. I was limited to a towel, a washcloth, and a bar of soap, apparently to prevent me from smuggling in the extra guest hidden in the trunk of my car.

Hoping the bookies wouldn't view me the same way, as a craven opportunist ready to skim whatever he could from the north's bounty, I headed for the racecourse a few miles away. Founded by Royal Charter in 1685, Down Royal is still surrounded by farmland, although the suburbs are marching toward it. The setting is so rural that rabbits are a nuisance. A three-foot-deep trench had to be dug, then lined with sharp stones, to keep the bunnies from tearing up the chase course. After parking, I had to walk across the course to reach the gate, surprised that the grass stuck up in clumps rather than being cut uniformly. When I tried to dig a heel of my boot into the ground, it barely gave an inch. Firm going, indeed.

Those thundery clouds over the Mournes had cleared, so the crowd was as large as anticipated that Friday afternoon, and in an appropriately festive mood. Having swapped the harried concerns of the business world for the freewheeling universe of chance, office workers were shedding their jackets, ties, and inhibitions, as jolly as kids playing hooky from school, but once more I caught a whiff of suspicion. Scattered on the main public bar were leaflets that warned of counterfeit bills. So many were in circulation that patrons were advised their money would be scrutinized closely before a drink was dispensed. The barmaids were unruffled, though. They were distracted, busy, and all dolled up, ready to be whisked off to Málaga if some joker hit the jackpot.

At the paddock before the first race, a hurdle for maidens, I recognized an old friend, You Need Luck, who'd lost twice more since Gowran Park. He was beautifully turned out and won a fifty-dollar prize for his groom, but I still couldn't bring myself to bet on him. His head sagged and his eyes looked guilty, fixed on the ground instead of bright with sublime images of victory. Young Vintage, a Noel Meade filly, was far more appealing, a brilliant babe strutting her stuff, but the halo around her was evident to everybody. At odds of 6–4, I had to pass on her and played Willie Mullins's Raikkonen, though not with much conviction.

I watched the race from the rail and saw why the hurdles take such a beating. Some horses only lifted their hooves a few inches off the ground—the merest nod toward a jump. The hurdle wobbled after they hit it, then snapped back into place, no more than a minor annoyance. To my astonishment, You Need Luck ran well and even took the lead seven furlongs from home. He had the race in his pocket, really, but at the second-last hurdle he jumped so far to the left, Barry Geraghty was in shock. It was as if the horse had just remembered an appointment in Hillsborough and had to get there as fast as possible. Geraghty grabbed his whip and sent You Need Luck on a crashing sprint to the wire, all too late. For his noble effort, Geraghty received a one-day suspension for careless riding.

Sentiment betrayed me in the third race. There, in a sudden and glorious blast of sunshine, was Andrew Leigh, Eamonn's teenage son, on Jessie's Slaney Fox, being led around the ring by his beaming father. They talked and joked as they probably did when Eamonn first put the lad on a horse, but all was not what it seemed. In fact, Eamonn worried about Andrew, who had just completed high school and had insisted on taking out an apprentice's license. "Last job I'd want for him," Eamonn had told me, knowing the dangers involved, all the bones that might break, even the young life that could be lost, but the only emotion on his face at the moment was a parent's bubbly pride.

How could I not back the horse? I put a hundred to win on Slaney Fox—and I wasn't being entirely rash, either. Andrew had won a fifty-grand handicap in September, and that was good for his confidence, although maybe not so good for Eamonn, who feared the kid was getting cocky. "Already thinks he's a pro," he'd grumbled. When Andrew moved early and let Slaney Fox dash to the front, I assumed he'd made a mistake, but the mare had plenty in reserve. He kept her in high gear down the stretch until she brushed a hurdle, lost her rhythm, and faltered. Down went Andrew in a heap, his share of the purse vanished in an instant. Eamonn frowned and shook his head, no doubt wishing his son had chosen a sane trade like plumbing.

ON MY RETURN to the hotel, I was delighted to find my towel hadn't been confiscated, and after a pleasant dinner I slept for a dreamless eight hours and woke refreshed and besotted with the familiar gambler's notion that today would be *the* day, all dismal memories of my losing bets having fled. But the morning sky was as black as tar, and soon the rain was spitting down, joined by a howling wind. The crowd at the track was different, too. I saw a few business folks around, but they'd been infiltrated by a hard-drinking gang of tough guys with copious tattoos and piercings, their hair reduced to nubbins or shaved off entirely to reveal skulls of terrifying dimensions.

The gang's focus was a row of large tents that billowed like the sails of a ship on a gusty sea. Each tent housed a little bar. The tents were already packed with guzzlers and a trifle sloppy underfoot from the rain and the beer sloshed on the floor. Not that the tough guys took any notice of the weather—no, half of them were in T-shirts to show off those tattoos, and I noticed a certain absence of teeth, as well. I could feel the punch-ups brewing, desperate battles to be fought over arguments nobody would ever remember. What a foul, mean-spirited afternoon! To make matters worse, only four horses were entered in the Nicholson Chase despite the generous hundred-thousand-dollar pot. The firm going on Friday had scared away most trainers. They'd be sorry now, because the track was turning to mud.

After Thurles, another baptism of sorts. I had a brief twinge of nostalgia for Golden Gate Fields, for palm trees and San Francisco Bay—okay, for California. Race-going was not supposed to be a version of Outward Bound, and yet it seemed to be in Ireland.

The Nicholson, run over three miles, lacked any drama at all, except perhaps for the trainer Arthur Moore, whose mud-loving Glenelly Gale outlasted the others. "Pure poetry," Moore remarked, rubbing it in. Meanwhile, the sky grew blacker, more bleak. I heard a drunk pester Paul Carberry, shouting, "Hey, Paul, got any tips?" as if Carberry didn't have enough to do warding off hypothermia. The jockeys resembled bog people. I could have squeezed a pint of water from my socks, so when Jessie scratched Intelligent from the Killultagh Chase, leaving just three horses, I called it quits.

Across from Down Royal is a golf course with an old-fashioned clubhouse, where a single-minded golf nut or a drenched racing fan can rent a cheap room. Simply for the opportunity to change my clothes, I rented one—a coffin-size cubicle—and after I was inside it, nobody else *could* get in, but it was dry and functional, at least. I had a cot, a small desk for working on the Great American Novel, an elderly TV, and a window with a view of a scrubby vacant lot. A man— although not a fat man—could live here quite happily, I imagined, albeit sexlessly and alone, but I was probably a bit delirious from exposure. In fact, my initial satisfaction faded fast, and I was so bored by the early evening that I looked forward to *The Evil Gun* on BBC2, featuring Arthur Kennedy as a maniacal killer.

On Sunday morning I hit the road right after breakfast (an egg, sausages, bacon, country butter in thick slabs, exactly what the doctor didn't order), eager to put the past behind me. By noon I was in Navan, a bustling town where the Blackwater and Boyne Rivers meet. It hadn't rained as heavily in Navan, so the going was still the dread "good to firm," and that was unfortunate because trainers would skip the Fortria, just as they'd skipped the Nicholson. Again only four horses were entered, including Glenelly Gale, who'd come over by van from Down Royal after a night's rest. He couldn't beat Moscow Flyer, especially after running the day before, but the cunning Arthur Moore reckoned he could place, which the horse did, adding another ten grand to his haul.

Well, Moscow, here we go, I thought as I waited by the parade ring. He was the first horse into it, doing his star turn and nodding to the fans. The other horses joined him soon after, but they were composed on a lesser scale, carved out of inferior material. "He's good enough if he's lucky enough," Eamonn said as they circled, tossing out an old racetrack cliché. Moscow still carried a few extra pounds, because he'd been out to pasture on his summer holiday longer than usual—and the grass was very good, full of juice—but he had already cut back on his feed voluntarily as he always did when he sensed a race approaching, mentally on edge.

In the Fortria, Barry Geraghty adopted a slight change of tactics. Instead of keeping a tight hold, he let Moscow go to the lead—a risky move since Moscow, unchallenged, might become dreamy—but it helped the horse to settle. "More relaxed," the jockey said later. "Not so jazzed up." He could have been heeding the advice of Frederico Caprilli, an Italian trainer of jumpers, who urged riders to interfere with their mounts as little as possible. "The rider should be at pains to allow the horse to jump with his natural movements," Caprilli wrote. In other words, the horse knows best, a principle Geraghty was applying. Only at the last fence did he shake up Moscow, who sprouted wings and was gone in a flash.

For Jessie, the Fortria was a relief. "Now I'll be able to sleep at night," she confessed. She'd been restless about Moscow. After his win at the Festival, he unseated Geraghty at Punchestown in April. (Horses "unseat" their jockeys when they jump awkwardly, and the jockey can't stay in the saddle.) That was Moscow's first race after the Queen Mother, so the accident had wiped the slate clean after three straight wins. Now he had a win and two more to go before it would be crisis time. But he couldn't repeat the pattern, could he? Three wins and then a loss? Jessie didn't think so. He'd run twice more before the Festival, she said. Frankly, I was worried—and superstitious, big-time. Moscow reminded me of the old Brooklyn Dodgers, who often came so close to winning the World Series, and then . . .

THE OPEN MEETING would go ahead as scheduled, I heard when I got home. John Nicholson's watering program had done the trick. I had a few days to recuperate before taking off for Cheltenham and needed them. After my dark night of the racing soul, in that coffinlike room with the Evil Gun mowing 'em down, I almost lost my faith in the jumps, but the afternoon at Navan had restored it with the inspiring spectacle of Moscow Flyer sailing over fences. I felt as if I'd been treated to a Bach sonata after many dreary hours of Salieri and had remembered that music truly does have the power to move us. That was the thrill of watching a great horse put on a show.

The Irish would send about twenty horses to the Open. Tony Martin was the trainer to watch, I decided after looking at the stats. His record at the meeting was superb, even better than Martin Pipe's—and Pipe had twenty-three winners from ninety runners in the past five years, a strike rate of twenty-six percent. The tally for Tony Martin was nine out of thirty in the same period for a thirty percent rate. Last spring, his Xenophon had pulled off an upset in the Coral Cup, one of the Festival's toughest handicaps. He didn't do nearly as well in Ireland, but he knew how to produce a big run on the day.

Pipe was fond of the Open because of the money, a hefty purse for every race. He was pictured on the *Post*'s front page, grinning like a man about to devour a T-bone with his bare hands. The bookies would profit, too, none more so than Paddy Power Bookmakers, the sponsor of four races, including the Paddy Power Gold Cup Steeplechase. (There are probably more gold cups on mantles in England and Ireland than anywhere in the world, I'd come to believe.) The capital outlay was significant for the firm, but so was the publicity, another wedge in the Power group's attempt to crack the British market, virtually closed to the Irish for decades.

The first time I saw a distinctive, emerald green Paddy Power sign, I assumed the name was invented, a bit of clever wordplay. That would suit the company's outrageous way of operating, always tweaking the public about such touchy subjects as religion and sex. Power had recently raised a storm with a pair of controversial ads offensive to certain constituencies—the aim of the campaign, no doubt. One featured a pair of old women about to cross a busy street, and quoted the odds for and against their success. The other showed a teenage couple on a park bench. Would the boy get his hand under her sweater (2–1) or under her skirt (5–1)? Such exemplary bad taste had the clerics and do-gooders screaming.

But I discovered there is a real Paddy Power, the son of a company founder and now its public relations chief, who has the gift of gab and chatted amiably with me before I left for Cheltenham. That he had a sense of humor was hardly a revelation. Bookies are inclined to be sober fellows on the pitch, but fun is a key element in the Power agenda, even though they're the first bookmakers to be listed on the Dublin Stock Exchange. "We're about entertainment," Paddy said.

"We want to enhance the experience of watching a sporting event," hence the ultraclean shops and plasma TVs. "Our ads push it to the limit without going over it." That was the in-house opinion, anyway.

In effect, the creation of Paddy Power (the company) represents another act of Irish bravado in the face of an English threat. In the mid-1980s, when the tax on betting in Ireland, a source of government revenue—bettors pay three percent on every bet now—was cut roughly in half, such major British bookmakers as Ladbrokes, Coral, and Mecca saw it as an opportunity to expand *their* market abroad, using "supershops" as a draw. "You'd take those places for a kip these days," Paddy laughed, "but a lot of Irish bookies were still working out of a front room at home. They wouldn't give you a glass of water for free, much less a cup of tea."

Caught napping, the local bookies fought back, led by David Power, Paddy's father, who worked on-course, and his partners Stewart Kenny and John Corcoran. All three men owned betting shops and sold off a few for the cash to compete against the invaders, although they hung on to their most profitable offices. They incorporated as Paddy Power in 1988, with Kenny, a promotional genius, assigned to run the company. "Stewart wanted to be Mr. Bookmaking," Paddy said. "He'd take action on *anything.*" A bold innovator, Kenny instituted the ploy of special and novelty bets. On a special, say, a punter might get his money back if his horse is second to a winner, while the novelties concentrate on politics and pop culture. Not long ago, Kenny retired from the company to study psychotherapy, his interest in the subtleties of the human brain apparently undiminished.

"The novelties don't generate much income," Paddy went on, "but they attract attention. We still try to be innovative. That's an edge we have over Ladbrokes, the only English competitor left in Ireland. They're too big and unwieldy to make quick adjustments." As if in proof, Paddy Power's turnover was up forty-six percent in 2004, with a profit of about $25 million despite heavy losses at the Festival (too many favorites won) and on the Grand National when Monty's Pass took the race, backed by every patriotic granny and child from Munster to Leinster. Anything at Cheltenham is huge for the firm, including the Open. "The Irish bet with the heart, not the head," Paddy said, "and they love to beat the English."

AT THE BIRMINGHAM AIRPORT, I picked up a rental car and drove to the Cotswolds, described in my guidebook as "preposterously photogenic." The area had the same prim neatness I'd seen in County Down, though even more refined. I passed apple orchards, dairy farms, chubby Old Spot pigs, and lots of sheep, of course, because the hills were once the hub of the British wool trade. The surrounding towns, picturesque but dowdy, bore names from a Monty Python skit— Stow-on-the-Wold, Moreton-in-Marsh, Chipping Norton. Tourists mob the Cotswolds in summer to admire the thatched cottages and Norman churches, basking in a quaintly reductive version of English country life. It's where you send your visiting auntie when you need a break, an arch London friend had explained to me once.

All the hotels in central Cheltenham were booked, as expected. Scouting around for a place to stay, I noticed some signs nailed to trees and telephone poles, way up high where nobody could tear them down. 59% OF THE PUBLIC SAY KEEP HUNTING, the signs read, not what I'd call an overwhelming majority and good news for the foxes. After an hour or so, I found a room at the Beckford Inn—a real room, too, and not another coffin. The Inn even had a skittles alley, where Falstaffian good times could be enjoyed on a summer evening. The Fenns, late of Birmingham, operated *en famille* and served a *Racing Post* with breakfast. Down the road, in the hamlet of Beckford, burly farmers in rubber boots carried in boxes of fresh vegetables, carrots and leeks with dirt still clinging to their scraggly roots.

The Open Meeting ran for three days over a long weekend, and when I entered the racecourse on Friday, I felt a silly sense of accomplishment, as a small-town art lover does on reaching the Louvre at last. My arrival franked my credentials as a punter and a fan, I believed. The size of the complex was a revelation. From watching the races on TV, with shots of sheep grazing on the hillsides, I'd formed a bucolic image of Cheltenham, but tons of concrete covered the track's five hundred acres, and the place was as urban looking as Yankee Stadium. Inside, the atmosphere was commercial, too, with many little gift shops, restaurants, bars, and even a pharmacy, should your losses make you sick to your stomach.

Though it was only noon, with the first race two hours away, the track was already humming. The crowd was unlike any I'd seen before. So many people were wearing tweed outfits that I wondered if those grazing sheep were being sheared on an assembly line nearby to feed an insatiable desire for the stuff. The folks were dressed almost identically, with a degree of conformity I hadn't observed since the 1950s, when the Man in the Gray Flannel Suit (not tweed) typified such conservative behavior. The silver-haired gents and fur-hatted ladies were genteel and sociable and gave off a distinct whiff of Old Money. Exquisite air kisses floated around like butterflies. Only when I learned that it was Countryside Alliance Day did I understand the House of Windsor fashion show.

The group had a booth on the grounds, where members were distributing literature in support of the hunt and a "rural way of life." As protection against the drizzly cold, I bought a baseball cap with LIBERTY & LIVELIHOOD stitched across the crown, apparently the Alliance's rallying cry. After trying but failing to be entertained by the Worcestershire Gun Dogs, who were dashing around in the paddock, I heard some distant music filtering up from the Cavern Bar, a dark, subterranean space, where a five-piece combo was coaxing the audience to sing along on "The Wild Rover." The Cavern, it seemed, was an unofficial meeting point for the Irish. Lads from Cavan or Mayo descended into the pit, blinked until their eyes adjusted, and lit up when they found the person they were seeking. "Finally! Finally!" cried one overjoyed fellow, hugging his long-lost pal. For an Irishman in England, there's no more comforting sight than another Irishman, especially from the home county.

I had no urgent need to sing along, either, so I went to the rail to check the going, designated as "good to firm (good in places)," rather deceptive as it happened. The jockeys later reported that the watered ground was slippery, and it got worse when the drizzle turned to rain. A stiff headwind was also blowing, and that sapped the horses' energy and nearly blew away my new cap. In fact, I blamed the wind for the poor showing of Dermot Weld's Lowlander, my bet in the second race. Though Lowlander was unbeaten in three starts over hurdles in Ireland, the horse came in next to last and cost me thirty dollars. Well, no matter, I thought. The Tony Martin factor was about to kick in.

The third race was a marathon four-mile chase. Martin's Royal County Buck had never gone that far, but neither had the other entries, so I put a hundred on him at 2–1. At the start, Uncle Mick and Rufius, two lesser lights, sprinted to a twenty-length lead, but four-mile chases do not reward such speed, and they both ran out of gas. Soon we had a duel between Ceanannas Mor and my Bucko, who smacked a fence two out and never recovered. Martin was dismayed and said he wished it hadn't rained, because Royal County Buck liked fast ground, a point I'd missed while studying the percentages. *The going is the most important thing.* I remembered J. P. McManus's advice, too late to do any good.

ON SATURDAY, Paddy Power was everywhere. His corporeal self was up in a sky box with the high rollers, while down below, in the modest territory I patrolled, the company's logo and banners were a splash of Ireland's green impossible to miss. Inside the race program were some prominent ads that posed a question I'd never thought to ask, "How does Paddy Power keep its customers so happy?" After a close reading of the text, I had my answer: Paddy Power takes risks, just as its customers do, so Paddy Power understands what it's like to be a customer! The logic was so irrefutable I suspected Paddy had a few former Jesuits on the payroll.

Yesterday's rain had softened the turf. The going was now "good (good to firm in places)," a plus for the Irish. I took out my betting book, a nifty little journal from Smythson of Bond Street, to check my accounts. The book (BETTING BOOK is stamped in gilt on the red leather cover) has five columns for recording wagers, labeled "horse," "bet with" (for the bookie's name), "odds," "win," and "lose." Even after the Bucko fiasco, I'd dragged myself up from the pit and was only down fifty dollars, so I believed I could do much better today, optimism being a disease easily contracted at the track. I avoided the first race, though, a steeplechase for four horses that shaped up as a rematch between Martin Pipe's Puntal and Brother Joe, stabled with the English trainer Phillip Hobbs.

The pair had met the week before at Chepstow, in Wales, where Brother Joe won by about thirty lengths. They would both carry the same amount of weight at Cheltenham, so I couldn't imagine a different result, nor could the fans, who sent off Brother Joe at even money. He and Puntal were locked together from the start and soon left the other horses far behind. While Puntal was traveling nicely, Brother Joe labored to stay close. It was like watching a man lift bags of cement. Each stride was another bag and extracted a further price. Toward home, Brother Joe hit four straight fences before falling, and that left Puntal in the clear. The fall was a very bad one. With a fractured shoulder, and in grave distress, Brother Joe had to be put down.

Whenever a horse dies in action, a chorus of naysayers can be counted on to criticize the "brutality" of the jumps game. This time it was Laura Thompson in the *Observer*. "Hideous cold thud to the heart when yet another beautiful horse crashes to the turf in a heap," wrote Thompson, "and the green screens go up to shield us from the sight—but not the fact—of death. That, in essence, is National Hunt racing." In essence? I found this hard to swallow. Never had I been around people who cared so much about their horses, and yet when I looked more closely at Brother Joe's record, I did see a cause for concern.

The horse had run an unlucky thirteen times that year, a huge number of races for a quality jumper. After finishing eighth in the Stayers' Hurdle at the Festival, he moved on to fences and won seven of eight chases from May through October. He never had more than a month off, although the year before he'd been allowed a five-month summer break. Unlike most chasers, though, Brother Joe was at his best on relatively fast ground, and the dry spell was a gift to him. He thrived on the conditions other horses hated, so he kept competing. But Cheltenham's fences are notoriously stiff, and a horse who isn't a handy jumper—Brother Joe wasn't—is liable to falter. If a horse is tired, the test becomes harder, and Brother Joe had every right to be tired. Had Hobbs and his connections made a bad decision? Or was it just bad luck? No one could say for certain.

A death at the track takes your breath away, but the Irish regained some color in their cheeks when they finally had a winner in the next race—Al Eile from John Queally's small, ten-stall yard in County Waterford. Al Eile had almost missed his appointment with destiny. The horse was supposed to leave Ireland by ferry on Thursday, but the sea was too rough, so he went home to Coolagh, a round-trip of almost three hundred miles, and returned to the ferry dock on Friday, only reaching Cheltenham at five in the morning on the day of his run.

The win was a feather in Queally's cap, but his horse's cover was blown, and he worried that Al Eile's owner might sell now. Small trainers have that problem. "All I can do is hope," he said.

Still, what a miracle! That an Irish horse should overcome adversity to bag a win against the English! Wasn't it grand? To judge by the celebrating, you'd guess that every Irishman had backed Al Eile, and maybe they did for all I knew. How else to account for the commotion? They spilled from the grandstand, wrestled free of the betting ring, and even surfaced from the dank recesses of the Cavern Bar to cluster around Jim Culloty, the jockey, and fondly pat Al Eile, whooping and thrusting their fists into the air, bursting into bizarre little jigs and booze-fueled arias, all invested in a wildly overstimulated group mania that might have been frightening if so much happiness weren't at its core.

With Al Eile's victory, the fans had bought back a measure of good cheer, so they were excited about the Paddy Power Gold Cup now. Risk Accessor, the only Irish-trained horse in the race, was bound to improve after his run at Thurles, too—a prep to sharpen him up, really, plus he had Timmy Murphy, the comeback kid, in the saddle. It's a fair bet that Murphy is the only jockey to ever do time at Wormwood Scrubs, a dump of a London prison. Not long ago, he had succumbed to the pressures of the rider's life, a hectic one that barely allows for a half-second of contemplation. If a rider is in demand, he spends the morning on the gallops. The racing day goes by in a blur, and the evening is merely about getting ready for tomorrow. It's a difficult balancing act, especially for the young.

Like most Irish jockeys, Murphy was almost born on a horse. His dad was a groom in Kildare, and Timmy started riding at seven or eight. He was an apprentice to Michael Halford first, and next to Michael Hourigan, a hard taskmaster who doesn't tolerate any monkey business. Being ambitious, Murphy left Hourigan to accept a job as stable jockey to Kim Bailey in England, but already the stress was affecting him. He was impatient and wanted to ride fifty winners his first season, so he tended to punish his horses, heavy on the whip. He asked too much of them and landed a number of suspensions.

By all accounts, Murphy is the politest of men, but also quite shy, and he slipped into the shy person's trap of drinking to help him relax and communicate. After a losing ride on Cenkos in the Nakayama Gold Cup in Japan in 2002, he began pounding down screwdrivers before his flight and got drunker on the plane, bothering the other passengers, groping a woman flight attendant, and peeing in the aisle—totally blasted, and totally out of character. He was arrested at Heathrow Airport and sentenced that July, his six months at Worm-wood Scrubs ultimately reduced to three. Not everyone would hire him after his release, but Hourigan gave him a second chance, and Murphy was back on top again, with Beef Or Salmon one of his plum rides.

In the betting ring, Risk Accessor was available at very tempting odds. As I squeezed through the crush, I saw that most bookies narrowly favored Fondmort, whose trainer Nicky Henderson is one of England's best, over Poliantis (Paul Nicholls) and It Takes Time (Martin Pipe), because the handicapper had treated Fondmort well. He would carry thirteen pounds less than the top weight Cyfor Malta (Pipe again), but Poliantis had beaten Fondmort at Cheltenham in April. Poliantis had a nine-pound advantage then, while today Fondmort was two pounds lighter. That was more math than I could handle, so I closed my eyes and bet fifty to win on Fondmort.

The race lived up to its billing. Ei Ei, a relentless front-runner, led the field away from the stands and through the first circuit of the track—the horses would go around twice—while Cyfor Malta sunk under all those pounds. Poliantis breezed past Ei Ei four fences out and seemed poised to pounce under Ruby Walsh. Risk Accessor, initially held up, was tracking the leaders as they came to the second-last, a tricky fence on a downhill slope. Horses accelerate as they approach it, and often misjudge the jump. Risk Accessor did just that, as did It Takes Time. They jumped the fence in tandem and collided, and down went Murphy and Tony McCoy.

At the same fence, Fondmort made his move. His springy leap shot him ahead of Poliantis, and there were five lengths between him and the other horses at the last fence. The result was never in doubt, but the drama wasn't over. After being pulled up past the finish, Poliantis staggered a little, as if his legs were jelly and couldn't support him. He was wobbly and dizzy looking. Walsh figured the horse must be feeling the effect of his strenuous effort, so he dismounted. The vets were called, and while they were administering some oxygen, Poliantis keeled over and collapsed, dead of a heart attack at the age of six. It was another blow for Nicholls, who'd had a devastating season so far. "I didn't think it could get any worse," he told the press, a gloomy statement that said it all.

LUCK IS A FREE-FLOATING THING, landing randomly and then departing, and Ruby Walsh wasn't having any at the Open. Every jockey understands the syndrome because it reflects the quicksilver nature of the trade. Despite their competitive nature, the Irish riders remain a close-knit fraternity wherever they're based. It isn't uncommon to see Walsh, Geraghty, and Carberry sharing a meal when they're camped at the same hotel for a festival. They may play golf or go on holidays together in the Caribbean. Walsh even bunks at Tony McCoy's house in Oxfordshire, a palatial spread with a framed flag from the eighteenth hole at St. Andrews pinned up over the fireplace. The flag is signed by Tiger Woods, an idol of McCoy's.

Ruby is a corruption of *Rupert*, Walsh's grandfather's name. It suits him, since there is a jewel-like quality to his riding. He has an exquisite sense of pace, knowing exactly how much energy his horse has left at any point. Preferring to take his time and creep through the field, he'll hook the leaders over the last few furlongs. His father, Ted, tutored him well, having been a good amateur jockey himself. I once asked Willie Mullins why Ruby stood out, and he replied, "Good racing brain," meaning the skill to read a race and predict how it will develop. He also raved about Ruby's physical strength and his determination. Add to that a bright smile and a distinctive patch of graying hair, and you had the makings of a star.

On Sunday, it looked as if Walsh would stay unlucky. He lost his first ride on Mr. Ed, producing the horse too late, a rare mistake. Probably Ruby kicked himself all the way to the weighing room, but in the next race he guided Thisthatandtother, a name to plague any race caller, to an easy win for the beleaguered Nicholls, his boss. Yet he truly earned his keep in the Greatwood Hurdle on Rigmarole, the top weight. The pundits in the *Post* roundly dismissed the horse, all but handing the race to Hasty Prince. Once more Walsh played a stalking game, only releasing the brakes four out and swiftly advancing. The pace was too much for Hasty Prince, and Rigmarole won in a driving finish.

Along with meals and holidays, jockeys share information, and Ruby Walsh gave Barry Connell a tip that helped Connell guide The Posh Paddy to victory in the Open Bumper, the meeting's last race. Of all the Irish amateurs on earth, Connell is the most unlikely, being a wealthy Dublin hedge-fund manager in real life. He has an awkward style, mainly because he didn't learn to ride as a child but rather in his mid-thirties when he began to buy horses. (He's forty-four now.) That's why he was on The Posh Paddy—he owned the horse and called the shots. "It's a disease," he once said to me about riding, although not one he hoped to be cured of any time soon.

From Walsh, Connell heard that the track was poached dry inside, watering or no watering. Ruby's advice was to keep wide for the better going down the back of the course, then swing over to the stand rail when he hit the stretch. Connell did exactly that and forced Richard Johnson, an old pro, to the outside on Alpine Fox, a move that surely won him the race. Barry's adrenaline high was memorable. "I was just delighted," he told me, still enthusiastic days afterward. "I kept thinking, 'What a bloody good horse!' And the cheering along the rail, the way they applauded me!" Here was every amateur's dream fulfilled.

Driving back to Birmingham for my flight home, I felt worn out from the intensity and the action of the Open. As much as I had enjoyed the wonderful racing, I missed the intimacy of the Irish scene. On the taxi ride to Dublin, I stared out at the city, so understated and village-like, and realized how attached I'd become to certain aspects of Irish life that had seemed curious at first, from the scurrying mail carriers to the gently indirect pattern of speech ("Could you not? Do you not? Would you not?") to the Irish School of Motoring with its claim that ninety percent of its clients pass the state exam, a statistic any American firm would bump up to ninety-nine percent, whether or not it was accurate.

I asked the taxi driver to drop me at the Merrion Hotel, a grand Georgian town house, where I was meeting Imelda for a late drink. This was our favorite place for an interlude away from the family, its public rooms hung with paintings by the Irish masters and peat fires burning in all the fireplaces at the slightest hint of a chill. With its old-fashioned charm, the hotel allowed us to imagine we were swells stopping for a spot of something before rounding the corner to visit Yeats or George Russell, who both had lived on Merrion Square for a time, possibly for a session at the Ouija board or a fevered discussion of the role of fairies in the Celtic Twilight. In other words, it felt good to be back. For a moment, the horses seemed far away, but only for a moment.

THE GREAT UNVEILING CONTINUED. Beef Or Salmon and Best Mate were finally coming out from under wraps, the first in the Oil Chase at Clonmel and the second in the Peterborough Chase at Huntingdon Racecourse, in East Anglia. To add some spice to the mix, Henrietta Knight was sending Edredon Bleu to Clonmel, an intriguing gambit since she rarely ran her horses in Ireland. The Oil Chase, at two and a half miles, might prove a trifle short for Beef Or Salmon, who was best at the Gold Cup distance of three-plus miles—although he had won the race once before—but the trip was ideal for Edredon Bleu and the pot was a good one, worth about forty-five thousand dollars.

So I was on the road again before I knew it, driving south past Carlow and Kilkenny to Clonmel, a lovely town at the foot of the Comeragh Mountains, in the valley of the River Suir. The streets were alive with people going to the races, because in Ireland a meeting is a special event—a carnival, a break from routine. Nowhere did I witness the air of drudgery that hovers over most American tracks, where the regular customers could be punching a clock at a factory they hated. Gambling makes the wheels go round in the land of the free, and though the Irish like a flutter, too, the horse is still at the center of things. Many folks would attend today simply for a chance to see (and later brag that they'd seen) Beef Or Salmon in the flesh.

Clonmel was really hopping. I felt sorry for the poor schoolkids in uniform lingering on the main street, who'd be faced with an uncool session of math or science after lunch instead of a trip to the track. They plucked at bags of potato chips and looked forlorn, denied a chance to join the record crowd of more than five thousand at Powerstown Park, the site of the course, where one Villiers Morton Jackson, an entrepreneur of the first order, built a grandstand in 1913, roped off the bookies in a special area, hired detectives to foil the pickpockets, and charged an admission fee of two shillings.

Despite Edredon Bleu's glorious campaign that autumn, the loyal Irish fans made Beef Or Salmon their choice. The two horses were in sharp contrast on parade, with Beef Or Salmon still gawky and adolescent, laid-back and pleasantly distracted by all the attention, while Edredon Bleu had the razor-sharp aura of a Realtor about to close a deal on a dynamite piece of property. And what a strange history the old fellow had! Only recently had I discovered that he'd won five times as a four-year-old novice in France, where a butcher was his trainer. It was awful to imagine what might have happened to him if he hadn't done so well.

Edredon Bleu was accustomed to the lead, but he didn't get it at Clonmel. The Premier Cat, a course specialist, stuck his head in front. That frustrated Knight's horse, who began pulling so hard that Jim Culloty had to rein him in. Beef Or Salmon, on the other hand, appeared to be daydreaming. He sauntered along at his own dawdling pace and jumped indifferently, without any verve. Timmy Murphy didn't push him, either, content to let the horse idle. His backers groaned and cursed as they pictured their money going up in smoke, but Beef Or Salmon fooled us by hitting his stride with three fences left. He seemed to find a purchase on the ground and gained momentum as rapidly as a ball rolling down a steep hill, and he might even have defeated Edredon Bleu if he hadn't botched the last fence and stumbled on landing, third in the end behind Arctic Copper.

After the race, Michael Hourigan was his usual peppy self and declared that he wasn't the least bit unhappy with the performance. Sure, Beef Or Salmon's jumping was a little "sticky," but this was the horse's first outing of the season. That shotgun burst of speed down the stretch hadn't escaped the bookies' notice, though, and they lowered Beef Or Salmon's ante-post odds for the Gold Cup to 8–1. (Ante-post wagers can be made weeks and even months before a race. The odds are usually far more generous than you'll get on the day, but if your horse is scratched or injured and doesn't run, you lose your bet. In effect, you're dealing in futures.) For Knight, the journey across the water was sheer bliss. Edredon Bleu was her first-ever winner in Ireland. He would be given a long break after his three courageous wins and would return to the track in the spring, she said—a plan she soon altered when a new opportunity presented itself.

In my room at the Fennessy Hotel in Clonmel, after a session of traditional music at Kitty O'Donnell's, I stayed up late reading Knight's *Best Mate: Chasing Gold*, a book that revealed as much about the author as it did about her famous horse. In some respects, Knight's childhood echoed Jessie Harrington's. Her father was a military man, too, and finished his career as a major in the Coldstream Guards, after which he turned to farming like Brigadier Fowler and kept horses, although he wasn't crazy about them and discouraged his daughter's fascination with ponies. Henrietta's favorite was a Shetland called Florian, who was "almost human" and had a bit part in the 1960 British film *Follow That Horse*.

As a girl, Henrietta showed an early interest in training. She entered her huge black donkey, Sheba, in the East Hendred Donkey Derby, riding him bareback across the fields in preparation. After high school, she bought Borderline, her first Thoroughbred, in 1964 for about a thousand dollars, plucking him from the advertising pages of *Horse & Hound*. She became a skilled eventer, but her parents wanted to introduce her to a broader social scene, so she was sent to London to meet eligible young men and join the debutante world. "Many of the parties were held in beautiful places," she wrote, sounding a Jane Austen note, "and even though I didn't enjoy them all, it was most educational, and I loved the food." Only years later did she meet her Prince Charming in the person of Terry Biddlecombe.

Subsequently, she enrolled in college to be a teacher of history and biology, and did her practice work in the rowdier districts of Oxford, where her pupils once locked her in a book cupboard for nearly an hour ("It was a claustrophobic experience . . .") and set booby traps to give her electric shocks. But horses were still her passion, and she opened a livery business in 1974 and progressed from there, taking out a National Hunt trainer's license in 1989. When Best Mate reached her ten years later, she was well established and had made many scouting trips to Ireland to look for racing stock, frequently in County Cork.

Yet it was in Kildare that she and Biddlecombe first saw Un Desperado, Best Mate's sire, a French-bred standing at Old Meadow Stud. That was in 1997, and they were infatuated with the stallion—big, proud, powerful, with superb conformation—and with his excellent record on the flat, agreeing that they'd love to have a horse he'd sired. Here Tom Costello entered her tale, and my ears perked up. Costello had bought Best Mate as a foal at a Fairyhouse sale in 1995, because he liked Best Mate's breeding—by Un Desperado out of Katday, a broodmare who later produced three other top-notch horses—and his "loose, easy walk." He paid about five thousand dollars after a brief but spirited round of bidding and turned over the foal to his son Tom Jr. to be broken.

Best Mate's life had been tough until then. He was only a month old when Jacques Van't Hart, the Dutchman who bred him, dispatched him and Katday to Old Meadow Stud for a stay, while Van't Hart was in Holland on business. The foal was so skinny and weird looking, having lost most of its hair from lying on wet ground, the stable lads nicknamed him Gonzo. They wondered if Gonzo would live or die, but as they nursed him on buckets of milk, his health improved. He was still undersized when he arrived at Costello's yard, so small and light most people could lift him up with one arm, but Tom

Jr. approved of his stride, his sound front legs, and "the nice head on him."

He was fit and in good health when the Costellos dropped him into a point-to-point steeplechase at Lismore in County Waterford, in February 1999. (Point-to-points are races for amateur riders, conducted on an improvised or temporary circuit in open country, from one point to another.) Often owners use such races as a showcase when they're ready to sell. Best Mate didn't win, but Knight, who was present, thought he jumped well and asked about buying him. Costello put her off until Best Mate had won, then let Knight and Biddlecombe examine the horse more closely. When they were satisfied, they suggested to Jim Lewis, who owns Edredon Bleu, that he make a purchase. Lewis negotiated with Costello, but the price he paid has never been disclosed because Costello, ever private, would never disclose it.

THE SATURDAY OF THE PETERBOROUGH CHASE began auspiciously, when the heavens opened and delivered a storm of biblical proportions. Most of Ireland was soaked and flooded, as were East Anglia and Huntingdon Racecourse. The rain came down hard and fast and foreclosed any lingering concerns about firm ground. At O'Herlihy's, the lads were clustered around the two gas fires, warming their hands and feet and shouting for hot port and brandy. Some customers had arrived early for the World Cup rugby final between England and Australia, and though they'd already endured a nail-biting match, they wouldn't budge till they'd watched Best Mate's first run in 254 days.

Knight had coddled her horse with infinite care, even dishing out his evening oats herself. After the Gold Cup, Best Mate had a two-month vacation on the grass, but in August he resumed the long, steady canters that build up the muscles needed for galloping and jumping. He also received a regular tutorial in dressage for variety's sake. A week before the Peterborough, he worked a mile or so up a hill and later spent time with Jim Culloty, who schooled him over fences. In between, he and Edredon Bleu, his bosom pal, grazed together in a field, wearing their horse blankets and looking like "two Little Red Riding Hoods," according to Ms. Knight. Her mother, I remembered, had written cute children's stories about animals.

Television is a deceptive medium, but I thought Best Mate looked even bigger and more rugged than Moscow Flyer, unsurpassable, with an attitude of utter authority. He met the criteria Irish folkore once held to be essential in a prize horse: three traits of a bull (a bold walk, strong neck, and hard forehead); three of a hare (a bright eye, lively ear, and swift run); and three of a woman (a broad breast, slender waist, and short back). Only two of his five opponents had honest claims, Valley Henry and Jair du Cochet, a French horse. I'd lost money on Valley Henry before, though, so I gave him a wide berth.

Jair du Cochet was more appealing. He might be the Big Bad Wolf to Best Mate's Little Red Riding Hood, I believed. Guillaume Macaire, his trainer, swore that his horse had no chance in the Gold Cup—not at Cheltenham, a course Best Mate owned—but at Huntingdon in the mud anything was possible. In an act of Gallic solidarity, Macaire chose to retain Jacques Ricou as his jockey, even though Ricou had been mocked in the English press last spring when he appeared to move too slowly on Jair du Cochet in a big race at the Festival, probably costing him the win.

The start of the Peterborough was very curious. As the tapes went up, the horses hesitated, as if they were stuck in a bog. When they did take off, they resembled infantry soldiers on a forced march. The pace was extraordinarily slow, but Ricou kept Jair du Cochet close to it rather than letting the horse lag behind, as he'd done at Cheltenham. Best Mate simply didn't respond. True, the ground wasn't to his liking, but his jumping, always precise, was very rusty. He blundered four fences out and never got on terms with Jair du Cochet. It was as though he were being deliberately cantankerous, upset with the difficult circumstances and unwilling to rise above them. It occurred to me that maybe Knight had babied him too much.

As usual, Henrietta hid her eyes during the race, but her husband later described it to her as "messy." Being a good sport, she didn't bother with excuses for Best Mate, although she could have. The bottomless ground was a horror; the distance of two and a half miles was short of the horse's ideal trip; and the pace was a full seventeen seconds slower than last year's race. Instead, Knight congratulated Macaire and confessed she had $150 to win on Jair du Cochet. She always backs the horses who might beat Best Mate, as if to put a hex on them, but the trick had failed her this time. As for the emotional Ricou, he shed a few tears of joy, his dignity restored before the dastardly English.

What did the future hold for Best Mate? Those at O'Herlihy's were of two minds. It would be silly to judge a great horse by a single dull run, T. P. Reilly felt. He cited some past champions who'd recovered after a lackluster debut, but it was also a fact that Best Mate had always won the first time out before. Moreover, he'd won on soft ground, too—not as mucky as Huntingdon, perhaps, but still testing. What concerned me most was his jumping, not nearly as fluid as usual. I wondered about his attitude, too. Had he been overly pampered, spoiled in the way of an egotistical movie star? When I recalled Beef Or Salmon's turn-of-foot at Clonmel, I thought it might still be possible for Hourigan and the Irish to steal the Gold Cup.

RAIN, GLORIOUS RAIN. All the trainers I knew were dancing around like Gene Kelly, able to implement their plans at last. Toward the end of November, the Irish sent six horses to the Hennessy Gold Cup at

Newbury in England, where the chief attraction was Strong Flow, Paul Nicholls's six-year-old novice chaser. "One of the best I've ever trained," said Nicholls, although Strong Flow was prone to mistakes. He fell in his first race of the season, but he recovered in a low-grade chase at the equally low-grade Newton Abbot track. I had watched the race at Boylesports and marveled at his ability. His entire being went into his jumps, every fiber of his body stretched to its elastic limit when he got it right.

He didn't get it right at Newbury, not immediately. He belted the ninth fence so hard his tail nearly sailed over his head. The fearless Ruby Walsh held on for dear life and later said the blunder was actually a help. Strong Flow calmed down and began to focus. From then on, the horse was in command and became the first novice to win the Hennessy in its forty-seven-year history, posing a question for Nicholls. Should he try Strong Flow in the Gold Cup, or wait for him to mature? Mill House, a similarly gifted six-year-old, had won the Gold Cup in 1963, but the next year he ran smack into a wall called Arkle, giving Nicholls some food for thought.

The following day, I went to Fairyhouse Racecourse to see Solerina, everybody's fancy in the Hatton's Grace Hurdle. Even I had a crush on the game little mare. She was a fluke, a case of lightning striking twice for the Bowes of Tipperary. They really were humble farmers, a father and sons who bred their own horses, often from cheap stock, and raced them under a permit held by James Bowe, the patriarch. He was primarily responsible for Limestone Lad, a heroic stayer, who had won the Hatton's Grace three times and could lay claim to beating Istabraq fair and square.

Solerina had a storybook background. Michael Bowe bought Deep Peace, her dam, for a pittance, but he still had high hopes because he'd long admired the bloodline. Her second foal was Solerina—a runty thing, a terrible disappointment. "I don't know what she is, but she's not a racehorse," Michael complained to his brother John. Her sire, Toulon, had won the St. Leger, a classic English flat race, so with that as bait, Michael tried to sell her by placing an ad in *The Irish Field.* There were no takers until John, who liked Toulon, made an offer. His mother had encouraged him to bid, yet another example of the intricacies of family life in the Irish countryside.

Even if Solerina never won a race, John thought she'd be a decent broodmare. At home, she was bored and showed nothing, but when Michael (now her trainer) brought her to the track, she blossomed and quickly ascended from bumpers to Grade One contests. She had a stall next to Limestone Lad, who was laid up with a bad tendon, and John told the *Field* that the old guy must be coaching the little mare, a trope to warm Henrietta Knight's heart. At Fairyhouse, Solerina swept the Hatton's Grace with her usual panache, bowling along in front and moving a step closer to a trip to the Cheltenham Festival for the Stayers' Hurdle.

THE TEMPTATION TO PLACE an ante-post bet on the Gold Cup was growing in me. Often at night, in the drifty moments before sleep, I went over the key races I'd seen and picked holes in the contenders. I agreed with Reilly that you couldn't write off Best Mate yet, but his jumping still bugged me, as did his light schedule—he'd have only one more race before Cheltenham. Strong Flow could be scary good, but also scary bad. As for Kingscliff, who was sneaking into the picture after winning a big chase at Ascot, I needed to know more before I could commit, but Beef Or Salmon . . . well, he had looked like the winged god Mercury at Clonmel, so I figured I should visit Michael Hourigan in Limerick and sound him out, never once giving a thought to Harbour Pilot, the darkest of dark horses.

DECEMBER

Glory Days

The perfection of a late-autumn morning at Lisaleen Stables in Patrickswell, County Limerick—trees blown free of their leaves except for a last few still clinging to the branches, the golds gone to umber now, a light frost on the grass, magpies squawking and sparrows chirping, and the *clip-clop* of horses returning to the barns after a gallop. I took a bracing belt of fresh air and felt the cottony dullness in my brain begin to lift. Creeping along a lane came Michael Hourigan in his SUV, fresh (or semifresh) from a tour of his yard. His window was open despite the cold, and his eyes were less bright and engaged than usual as he jumped down from the driver's seat in his rubber boots.

"What time did you get home last night, Michael?" I asked him.

A dour look. "A quarter past," he said.

"Past what?"

"I don't know."

Hourigan and I had attended a public forum at the Dunraven Arms Hotel in nearby Adare the evening before. I went out of curiosity, while Michael was dispatching a duty. The event, sponsored by Horse Racing Ireland (HRI), a government body that funds and administers the sport, was an attempt to get some feedback from the fans, and it drew a large, vocal, opinionated group. To orchestrate their comments,

HRI had enlisted Brian Gleeson, a racing analyst on Irish TV, who has the earnest, pink-cheeked face of a choirboy. Gleeson performed the job with an Oprah-like aplomb and passed a cordless mike to a senior citizen, who fired the opening salvo and griped about having to pay so much to go to the races at Listowel. "And I'm Listowel born and bred!" he said bitterly, yearning for a discount he'd never get, not in a million years.

His contribution set the tone. Ticket prices were too high (about twenty dollars on an average race day, more for major festivals); the food was bad and the drinks expensive; and the amenities were few. "There isn't even a seat to sit on if you bring a lady or a girlfriend," another man said, implying that a girlfriend couldn't, or shouldn't, be a lady. All this amounted to pie-in-the-skyism, I thought, since it was an unwritten law of the universe that every racetrack, like every airport and ballpark, screws the patron. You might as well bitch about having a nose.

Toward the end of the evening, Gleeson nailed Hourigan, who was trying to sneak out a little early. "Don't you go anywhere, Michael Hourigan!" he cried. "Not until I ask you about Beef Or Salmon."

"The horse is grand," Hourigan said, as noncommital as ever.

"Were you satisfied with his run at Clonmel?"

Hourigan confessed some unease. "I kept wondering, 'Who's asleep? Timmy or the horse?'" But he assured Gleeson that Beef Or Salmon was fit and healthy, although he noted that his horse would have to jump "quicker" to win the John Durkan Chase at Punchestown, his next big engagement.

After Gleeson's closing remarks, we joined a mad stampede for the hotel bar. Such formal proceedings foster a terrible thirst in people, and everyone was delighted to ditch the constructive criticism and talk about races and gambling. The Irish hate to say good night, so when I heard the first few bars of off-key singing, a sign that the session was gathering steam, I went to bed. It was about one o'clock, but Michael was going strong and kept at it until the last revelers straggled out, just before dawn. Now his nose was snuffly, and his stomach was grumbling. "I'm still fairly full of drink," he muttered, leading me into his kitchen so we could warm ourselves by the stove.

Hourigan has the self-made man's outsized and justifiable pride. His yard, just shy of a hundred acres, was raw land with only a run-down cottage on it when he bought it in 1985. "Nobody had lived in that cottage for fourteen years. Two rooms up and two rooms down, go bump your head! Anything you see here, we've done," he said of his spacious, commodious home. "The price was about a hundred thousand dollars. I had the ten thousand for a down payment, but no idea where I'd get the rest. For a time, I thought about backing out of the deal. I had cold feet, like a fella about to be married. Jaysus, where am I going to find a hundred grand? That's what I kept asking myself. I hadn't a clue!

"You know who saved me? Jerry O'Connell!" He slapped the kitchen table for emphasis. "He's a bank manager and my best friend. He saw to the loan, all right. He gave me a chance and authorized my overdrafts. Let me tell you something, I'm a big spender! If I make five thousand selling a horse, I'll spend twenty. If you come to me to buy a horse and decide against it, I'll spend your money anyway!" His eyes were merry again, the previous night's pints burning off like fog. "My overdraft *never* drops below fifty grand. I was laid up in bed one time with a bad back, and Jerry called to ask after me and said to my wife, 'Nothing wrong with his hand, though, is there, Anne? He's still writing those feckin' checks!' "

Soon to be fifty-six, Hourigan was on a roll and began reflecting on his past. He is the last of four children; two others had died at birth. He rued the loss of his father, a cattle dealer and notorious carouser, who dropped dead suddenly at sixty-seven. "It was like the end of the world," he said sadly. "So unexpected! He never saw me train a winner. I still regret it. When I was fifteen, sixteen, I was a thick fucker and thought my father was stupid. But he wasn't. Ah, well, every kid thinks his father's stupid at that age." He cut thick slices of brown bread, slathered them with butter and strawberry jam, and ate hungrily, the crumbs cascading down his chin. "I was small as a child and a young man," he said, meaning slight, "and I was not very good at school. Would you believe I couldn't read or write when I was thirteen?"

"Amazing," I said. I was on the edge of my seat, in the grip of his tale.

"My parents sent me to Rockwell College, to the holy fathers, and when I completed my schooling on the seventeenth of June 1962, I joined Charlie Weld as a stable lad on the Curragh on the seventeenth of August. I was fourteen years and eight months old, and the ideal size for a jockey. I could do a hundred pounds easily, but I was just terrible. Terrible! Why? Because I was a *big* coward. In all my time as a jockey, I rode just nine winners on the flat and four over jumps. The last was Ballybar at Cork in a novice chase, and the crowd cheered for me. They must have been in shock!" He buttered another slice of bread, his fourth, and sent more crumbs to flying. I got a kick out of this Hourigan, who gobbled up life in appreciative bites.

"My family owned a grocery store and bar," he went on, "and when I took it over, I changed the name from Hourigan's to the Horse and Jockey Pub. That's when I started training, but I didn't have a winner for six years. Six years! And when I did win, wouldn't you know it was on St. Patrick's Day? That was in 1979. The problem was, I was always selling off my horses. I used to pray I'd have a five-year-old someday, because the three-year-olds were gone before they were four. I had to make ends meet, you see." The bar catered to travelers, an itinerant band formerly known as tinkers, or tinsmiths, and they were good customers, although boisterous. They sucked Michael into poker games and betting on horses and dogs. "Gambling!" he shouted, as if I'd stuck his hand in a flame. "I tried it, all right, but I was a bad man for it. Put your money where your mouth is, and you'll lose your money."

Over time, Hourigan began to have some winners, but his fortunes really improved when he bought Dorans Pride, known as Padjo around the stable, and sold the horse to Tom Doran. Dorans Pride won twenty-six of his sixty-one races, among them the Hatton's Grace, the Irish Hennessy, and the Stayers' Hurdle at Cheltenham, and also placed twice in the Gold Cup, but his life ended in tragedy when Hourigan brought him out of retirement at the age of fourteen, well into his fifties on the human scale of aging, to compete in the Festival again. In the Christie's Foxhunter Chase, he fell at the second fence, broke a leg, and had to be destroyed. This was still a sore point for Michael, who was accused of neglect and worse in some quarters.

"Nobody knew Dorans Pride better than I did," he asserted in his own defense. "He was restless at pasture and deserved one more chance. He wasn't happy doing nothing, that's for certain. Well, I've been lucky, anyway, haven't I? Better trainers than me never had a horse like Dorans Pride."

All the while we talked, I tried to steer Hourigan toward Beef Or Salmon, foolishly seeking the sort of inside information I distrusted, but when he wasn't regaling me with stories, he was fielding calls on his cell phone. "No, no I got knocked off my pedestal," he corrected one caller. "Noel Meade's in front now." Meade had just overtaken him to rank first among Irish trainers in terms of money earned. Actually, I was mystified that Michael did so well, since his strike rate hovers around ten percent and dips even lower at large tracks. At Punchestown, for instance, he'd had only three winners in 116 runs since 1999.

The reason for such discouraging figures, I learned, is that Hourigan uses races as a training tool. He knows a quality horse from day one, he said, but with most others it's a matter of finding the right level, something he can only do by trial and error. That's part of it, at least. The other part is that he still trains some nags, a job that requires tact. "You can't say to an owner, 'Your horse is no good,' because he won't believe it," he explained. "You can say, 'Your wife is cheating on you,' and he'll believe that, but he won't believe his horse stinks." Hourigan enjoys winning with a cheap horse, but his ultimate thrill is to capture a big race on the flat. "I did it once with Discerning Air at the Curragh—a fifty-grand handicap!" he bragged. "A National Hunt trainer kicking them up the arse in their own backyard! I well and truly celebrated that day!"

Remembering our chat at Tattersalls, and how he had rejected that yearling after a cursory inspection, I asked how he goes about shopping for horses at a sale. He just flips through the catalog, he said, and turns down a page if he sees a horse who is related to a nice one in his yard, but he'd never buy a horse on that basis alone. He watches for a glimpse of possibility, even a "come hither" look. As I guessed he might, he compared it to falling in love and recounted how he fell for his wife the first time he saw her, when Anne was playing tennis in a short skirt on a summer night. She was just fifteen, and though he was a little older, he pursued her, and they've been married for thirty-two years now and have five children.

"Boy, girl, boy, girl, boy," Hourigan recited, charmed by the symmetry. "Mark, the youngest, is ten and riding ponies now. I could be his grandfather! My friends call Anne 'the Queen.' When we go for drinks at the Woodlands House Hotel, they ask, 'Will the Queen be along?' We do everything together."

"With Beef Or Salmon, what attracted you?" I asked. "It couldn't have been his pedigree."

"Pedigree isn't everything," Hourigan replied. "Buying a horse isn't like buying a car. If you want a Ferrari, you can open the bonnet and look at the engine. You can take it apart and check it all over, and you'll know it well and truly is a Ferrari and capable of doing what a Ferrari does. But a horse? You can't take a horse apart. Sometimes a horse with a wonderful pedigree turns out to be a duck. Can't even get out of its own way! But if they're well-bred and trained properly, their pedigree comes out at some point."

"And if they're not well-bred?"

Hourigan laughed. "My friend Mick Easterby says, 'I'll gallop some pedigree into the fucker!' "

The break from work and the generous serving of bread and jam had boosted Michael's energy, and he was firing on all cylinders again. "Five o'clock I must have got in," he moaned, amused by his own antics. Ordinarily, he's out in the yard by six-thirty or seven, but he'd stayed in bed this morning to nurse his head. "The stable lads notice those things. They'll be gossiping about me, saying I was out on the town, same as I did when Charlie Weld was late. You have to show your face at the regular hour," he confided, "and then you can go back to bed. Only if you do, you must keep the bedroom curtains open. Very important! That stops the lads from yappin'."

Around noon, some visitors from Canada arrived. They were touring Irish yards, doing some hunting, and thinking about buying a horse or two, and that was enough for Hourigan to start pitching his wares, but the bloodstock agent in the party had also been at the hotel bar until the wee hours and looked so green around the gills that he probably couldn't have ordered lunch, much less handle a business deal. When Michael saw the writing on the wall, he showed them around his yard instead, while I tagged along. We saw his three gallops first—a four-to-five-furlong gallop of wood chips, a three-furlong circular gallop, and a new all-weather gallop of sand.

"I can do anything with it," he said, snatching up a handful and sifting it between his fingers. "I can make it fast or soft, and the only tending it needs is some harrowing."

Next, he moved us along to a seedy two-story building. "There's my hotel," he said cheerfully, ignoring its decrepit condition. "Some good jockeys have come out of there—Timmy Murphy, Adrian Maguire, Shane Broderick, Willie Supple. Course, it wasn't such a nice place in the old days. The rain would come down the walls at night, and the lads would wake up and shove their beds away from the wet. It's dry now, though, and it has central heating. Well, I did all right by them, anyway. When I see potential, I encourage it. What a good jockey needs is an old head on a young body."

Soon we were in the barn area, with horses all around us, either starting for the gallops or just coming back from them. Grooms were bathing those who'd finished their exercise, and the crisp air was pungent with the smells of soap and manure, each sharply defined. We were in a vibrant, tactile, physical world constructed out of dedicated daily labor. Its constants were fixed, and that had the effect of banishing confusion. Everyone knew exactly what was required of them. Certainly, Hourigan was a model of clarity in his role as our tour guide, walking us to a little stream overhung with sheltering trees.

"This is the greatest thing I've ever done, without a doubt!" he crowed. He'd poured some concrete to form a dam and create a deep pool, where up to six horses at a time can have a soak. The gently flowing water cools their hot legs and shins, and they can have a drink at their leisure. "Sometimes I leave them in overnight and collect them in the morning."

The last item on the tour was an indoor swimming pool comprising two concrete rectangles, one inside the other, to make a four-sided lap pool. A horse was in for a swim, and blowing hard. He had two longish ropes attached to his bridle, one for each of the grooms who tugged him along, treading on the concrete. "Go, boy!" they encouraged the struggling horse. The swim was equal to a good gallop, Hourigan said, and especially helpful for horses who have bum legs. "I used to be the only private trainer in Ireland to have a pool," he told me. "I spent fifty-odd grand on it, when I should have spent the money on a new house. That's what my wife wanted, anyway, but she never protested." He grabbed my elbow and whispered an aside. "When you're young and ambitious, you do some stupid things."

ON THE FIRST SATURDAY in December, I bellied up to the bar at O'Herlihy's to watch Moscow Flyer in the Tingle Creek Steeplechase at Sandown Park in Surrey. Tingle Creek—the horse, that is—was a foot-perfect jumper, who never fell in a race. My friend Reilly supplied this bit of trivia, proud of his expertise. He scoured Dublin's back streets for his racing collectibles, and when I told him I was going to Punchestown on Sunday for the Durkan Chase, he quoted four lines of an old poem from memory. "A loud hurrah for Ireland, boys / And louder for Kildare / And loudest of all for Punchestown / For I know you all are there." What a show-off, I thought, but I was impressed.

"Very strong performance, T.P. And will you not join me tomorrow?" I asked, in my newly adopted indirect style.

But Reilly had no interest in Punchestown. It's too big and roomy for him, and he feels lost, a stranger in a strange land. "You go out there," he griped, "and your cousin will be there, and you'll never meet unless you have a map. Or one of those mobile phones!" He prefers the urban confines of Leopardstown, where no family link goes unforged. "So what grave secrets did you pry out of your man Hourigan?" he asked.

"Beef Or Salmon's in the Durkan, for sure," I said. "But he's got to jump quicker if he expects to win."

"That's the whole of it?"

I shrugged it off. "When you're old and ambitious, you do some stupid things."

He hit the volume button on the TV clicker, so we could hear Jessie

Harrington being interviewed at Sandown. Ever good sports, the British were praising her for sending Moscow to England to battle Paul Nicholls's Azertyuiop, his main rival in the Queen Mother, rather than taking an easier road at home. The Irish purse money would be as good, if not better, and the competition softer. "Horses are there to be raced, and for the public to see," Jessie said, earning an A-plus in media relations.

By coincidence, Henrietta Knight had just earned a D-minus. She had let it drop that she might ship Best Mate to Leopardstown—in Ireland!—for the Ericsson Chase over Christmas and pass up the illustrious King George VI at Kempton, in England. Was *she* taking an easier road? I was suspicious, but Reilly thought Knight was being clever. "Best Mate never liked the going at Kempton," he said. In any event, the mere mention of the potential trip—a desertion, an outrage, even a betrayal—already had angry Brits writing carefully reasoned (though mildly threatening) letters to the *Post* that read like legal briefs.

At Sandown, Moscow Flyer went off at 6–4, but I'd backed him earlier at 13–8 and counted it as money in the bank despite Azertyuiop's presence—and it was, although the pace was too slow to bring out Moscow's best. He took the lead at the head of the stretch and soon had the others beaten, although he got a little lazy and needed a couple of cracks from Geraghty to wake him up. The horse would run next at Leopardstown's Christmas meeting, then rest up for Cheltenham, Jessie said, and I wanted to shout, "Don't do it, Jessie," still superstitious about Moscow's indelible pattern of three wins and then a loss. The Queen Mother would be his dread fourth race.

On Sunday, I did go to Punchestown for the Durkan Chase. Originally developed by the Kildare Hunt Club, the racecourse held its first recorded meeting in 1824. Punchestown *is* roomy, but that pleased me, maybe because I had no cousins to find. As at Cheltenham, the setting was pastoral with sheep on the hillsides. I'd seen an old engraving that showed several tiny black-clad figures perched on such a hill. They were priests stealing a glance at the races. A diocesan statute prevented them from attending in person, and it wasn't rescinded until the 1970s. The only other notable thing I knew about Punchestown was that Harry Beasley, a famous jockey, rode a winner there at the age of seventy-two.

Vowing not to bet on Beef Or Salmon just because Hourigan had charmed me, I adopted a trick from Reilly and judged the six horses on parade by their looks. Only three spoke to me. Knife Edge was handsome, but he was probably outclassed. Tiutchev, the sole English horse, deserved respect because he was from Martin Pipe's yard, and Pipe seldom bothered with Ireland. An old-timer of ten, Tiutchev was as buffed up as a bodybuilder with perfect pecs and abs, but Beef Or Salmon acted goofy again, all gangly and teenaged, too distracted for his own good. His speed alone wouldn't win him a Gold Cup. He had to jump as well as run.

Still, the crowd backed him heavily. Their intuition proved correct, largely because of Hourigan's advance preparation. With Timmy Murphy, he had walked the course before the race and found it so chopped up on the inside he opted to keep his horse off the rail. From three fences out, the Durkan was between Tiutchev and Beef Or Salmon, who needed reminders with the whip. Tiutchev made a hash of the last fence, so Beef Or Salmon's triumph wasn't clear-cut, but Hourigan didn't object, not even to the man in a Santa Claus costume, who insisted on hugging him a good three weeks before the gesture would be appropriate, and maybe even fun.

THE IRISH ARE FOND of launches, so whenever a new play, art exhibition, restaurant, hair salon, auto parts store, tire center, or whatever opens, you can count on a cheerful party with a dignitary present to extoll its virtues and wish it Godspeed. When I heard that Paul Carberry and Barry Geraghty were going to launch a refurbished Bambury Bookmakers shop in Ashbourne, in County Meath, I put the date on my calendar. Though Geraghty currently had the hot hand, Carberry is reputed to be the best natural horseman in Ireland, and I hoped to meet him and have a talk.

Traffic strangled the main road in Ashbourne. Blocks of housing covered the fields where crops once grew, another country town tipping over into suburbia. The Bambury shop had a piece of hand-lettered cardboard in the front window, half-collapsed and folded in on itself, to advertise the launch. That gave me pause, but the shop looked jaunty inside with new TVs and carpeting and a new wood floor agleam with fresh possibilities. About twenty gents, most of them elderly, were waiting for the festivities to begin, but I had a feeling they would have been there anyway, like potted plants, without any eminent jockeys to entice them.

Carberry was the first to arrive, his right thumb in a bulky cast. He'd fractured it in a recent fall at Fairyhouse when his whip banged into it, a freak injury. He hated to lose any rides, but he'd be on the sidelines for a couple of weeks. Soon to turn thirty, he was about to enter the danger zone for jump jockeys, where each new blow takes an increasing toll. His weight wasn't a problem, and his job as a stable jock for Noel Meade was secure, so he had no reason to be alarmed yet. In fact, he was as relaxed as a college kid in jeans and an Izod sweater, and I assumed Geraghty must go to the same school because he was dressed almost identically, right down to the shiny black loafers with silver buckles.

Seeing them up close, I realized how tall Geraghty is for a jockey at five feet nine inches, and how strong in the upper body. He rides at 147 pounds and can starve and sweat off three of those, but his normal weight is around 154. Where Carberry seemed at ease and agreed to have a drink afterward, Barry was anxious to complete the gig and hop on a plane to England to ride. He was even toting a set of silks on a hanger. Fame had Geraghty in its grip, but he deserved the recognition. The Irish had six winners at the Cheltenham Festival last year, and he'd been on five of them.

Jimmy Findlay, the shop's owner, had married into the Bambury family. He was bustling about and urging his clients to hit the buffet. "Come on, lads, don't be shy, help yourselves, I'm not going to bring it 'round to you," he scolded, but the lads held back, maybe suspecting a previously unknown bookies' trick that would cost them some money. The launch itself was short and sweet. A "personality" I didn't recognize contributed some patter, and the jockeys answered a few questions without revealing anything of value to a punter. Geraghty was awarded two hundred euros for a charity bet and selected Keen Leader in the Ericsson, a horse of Jonjo O'Neill's he'd just won on at Haydock.

That was about it, except for the obligatory photo op and Findlay's introduction of a potted plant named Frank ("I inherited him when we bought the shop in 1990"), who was the oldest codger in the room by a decade, no mean feat. Frank stepped brazenly into the picture, as if he were the jockeys' patron saint. While Carberry schmoozed with the crowd, Jimmy introduced me to another old guy and said, "Any idea who this is? Arkle's groom! Isn't that right, Joe?" But it wasn't right. "I was *never* Arkle's groom," Joe sputtered, "but I worked for the Dreapers for fifty-two years." He was upset that Arkle always got all the glory and started listing some other good horses from the yard, but the din in the shop drowned him out.

After a while, Carberry and I left for the Ashbourne Hotel next door. The quiet bar features portraits of horses etched in glass—Prince Regent, Mill House, and yes, Arkle, no doubt to poor Joe's dismay. I felt a little relieved to be gone from the launch, and I imagine Paul did, too. He can act the part at such dog-and-ponies, but it doesn't come easily or naturally. There's something of the loner about him. He ordered a Bulmers cider and tapped out a cigarette with his bandaged hand. His thumb was healing fine, he told me, and he would be back in time for the important Leopardstown meeting at Christmas.

"I can still hunt, anyway," he said, with a grin. He loves hunting, even more than riding a race. He keeps eight hunters at his home place and rides out with the Ward Union Hunt Club, established in 1854, twice a week. Between sixty and eighty of the club's one hundred or so members follow the hounds across the rolling countryside of Meath, tracking a stag that's been given a twelve-minute head start. The stag is never killed, only cornered and returned to the club's park, where it joins in the Ward Union's breeding program. "I like the speed, the unpredictability," Paul said, plus there are so many different obstacles to be jumped—hedges, walls, ditches—and so many instant decisions to be made. The journey is slightly mysterious, too, with the destination not plotted in advance. "You don't know where you'll wind up," he added, "except it's usually by a pub." He was the club's honorary whip, who assists the huntsman in controlling the hounds, and as puffed-up about it as any of his big-race wins.

Glancing at his thumb, I asked about his injuries. I was becoming a collector of griefs, fascinated by the inventory of pain a jump jockey endures. "Do you have all day?" he replied, with a smile. He'd broken a leg three times, his ribs, and both his wrists. The docs removed his spleen after a horse kicked him in the back, but those were just the most severe damages in a list he could, but wouldn't, elaborate on. He felt it would be dishonorable, I think. Honor was a concept you could truly apply to Carberry. He has the bearing of a shy, laconic sheriff in an old western, the man of principle who runs the black hats out of town.

Like most riders, Carberry started early, still in his teens. His father,

Tommy, a great jockey who later became a trainer, won the Cheltenham Gold Cup three times and lost a fourth through disqualification, and also won a Grand National. (Paul won his own Grand National in 1999 on BobbyJo, trained by his dad.) Tommy arranged for his son to be apprenticed to Jim Bolger, a flat trainer known for being tough on his apprentices. Bolger's lads aren't allowed to drink or smoke, and they go to church on Sunday or else. "Your daddy definitely doesn't like you," Bolger warned his new arrival, but Carberry survived the regimen and even managed to sneak in a cider or two.

Though Paul was light enough for the flat, he found the races too boring and preferred the jumps. At the age of twenty, he tried riding for Sir Robert Ogden in England for a time, but that didn't suit him, either, not with all the commuting around the country and racing almost every day, as the English do. (In Ireland, there are races four days a week, at most.) "I missed my hunting," he said, implying that he missed his home and family, as well—he has a brother and a sister who are both jockeys, one a pro and the other an amateur—so when Noel Meade offered him a job, he settled for a lower profile and a slower pace of life.

The move didn't hurt him financially. Both he and Geraghty were about to pass the million-dollar mark in prize money. The standard fee for an Irish jockey is about $140 a ride, plus eight percent of the purse should he win or place. (There is no show betting, but two, three, or four horses can place depending on the size of the field.) Carberry's agent carves off ten percent, and he pays a valet to care for his silks and his tack. As much as he loves to ride, he admitted it can be difficult to climb aboard a horse who's a poor jumper. Maiden races also spook him a little because the horses are so green, but he tends to worry most about dodgy jockeys. "Plenty of those around," he said.

"Any jockeys you admire?"

"A few."

"Want to name them?"

Reluctantly, as if the subject were as undignified as his list of injuries, he cited Ruby Walsh. "Ruby knows where to be in a race, the best possible position, and how to save ground. And how to keep out of trouble." Trouble can lead to a fall.

"Can you tell when a fall is coming?" I asked. "Any signal from the horse?"

"None. It's always unexpected," he said. "There's never any time to think. All you can do is cover up and protect yourself."

Carberry only travels to England for the major races these days, so his work schedule is fairly routine. He does a bit of schooling for his boss, rides out on the gallops some mornings, and goes racing on Thursday, Saturday, and Sunday. "That leaves you a lot of free time."

Another smile. "Not enough."

"What's the downside of the job?" I watched him take a slow sip of his cider, still closemouthed as the seconds ticked by. He couldn't find a downside, really. "I guess that's the answer, then," I said, and he nodded.

Outside, the afternoon had turned balmy, with just a few high clouds in a bright blue sky. It was so pleasant Paul thought he'd go for a ride on one of his hunters. I was curious why he was so attached to them, what made them so special, and he considered for a moment and replied, "Guts. They're bold and fearless," the very qualities that separate a jump jockey such as Carberry from the rest of the pack.

THE GOLD CUP, all but ceded to Best Mate in October, was up for grabs by mid-December. Insidious reports in the papers spoke of the champ's "slipping crown," an insult Henrietta Knight didn't take lightly. Young Kingscliff, only six and being promoted as a legitimate challenger, had moved onto center stage after winning two more chases in England—one at Wincanton by seventeen lengths, followed by a victory at Cheltenham in the Tripleprint Handicap, proving he could handle those stiff fences. "I didn't know how good he was before today, but today I got the answer," said Robert Alner, his trainer, whose garbled syntax betrayed his excitement. Alner had won the Gold Cup with Cool Dawn in 1998.

Cheltenham, Cheltenham. The word cropped up twenty-six times in the first ten pages of a recent *Post*, causing a reader to file a letter of protest. A few diehards were still ranting about Knight's possible avoidance of the King George VI, too, while Knight, who wasn't used to such criticism, had started making belated excuses about the Peterborough, blaming the bottomless ground, as treacherous as quicksand by now, and its disastrous effect on her horse. Fortunately, Matey had recovered from his trauma and was quite well again, thank you, although busy shooting a TV documentary with Jim Culloty in a supporting role. "Best Mate has an audience most days," Henrietta sniffed. "He enjoys being a star."

Across the ocean in France, Guillaume Macaire was biding his time. Scarcely the type to compare his horses to fairy-tale characters, he worked them hard and steadily, as tough-talking as Jean Gabin in an old gangster flick—none of that three-races-a-year crap for him. He could be cutting and disdainful, even of *his* stable star. "Jair du Cochet is the most stupid horse in the world," he told a British reporter. "The slightest change in his program, and he flips! He has done some very silly things, and I am on edge worrying about him. Best Mate scares me in the paddock. He walks around with the command of a lion. He is not an ordinary horse."

Was this an honest assessment, or merely Gallic subterfuge? Macaire kept his Gold Cup intentions hidden. And where did that leave Beef Or Salmon? A week after the Durkan, Hourigan ran him in a chase at Cork as tune-up for the Ericsson, and his horse fiddled a win despite more sloppy jumping. My urge to place an ante-post bet was dribbling away, as were my hopes for the Beefster. That same weekend, pretty Solerina added to her string of pearls with the Tara Hurdle at Navan, while at Fairyhouse Barry Connell let a professional ride The Posh Paddy in a maiden hurdle, but Paddy must have missed his master, because he finished a well-beaten fifth.

Wheels within wheels. The clarity I expected to have after almost three months of study and travel still eluded me. There was a pie cooling on the windowsill—apple, blueberry, seriously rich and tasty—but whenever I grabbed for a slice, the window slammed shut on my fingers. Was Kingscliff the real deal? Could Best Mate turn it around? Picking a Kentucky Derby winner looked simple by comparison. These were horses, not colts, and they'd been racing for years through many ups and downs, plus they trained at private yards essentially in secret. What to do? I needed some help before going to Leopardstown at Christmas, so I checked in with Ted Walsh, Ruby's dad, who's the ultimate insider.

WALSH'S FARM IS IN KILL, in County Kildare. I arranged to meet him there at noon, but he was on the Curragh exercising some horses when I arrived. "Why do racing people make appointments?" his wife, Helen, asked. "It never works out." She invited me to wait, but rather than sit like a lump on the couch, I went to town—killing time in Kill, as it were—reflexively bought a *Post*, ordered a sandwich and a pint at the cozy Dew Drop Inn, and listened to Shane Magowan singing "Fairytale of New York" on the radio. An hour later, I returned to the farm, but Ted was still missing in action, so I became the lump I had tried to avoid becoming, seated before a TV tuned to the races at Folkestone, in Kent.

Ruby had three rides there that afternoon, all for Paul Nicholls. He won the first race on Lord Lington, and as he was going to post for the second, Ted popped through the front door. He's a compact ball of fire, outgoing and outspoken, and he wasted no time on introductions, flopping into an armchair and asking for my paper. "What number is Ruby on?"

"Three," I said. "Harapour."

He ran a finger down the page. "Black and white," he said, noting his son's colors. Helen came in from the kitchen for the race, as did Ruby's sister Jennifer, who acts as his agent. Sometimes when the Walshes can't get a race via their satellite service, they dash down to Kill's only bookie joint to see it, and that causes a feeding frenzy among the neighborhood punters, who figure the family's there to bet on the kid and plunge accordingly.

Today, it was clear that Harapour had no chance in the Mr. & Miss Kelly Regan Birthday Novices' Hurdle, a Grade E contest (or nagathon), so Ted hit the mute button. "Fire away," he said. As Irish TV's most respected commentator, as well as a trainer and a former jockey, he is used to such attention. He told me he's from Fermoy in County Cork, where his father owned a pub, did some farming, dealt in horses, and raced them in point-to-points. Ted had worked with him and took over the present yard when his dad died in 1990. He doesn't regard training as a precious or esoteric art, just a job like any other.

"If you get a decent horse, the trick is not to mess it up," he claimed. "Ninety percent of our trainers are equals. Only ten percent are lacking. But this life isn't simple. Don't do it if you don't like it. If an owner wants to go to Thurles on a rainy Thursday and watch his horse finish feckin' ninth, you've got no choice but to agree."

The phone rang. It was Ruby calling from Folkestone. He still relies on his father for criticism and advice. Ted apologized for missing the first race. "I didn't see it, but you won. Good man, good man!" After hanging up, he said, "Ruby's at the top of the game, and he enjoys the buzz, but it's risky at the top. Some jockeys prefer to stay in the comfort zone, and they can last for years at the second or third level. It's safer. But if a top jockey slips, he falls all the way to the floor, and he won't get up again." In fact, Walsh believes the National Hunt itself is in trouble, too dependent on government support for its survival. To build a bigger audience and attract a younger, increasingly sophisticated crowd, the tracks have to improve their facilities.

"We're on slippery ground," he warned. "Nobody wants to eat bad food and drink overpriced beer when their feet are all wet," an argument I could support from personal experience. "Not long ago in Ireland, when you checked into a hotel, you asked if the bathroom was on the landing, so you wouldn't have to deal with the stairs. Now you wouldn't stay in a room that doesn't have a bathroom. What the National Hunt needs is a Paschal Taggart, someone with a business head and the common touch. He's the most innovative, down-to-earth entrepreneur I've met!"

Taggart is Ireland's greyhound chief, lauded for taking a mug's game and turning it into a lucrative enterprise by offering more bang for the buck at dog tracks—great meals, terrific service, casino-style glitz, and so on. Ever in search of low-rent kicks, I once tried to reserve a table for a fixed-price dinner at Shelbourne Park, Dublin's upscale venue for hounds, and wound up on a three-month waiting list.

Tossing out Taggart as a role model is the kind of loaded remark that gets Walsh in hot water on TV. He started about thirty years ago, while he was still riding as an amateur, and beat out a half-dozen other candidates after a series of auditions. He thinks his honesty helped, as did his inside knowledge of the sport. "Before it was like the news," Ted said, waving a hand dismissively. "Actors read the script, but they didn't know fuck-all about racing and couldn't answer a simple question." He was a little too direct at first, though, and had to acquire a knack for diplomacy. He gave me an example. "If a jockey screws up, you don't say, 'What an awful ride!' You put it this way instead, 'I believe he's had better days.'"

Walsh credits Tim O'Connor, his old boss, with teaching him how to be a better broadcaster. "Four trainers are in the parade ring, okay?" he asked, recalling one such lesson. "It does no good to say, 'And there's Paddy Mullins, the trainer.' It could be any of them! You have to say, 'And there's Paddy Mullins *in a trilby!*'" O'Connor also prompted him to tailor his remarks to the image on-screen. "Say there's a picture of a Mercedes, and the camera shifts to a red schoolbus. Tim told me, 'That's when you stop talking about the Mercedes.' I didn't understand, I said, 'But I didn't finish with the Mercedes, Tim.' And he said, 'I don't care, Ted.' And a producer added, 'Just talk about the feckin' schoolbus, Ted.'"

"So you're comfortable with it now?"

"Ah, yeah, I enjoy it. Racing's been good to me, and I wouldn't knock it, but I don't give a shite about the establishment. I'm a friend of the real National Hunt enthusiasts," he continued, loosening up. "I don't have much interest in the gambling side. Even when I rode, it was never about the money. I was as thrilled to win a maiden race as a big handicap—bar Cheltenham, of course. That's the be-all and end-all of the jumps. The winner's enclosure is like an amphitheater, and you don't have hundreds of fans, you have thousands. They're the most appreciative on earth, too, that mixture of the Irish and the English. When you head for the enclosure, the crowd parts like the Red Sea. Isn't that the one Moses parted?"

"It is."

Ted could barely contain his exuberance now and reached for a more vivid comparison. "It's like walking into this huge cauldron of cheering people! There's no greater atmosphere anywhere. Nothing else in the world compares to it!"

With the mention of Cheltenham, my thoughts turned to the Gold Cup. "Can Best Mate win there again this year?"

"Absolutely," he said, without hesitation. "He has all the attributes. He jumps, he stays, and he has a turn-of-foot. And he loves Cheltenham."

"Any idea what Jim Lewis paid for him?"

"Around a hundred grand, I'd guess, but it's only a guess. Tom Costello doesn't boast about those things. Costello is the king of dealers. He's produced more top-class racehorses than anyone else in Ireland. Did you know Kingscliff and Strong Flow both came out of Costello's nursery? Two more Gold Cup winners, maybe. Tom's a lovely fellow, but he's not in good health at the moment."

Kingscliff and Strong Flow. Every horse this mysterious man touched was a potential champion, it seemed. Walsh has been a friend of Costello's for ages, and he described how Costello operates. "There are breeders, you see—small farmers—who don't go to the sales, because they hate all the claptrap," he said. "Tom knows them all, and he knows from the stallion masters in the area the pedigrees of their foals. Take Un Desperado, say. Tom will know Un Desperado has covered a mare over at Mike Smith's farm, so he'll arrange a meeting. And maybe Smith will have some other nice foals, as well—a Be My Native, or a Supreme Leader.

"Mike Smith will have a price in mind, maybe thirty-eight thousand for the lot. Tom will dwell on that and write a check for twenty-five thousand. Probably Mike won't accept, so they'll have a pot of tea, and Tom will write a check for twenty-eight thousand. Sooner or later, he'll close the deal at a price he likes. In the old days, Tom paid cash to the farmers who didn't trust banks. He'd have a wad of bills in a satchel. And he's a master of psychology, too. If a buyer suspects he has a special horse, Tom might say, 'I do, but I don't want to sell it,' and that drives up the price. Or he'll play off one of his sons. 'Tom Junior believes that horse jumps like Best Mate,' he'll say, 'but I don't think so.' His horses are always beautiful jumpers. When the Costellos put a horse through its paces, it takes the sight right out of your eyes."

I wanted to know more about Costello, but it was almost three o'clock, and Ted still hadn't eaten lunch, so I joined his family in the dining room. I reckoned I'd never lived in such a hospitable country. On a wall, I saw a framed photo of Ruby on Papillon, Walsh's Grand National winner in 2000, but that was the only racing-related item around. Some trainers are workaholics and don't have a life beyond the horses, but others develop outside interests, as Ted has done with travel.

"I love America!" he bellowed, when I told him where I was from. He spent two years there in the mid-1950s, when his parents immigrated to the States. His father worked with Mickey Walsh, his brother, who trained jumpers and entered them in shows at Madison Square Garden. The Walshes passed their summers in Queens Village in New York, then moved to North Carolina during the winter, a peripatetic existence that didn't suit them in the end.

As I was shoveling in some ice cream, I realized we hadn't gotten around to the Christmas meeting at Leopardstown at all, but Ted assured me I didn't need any special instructions.

"You'll have a grand time. They take a horse to heart there," he said, clearly a high accolade. "They clap to the horse. The horse is the hero."

"And the horse knows it?"

"And the horse knows it," Walsh repeated.

THE SKY OVER DUBLIN BAY was a flinty gray on the afternoon I visited Leopardstown, a week before the Christmas festival. The temperature was in the low thirties, and the Dublin Mountains, looming up behind the grandstand, were almost black in the stormy light—brooding, foreboding, the stuff of bad romantic poetry. Tom Burke, the track's racing manager, was in his office, a cubbyhole piled so high with cardboard boxes I had to sidle this way and that to reach him at his desk. The desk, too, was buried under papers, so that the overall effect was of a place under siege, although Burke had the calm look of a veteran used to surviving in the trenches.

"Feels like snow," I said, shivering as I unbuttoned my overcoat.

Burke looked horrified. "Don't say snow."

The fickle Irish weather was his enemy these days. The Christmas Meeting begins on Boxing Day and is the track's biggest earner, but Burke needs the heavens to cooperate if he's to bring it off. The heavens don't always oblige. In 1995, he lost all but one of the meeting's four days because the ground froze solid, and that could happen again. Anything could happen, really, so Burke's sleep was restless. Whenever he felt in control of the situation, all systems go, Mother Nature knocked him off balance with some torrential rain, say, or a pounding of hailstones. If frogs dropped from the clouds, Burke probably wouldn't bat an eye.

"There's always a new trauma waiting," he said, a verity he's mastered after sixteen years on the job. Leopardstown is insured to cover any weather-related losses, but the policy is expensive, and a canceled meeting is also costly in terms of goodwill. Grumpy patrons blame the track for depriving them of their holiday treat and consigning them to a dish of cold plum pudding with the in-laws.

Burke had a phone call to make. To keep me occupied, he handed over a brief history of the racecourse, prepared for its centenary in 1988. The two-hundred-acre site, chosen for its scenic qualities and its access to a railroad line, once housed a leper colony, hence the devious permutation "Leopardstown." In the 1860s, an order of Benedictine monks from England bought the land for a charitable model farm to introduce the latest agricultural technology to impoverished Irish farmers, but they went belly-up when the Father Superior spent too much money on machinery.

After that, some Dublin businessmen acquired the property. Their idea was to build a track that would be a rough replica of Sandown Park. The gates opened in August 1888, on a date chosen to coincide with the Dublin Horse Show, to a crowd estimated at fifty thousand. People poured into Foxrock Station by train on the old Harcourt Line, but the bridge to the course was only three feet wide and almost collapsed under the crush. The roads were so jammed some fans never reached Leopardstown at all. The turnstiles couldn't cope with the pressure, either, and malfunctioned. The main entrance was too small for horsedrawn carriages, while Mr. Street, the caterer, was singled out for abuse in the papers and trashed for serving such "execrable food."

His call completed, Burke asked for the book and flipped to a favorite page. " 'Disgraceful bungling,' " he read aloud, with a fair degree of drama. " 'That a number of lives were not lost must be ascribed to a miracle rather than to any precautions on the part of the management.' "

"The press was a lot harsher in those days," I volunteered.

"Obviously." Burke, it seems, has a dry sense of humor, but I could see how he might lose it in the run-up to Christmas, while he was putting in sixteen hours a day. His duties were manifold. He was responsible not only for the state of the ground, but also for the printing of race programs and the posting of sponsors' signs. He had to liaise with the police over traffic control, still a problem, and massage the egos of corporate honchos with private boxes. All the fences and hurdles had to be checked and repaired if necessary. The course does have very good drainage, so the principal threat to the meeting was a severe frost, such as the one Burke experienced in 1995.

Maybe it was the paragraph I read about the Benedictines, but I thought Burke had a monkish aspect as he bent to the work on his desk. His office had the feel of a cell, and no doubt he muttered a prayer or two about the weather. The stress was most intense on Christmas morning, he said. One of his younger children—he has eleven, and they range in age from four to twenty-five—would wake him early, just after dawn, and if Willie Gibbons, his track foreman, reported any trouble, he'd hurry over for an inspection. But if the day was benign, he'd attend Mass, enjoy his Christmas dinner, entertain some guests, and retire around ten o'clock, surely counting his blessings.

TWO DAYS BEFORE CHRISTMAS, Henrietta Knight put a lump of coal in British stockings and added to Tom Burke's stress by announcing that Best Mate would forgo the King George VI and compete in the Ericsson Chase at Leopardstown. The Irish ground was softer and safer, she said. Furthermore, Matey had never liked Kempton, because it was too quick and had once given him sore shins and shoulders. Michael Hourigan welcomed the challenge on Beef Or Salmon's behalf, while the wily Guillaume Macaire, whose Jair du Cochet was in the King George—and whose chances were now much improved—remarked slyly, "Well, it isn't bad news, is it?" although Macaire was in for a surprise.

I was on my way to O'Herlihy's when the story broke. The pub was in fine holiday fettle. A diligent staffer had dug out a few old decorations from an attic corner, and they matched the antique tenor of the place—some tiny plastic wise men, cardboard angels missing their wings, and a strand of glittery letters wishing everyone a Happy Christmas. In honor of the season, the regulars were defying their ordinarily inflexible routines, stopping in at odd hours and standing or sitting in spots other than their normal ones, and that had resulted in a topsy-turvy effect. They were compelled to talk with people they'd been avoiding all year and were reminded of the reasons why.

T. P. Reilly sat at a table, with his dog Oliver snoring at his feet. He was excited about Best Mate coming to Leopardstown, yet suspicious about Knight's motives, more so than before. He was beginning to share my doubts, although from a different angle. You can never trust the English, that seemed to be the gist of it. "The harse is not right," Reilly said darkly. "Your woman lives in mortal fear of Jair du Cochet. One more beating, and she'll be pulling out her hair."

"Maybe she's afraid of Strong Flow," I said. Paul Nicholls was still considering the King George for his horse, although he leaned toward the less competitive Feltham Novices' Chase on the same card.

"Now there's a proper animal," Reilly raved. "Jumps like a bloody stag."

"Except when a fence gets in the way."

"Ah, he's still learning. Strong Flow has Gold Cup written all over him, next year if not this one. Have another, will you?"

I had another Guinness, a guilty pleasure at midafternoon, and basked in the atmosphere of bonhomie. Peace on earth, goodwill to men, that sort of thing. The faces along the bar had a rosy burnished glow, teased out by the beer and the whiskey, and as I sipped my pint, I thought dreamily about my travels and all the people I'd met, struck again by the relative purity of the National Hunt—purity always being relative—and how the love of the game colored and enriched the lives of those who cared for the horses, a simple but powerful equation.

Dubliners do Christmas with a vengeance. On Grafton Street the next morning, I joined the throng of last-minute shoppers, each on a special mission, searching for the right digital camera or a choice pair of woolly red socks for Uncle Fergal in Ballymurphy. Ornaments, tinsel, they danced on the breeze. The air was crisp, the sky sparkly. A little boy was belting out "Silent Night" for his supper, while coins clattered into the bucket at his feet. From the Brown Thomas department store wafted the scent of a thousand perfumes, the very aroma of a harem. Somewhere, in one pub or another, I was certain Shane Magowan could be heard singing, "Got on a lucky one, came in at eighteen to one . . ."

At Sawers Fish Market on Chatham Street, I bought a side of wild smoked salmon and a dozen Dublin Bay prawns still in their shells, like little lobsters, to be pan-fried with garlic and shallots, then served with crusty bread to mop up the juices. It was Sheridans for cheese, Gubeen and Durrus from Ireland, plus a wedge of Gorgonzola and a tub of mozzarella *bocconcini* in olive oil spiked with flecks of red pepper, perhaps the handiwork of an artisan in the Apennines, snow falling there now and the poor artisan—underpaid, undervalued, his horse a loser at Grosseto—trembling in his icy studio when the village beauty knocks on his door with a bottle of grappa under her arm, saying in a husky whisper, "*Buon Natale, caro.*"

Our Christmas tree came from the Wicklow Mountains, freshly cut and still smelling of the pine forest. A neighbor's son delivered it. Matt is ambitious, a real go-getter, and his tree business would earn him enough for a trip to New York over the summer, when college was out—to the Hamptons, no less, where he'd seek his fortune on the golf courses. He'd done his research and knew what a caddy could make at the better private clubs (if the tips were as advertised), and though he ultimately got stuck in a ratty trailer in Montauk swabbing out rowboats, he would be the first to tell you what a grand time he had, another Irish youth who'd crossed the sea to commit his American adventure.

The ham and the turkey were on order from our butcher. That was another Irish tradition, Imelda had explained during our first Christmas together. Why both? I couldn't understand and thought she must be joking until we made the rounds of parties, where hunks of pig and bird were heaped on platters. Salt beef was another new one on me, a pricey seasonal delicacy and as tough as shoe leather, but our guests ate it without objection, just as I'd done as a kid when my mother served us stinky lutefisk she ordered by mail from Minnesota, a tribute to her Norwegian ancestry.

With the tree up and dinner in the oven, Imelda and I walked to town for a drink at the Shelbourne on Christmas Eve. Always at the hotel she met someone she knew, often a friend she hadn't seen since her school days, Dublin being small and the lives of its residents intricately linked, with no secret ever truly secret. And so it was that night, a medley of merry introductions, and when we left the streets were filled with couples and families on their way home, some of them singing carols. Horse cabs trotted along the fringes of Stephen's Green, and we heard laughter ringing out like bell tones from the bundled-up passengers, a complement to our own jolly mood.

Christmas morning broke mild and breezy, with a spattering of rain. I remembered Tom Burke and wondered which of his eleven children had rousted him from bed, and if the absence of any frost would grant him an untroubled day. I hoped so. Lying in bed with Imelda beside me, I was filled with good wishes for all mankind, as silly and trite as that may sound, thinking that we all deserve big plates of turkey and ham at a table with those we love at least one day a year. I'd been around long enough by now, and had certainly seen enough, to cherish such rare full-hearted moments and accept them for what they are, a gift.

ON BOXING DAY, the ground came up soft but testing at Leopardstown. I couldn't rouse myself from a chair by the fire and stayed home to watch the King George VI, suffering from a familiar post-Christmas sensation of being stuffed and never in need of any food again. Two words, *Edredon Bleu*, rattled around in my numbed brain—"blue eider-down," a comforting image on a cold winter day, maybe even to Guillaume Macaire, the French tough guy, who looked to have the race sewn up with Jair du Cochet. Macaire might have viewed Henrietta Knight's gesture of sending her second-best horse to Kempton as a sop to her outraged fans, as many did.

For me, the matter was not so clear. Edredon Bleu had tried the race once before and failed to stay the three miles, but his season had been so spectacular, with each win an admirable endorsement of his ability to surpass himself, that he might do it again. Then, too, Knight was so finicky about her horses I couldn't imagine she'd risk one of her best just to placate the outraged Brits. With that in mind, I went to Boyle-sports, where Edredon Bleu was on offer at 25–1, and promptly bet on Fondmort because I'd won some money on him at the Open Meeting. I blame the ham and the turkey.

Best Mate's desertion was a hot topic, of course, and Tony McCoy took a potshot at Knight after winning the first race. "I don't want to start a controversy," he said, lying through his teeth, "but it's beautiful ground. I'd like to ride Best Mate over it." Actually, McCoy had ridden Best Mate twice in the King George, substituting for Jim Culloty, and he'd even won it in 2002. But Knight had been critical of McCoy in her book, suggesting the champ's aggressive style didn't suit her sensitive horse. Best Mate was so smart and capable, she implied, that a jockey only had to sit on him—a notion that McCoy, with his king-size ego, found galling.

The King George might have been more competitive if Paul Nicholls had thrown in Strong Flow at the deep end, but he chose the Feltham instead. Again Strong Flow demonstrated his potential when he jumped well, giving the fences plenty of air, but he also jumped horribly at times, taking off far too soon. He smacked two fences squarely, stuck out a single leg on landing, and remained upright long enough for Ruby Walsh to regain control and pursue Ballycassidy, who had jumping problems, too, veering to the left. Strong Flow needed a super jump at the last fence, and he got it to win. The look on

Ruby's face combined relief and disbelief, the standard emotions of a survivor.

Jair du Cochet was installed as the King George favorite, as expected. First Gold and Swansea Bay also attracted some money, but Edredon Bleu remained a long shot. As usual, the old fellow shot to the lead at the start. Just a week shy of his twelfth birthday, he looked as frisky as a colt. Going along with him was First Gold, who'd won the race in 2000, but Jair du Cochet, once accused of stupidity by Macaire, seemed to be living up to it. He showed no interest in the race and lagged behind the field, clipping the fourth fence and nearly landing in a ditch. It wasn't a terrible mistake, but Jacques Ricou almost took flight and never recovered, unlike Ruby Walsh. Soon Jair du Cochet was pulled up, and Ricou was greeted with another round of catcalls and scorn.

The useless Valley Henry—I never forgive or forget a horse who has cost me some money—was a faller, and so, too, was Le Roi Miguel. The suspect stayers, those who couldn't handle the distance, began to unravel at the fourth-last fence, Fondmort among them, and First Gold flattened out, so Edredon Bleu seized the lead on his own. He was still full of run, but Martin Pipe's Tiutchev, the near-master of Beef Or Salmon, came on to challenge. Nobody is better than Tony McCoy at squeezing the last scrap of energy from a horse, but Tiutchev simply didn't have enough left. Edredon Bleu rallied for a crowd-pleasing win, every bit as brave as his trainer, who had the courage for once not to cover her eyes. "Hiding in the bushes has not brought me much luck lately," she said, "so I stood by the railing and watched it."

DEEP POCKETS. Those were the words that rumbled through my head on Saturday, when I did forsake my chair for a trip to Leopardstown. Paddy Power was sponsoring all the races on the card—very deep pockets, indeed—including the big one, a steeplechase worth almost two hundred thousand dollars. Often I imagine another life for myself, lost in the dream of eternal return, and if I were to be reincarnated as a major-league bookie, I doubt that I'd complain. Twenty-seven horses would be after the prize, but I only cared about the "Dial-a-Bet" chase, a celebration of your phone as a gambling tool, where Moscow Flyer would face a field of five. For once, I'd will myself to root against him. My superstitions had flared up, like a case of hives.

Leopardstown has the feel of an American track. Trees and mountains, yes, and a glimpse of Dublin Bay, but there's a slick, sleek pace to the action that pulls in the urban cream, young people from the city center just six miles away. The parking lot was full of fancy cars, but I also saw aged buses that had carried fans in from the country, often older folks flat-capped or trilby-topped. Among the crowd, too, were tour groups from the north, Belfast and Derry lads who'd had a few on the ride down and were fanning the flames with cider and beer. For the moment, Ireland was the center of the jump-racing universe, and the "buzz," as Ted Walsh called it, had us all tingling.

I felt the buzz when I went through the gate, past a cash machine where a long line had already formed. How strange, I thought. Had everyone forgotten that they'd need money at the track? Then I remembered Elizabeth Bowen ("distress, miscarried projects . . .") and understood. Many were the mysteries, and I met with another just ahead—the Leopardstown child-care center, a Jerry Springer–type mobile home, where a kid could be deposited for the afternoon, although a forcefully worded sign warned, COLLECTION IMMEDIATELY AFTER THE LAST RACE. Had tapped-out parents left behind their children in the past? And what had become of the orphans? Sold off as camel jockeys? The mind boggled.

Through the crowd I went, and here was another amazing sight. A really, really, really old man—nearly a hundred, maybe—sat on a folding chair beneath a TV lodged on a shelf that jutted out from a pillar. For this privilege, he had paid an entrance fee of twenty-five dollars, even though he could have watched the races at home for free. But no, he liked being where he was, a boulder in the river of human beings that had to split into side channels to get around him. With his plastic spoon, he was eating what appeared to be a bowl of soup, missing his mouth occasionally but not bothered by the error. How stunning that the old guy was so content! He didn't want to be anywhere else. The buzz had stung him, too.

I ducked into Jodami's Bar, where some high school jocks pressed into part-time service were doing the pouring. They acted cool and stored up incidents of adult misbehavior to retail later to their pals. The meet-and-greet dance that Reilly so treasured was in full swing, with Cousin Jimmy shaking hands with Uncle Tommy, while Aunt Maeve nattered about her piano lessons to Niece Fiona. The various clans were conducting their ancient rituals, the Kellys and Mahoneys, O'Neills and Hickeys, with the ladies in bright new Christmas frocks and the fellows sporting their new red ties. In the midst of the babble, I sipped my wine, still too stuffed from the turkey and ham to stomach a pint, and thought about Moscow Flyer.

Apart from the prospect of winning or losing a bet, why should anybody identify with a horse, especially a person like me? I've only gone riding a few times in my life, and then somewhat reluctantly, fearful I'll be thrown, a paranoid delusion similar to the fear that I'll be trampled around the barns or stables. Ample material for the corner shrink, all right, yet through the years I've latched on to some racehorses with a startling fervor—the great Alydar, for example. Though Affirmed defeated my colt in three Triple Crown races, I am convinced Alydar was better, and nothing can change my mind. It's the same syndrome that compels otherwise sensible folks to root for the Chicago

Cubs or worse, buy a used Fort Wayne Pistons' jersey on e-bay. With Moscow Flyer, I sensed a kindred soul. Weirdly, irrationally, I felt my fate as a gambler was linked to his, so when he won the Dial-a-Bet by miles, I knew in my heart he'd never win the Queen Mother, and that I, too, might take a beating at Cheltenham.

REDEMPTION WAS THE THEME for the Ericsson Chase, held appropriately on Sunday. Best Mate threw off so much star power that more than nineteen thousand people bought tickets to see him. Not that he was the only attraction—Pizarro and Sacundai from Edward O'Grady's yard, both Cheltenham hopefuls, were also out to polish their tarnished reputations. The weather was ideal, very cold and clear, with the last traces of frost melting. The drying ground wasn't so testing anymore, described instead as on the easy side of good, so there would be no reason for excuses.

In a reversal of boxing protocol, Best Mate entered the paddock first, the champ preceding the challengers. He looked splendid, elegant, regal—like a lion, as Guillaume Macaire had put it. He seemed delighted to be alone and on parade, accustomed to being loved at home and adored in public. He was clearly attached to his groom Jackie Jenner, who also cares for Edredon Bleu, and nuzzled her once or twice. She knows all his quirks (he only likes his tail and mane brushed, for instance) and often rides him out. She was on him the day he had an accident that could have ended his career, when he stepped on a rusty nail on a bridle path. The nail missed his navicular bursa bone by a fraction of a centimeter. Matey, the vets said, had been lucky.

Henrietta Knight soon joined her horse, as did Terry Biddlecombe and Jim Lewis's gang. They had a studied nonchalance, that McManus-like talent for concealing their emotions. Biddlecombe may have a heart of gold, but he had the look of a rough customer. By contrast, Knight projected an aura of innocence and sweetness. I felt I could trust her with my darkest and most damaging secrets, even that any hideous thing I confessed to her wouldn't shatter her composure or alter her positive attitude toward life. I wanted Henrietta to approve of me and tell me I was a decent guy, so I understood why her Oxford pupils had stooped to giving her electric shocks.

The ever-increasing Irish part of me wished Beef Or Salmon wouldn't let Michael Hourigan down. The bookies made the horse second-favorite to Best Mate, who went to post at 8–11. (The bookies' handle on the Ericsson was more than a million dollars, most of it on Best Mate, so they took a bath.) In spite of such wishes, I couldn't bring myself to back Beef Or Salmon. He still had that distracted air of youthful inattention, while Best Mate grasped the exact nature of his mission. When he hit the track, he showed no hesitation. Instead, he was off at a trot, tossing his head about and eager for the action to start.

For Best Mate, the race was a cakewalk. His performance blew to shreds all the theories about his deteriorating condition. Jim Culloty allowed him to travel along at his own speed, in no hurry—Culloty was unruffled, a picture of calm. There was no point in chasing Batman Senora, the leader, because Batman began banging fences right away, bungling the third and crashing into the fourth, as if he'd been assigned to demolish it. With the Batman fading, Tony McCoy on Colonel Braxton forced the pace, but Culloty still didn't flinch or make a move. As I suspected, Beef Or Salmon ran no race at all. In fact, something was wrong with him. Timmy Murphy smacked him on the shoulder at every fence, but it did no good. The horse didn't respond.

So Colonel Braxton pressed on, with McCoy digging in, but Best Mate was relentless. He tracked the Colonel from a leisurely distance, second or third, and approached each fence as he might a divertissement, not an obstacle, jumping over them flawlessly, in a rhythm all his own. When Culloty finally let him go, he vanished in a flash, as though he'd been waiting for that very moment as a child waits for Christmas in a state of suspended animation, and now he was released and running free. His official margin of victory over Le Coudray was nine lengths, but it could have been forty if Culloty had pushed him.

"As good a feeling as I've ever had on a racehorse," Culloty said afterward. Though Knight was front-and-center to unsaddle Best Mate, her courage had deserted her again, and she had listened to the call of the race in a parking lot rather than watching it. The applause that greeted Matey on his return from the track was extraordinary. "I've never heard the Irish cheer an English horse like that," Willie Mullins said to me, but Best Mate was only technically from England—on loan, as it were—since he'd been born and bred on the Auld Sod.

Lost in the uproar were the fine efforts of Pizarro and Sacundai, who also redeemed themselves. In the Grade One Neville & Sons Chase, Pizarro hung on to defeat Knight's Rosslea, a boost for his trainer after the horse had been pulled up in the Drinmore, his last race. Under top weight, Sacundai beat a strong field in the Christmas Hurdle and was once again listed as a Festival worthy. For Edward O'Grady, it was a pensive afternoon. Had Pizarro's jumping errors killed his chances in the Drinmore, or had O'Grady made a training mistake? "I honestly don't know," he said, after thirty-two years on the job. "I'm a slow learner."

ON MONDAY, I was at Leopardstown again for the Bewley's Hotels December Festival Hurdle, a Grade One over two miles. An unusually spirited race, it featured such first-rate Irish hurdlers as Back In Front, Hardy Eustace, and Solerina, along with Jonjo O'Neill's Rhinestone Cowboy, a favorite for the Champion Hurdle at the Festival, but none of them figured at the finish. Instead, the race was between two long shots—Flame Creek from Noel Chance's yard in England and Jessie Harrington's Spirit Leader—until an even longer shot, Golden Cross at 66–1, zipped past them like a greyhound to capture the prize on his first run of the year, with Spirit Leader second.

That shouldn't have shocked anybody, since nothing in racing is quite what it seems. While reading Richard Holmes's *Sidetracks* recently, I'd come across an account of Théophile Gautier's visit to Royal Ascot in 1842, a high point on one of his periodic trips to London. Gautier was enthralled by the sights. He celebrated the "vegetable velvet" of the turf where the "cherry-red horses" ran, while the brightly colored jockeys' caps resembled "poppies, cornflowers, and anemones carried away on the wind." Our Frenchman waxed poetical about the flock of white pigeons that flew about the course, too, only to hear later the birds belonged to the bookies, who used them to carry odds and results to their associates around the city.

Deep Freeze

For Irish trainers, the New Year began with some distressing news. An equine virus was sweeping through their yards. It was a devastating one, too, and sometimes undetectable. Horses scoped clean and then ran badly, as Beef Or Salmon had done in the Ericsson, sick and gurgling because of the mucus in his throat. "He'll be grand in a few days," an optimistic Michael Hourigan told me, a better prognosis than Paul Nicholls delivered for Strong Flow, who had cracked a knee bone in his near-foreleg in the Feltham. Whether or not the fracture was due to his sloppy jumping, Strong Flow's season was over, along with any chance that he might duplicate Mill House's feat in the Gold Cup.

Noel Meade's yard was the hardest hit. On the Monday before Christmas, he had eight horses with fevers; on Tuesday, sixteen; and on Wednesday, forty-five. Meade went ten straight days without a runner, and that dealt a whopping blow to his operating costs. Jessie Harrington was also affected. The bug had knocked out Imazulutoo, her Festival hope who'd shined at Gowran Park, but she still had Moscow Flyer to cheer her up. There would be no more prep races for Moscow. He would go directly to the Queen Mother despite what I now thought of as the Pattern, a malign condition from the annals of science fiction.

It's crucial at any yard for "trouble to stay outside the door," as Eamonn Leigh liked to say. Trouble in the form of a virus can be a nightmare, multiplying with astonishing speed and ripping through the barns like wildfire. Infected horses must be isolated, and all the others checked daily for coughs or dirty noses. The hours around breakfast become supercharged. This is when you hear the bad news, as Martin Pipe put it—that your best horse just broke a blood vessel on the gallops, say. With a bug, the stakes mount. Every horse is susceptible, and they don't always recuperate quickly.

In the *Post,* I saw that Andrew Leigh was still hustling rides. He had a promising one coming up at Thurles, so I was tempted to go. That would make me a pervert rather than a philosopher in the eyes of Voltaire, but a horse fancier always has an excuse. After the holiday banquet, the National Hunt was a meager meal in early January, mostly burgers and very little prime rib. Trainers were saving their big horses for the valuable races on the weekends. If you craved some action during the week, you had to lower your expectations. You had to consider Thurles.

Once bitten, twice shy. Here was another maxim I recalled on the train ride to Tipperary, looking out at fields layered with frost, Ireland's deep freeze. The same old bookies sat across from me, as weather-beaten as their satchels. True winter had arrived with bone-chilling winds, peltings of sleet, and light snow high up in the hills. All the talk in the papers about a false spring caused by global warming went into the garbage can. Well, I reassured myself, it isn't raining, at least. I'll be cold, but not wet. I felt a twinge of sympathy for the jockeys, though, when I remembered a remark of Paul Carberry's. "No matter how cold it is outside at Thurles," he once said to me, "it's colder in the weighing room."

Thurles on a cold, dry day was pleasant, really. Even pretty, a little. Once more the elderly crowd made me feel youthful, and with a bounce in my step and a hot whiskey in my belly, I bagged a couple of bets before Andrew Leigh's race, a three-mile hurdle, rolled around. Leigh was on Sixtino, the people's choice, who had "won on the ice at St. Moritz," according to the *Post*. Had the horse worn skates? Clearly, my knowledge of the jumps was still incomplete. But Sixtino also had two wins in Ireland, not on the ice, so I had to take him into account considering the quality of the opposition.

Sixtino faced a veritable bevy of nonwinners. Only the whim of an owner or a trainer kept these nags in competition. Like the supposedly gifted children who flunk every exam, they were being indulged. Moreover, they were untried at the distance and could not be expected to abruptly find their form. Any horse who could stay on his feet and last for three miles had an honest shot, and since Craigmor Hero had performed that marvel (although not much else), I cast my lot with him. The race set up just as I figured it would. Most horses were sucking wind after two miles, and that left Sixtino and Craigmor Hero to slug it out. The ensuing battle, hardly epic, devolved into a photo finish with Craigmor Hero in front, a belated Christmas gift I collected at 10–1.

I was sorry for Andrew, but happy for myself. The trip back to the city was sweet. Having neglected to bring along Paddy Kavanagh for company, I picked up the *Post* again, but I'd read all the articles about horses and flipped to the greyhound pages I normally skipped. The classified ads offered Super Pups for Sale and, less ambitiously, Quality Pups for Sale, and Greyhounds for Under 500 Pounds ($900) in the bargain basement. I wondered what it would be like to own a dog, and if the fall from grace would be truly spectacular, although I guessed not since Noel Meade, a classy guy and a member of the Dog Gone Syndicate, held an eleventh share of a hound known as Springwell Arctic.

Unfortunately for Meade and the other trainers, the virus continued to spread, and there were fears of an epidemic. Dr. Ned Gowing, who owns and operates Anglesey Lodge Equine Hospital on the Curragh, understood the situation well. He was so busy with sick and injured horses I had difficulty connecting with him, and when we did manage to speak and set up a meeting, I made sure to get to Kildare early and had a quick lunch at the Stand House Hotel, where there's a collection of racing memorabilia to rival Reilly's. Upstairs, I saw a photo of Arkle (yet again) and Tom Dreaper, who was petting his forehead and chomping on a pipe, as if the pair were hatching a plot to spring at the Gold Cup.

The lodge, I discovered, is a white, one-story building opposite the racecourse, more like a ranch-style house than a hospital. A horse trailer was parked next to a vacant paddock, and a glum man in the filthy clothes of an overburdened groom paced around, evidently on edge about his appointment. My wait for Dr. Gowing—or Dr. G., as a staffer affectionately called him—wasn't long. A big, easygoing, snowy-haired man, he has the sort of benevolent presence that often earns an endearing nickname from coworkers. He seemed tired at first, as if talking with me didn't rate very high on his list of desires, for which I couldn't fault him, but he slowly warmed to the subject of veterinary medicine. It was his life's work, after all.

Dr. Gowing was familiar with the virus plaguing the yards. He hadn't heard of anyone identifying it specifically, but he assumed it was a respiratory strain of influenza and quite contagious. The virus could be detected before a race about seventy-five percent of the time through a blood sample, but it stayed dormant in the other cases. Triggered by stress, it bloomed during a race, causing the horse to falter as Beef Or Salmon had done. There was no set recovery time. A horse might need a month or six weeks, depending on the symptoms—faster with a mild cough than with a full systemic infection. (Imazulutoo was still sick in March, in no shape for Cheltenham.) Rest and antibiotics were the only cure. "The economic losses are huge," Gowing said. "I shudder to think of them."

Viruses come and go, of course, and Gowing ordinarily deals with a garden variety of basic injuries. For jumpers, a bowed tendon is the most common. The doc believes the length of the races, and the pressure that exerts on tendons, is responsible for the damage. A bloody nose is also a common complaint. But what about fallers? Those crashes looked so bad I imagined he must have a whole hospital wing filled with patients whose legs were bandaged or in plaster, but he doesn't. "The soft ground protects them," he said. "It cushions the fall."

In the old days, trainers would come to Gowing worried that a horse might have a heart murmur, and he would do an exhaustive exam to see if it were true, but today there are simple diagnostic tools to detect such problems. Among the easiest ways to assess a horse's health is by its weight, he told me. During a race, a horse can lose up to twenty pounds while sweating, but should put them right back on through rehydration in three or four days. If the horse doesn't, there's a problem, most likely something latent.

"Where's the fun in this?" I asked, an angle I'm always exploring, and he blinked as if startled by the question, one he might never ask himself, and laughed. "Every day is different. You're never bored."

"Not even with horses? You're still fond of them?"

"Well, why wouldn't you be?" His fondness aside, he confessed he'd never been much of a rider himself, although he admired Ireland's brave jockeys. I painted him a picture of Paul Carberry tearing across the countryside on his hunter, leaping over stone walls and thorny hedges, as wild and willful as Black Jack Dennis. "That would be a very dance," he said appreciatively, then rose to show me around the hospital, moving with a big man's shambling gait. Like Michael Hourigan, he started from scratch in a cottage that still stood by the road, and he, too, was proud of his achievements.

Now Gowing has a pristine room for his lab work and also two surgeries, one for the messy stuff such as colic and abscesses and the other for orthopedic jobs. The horses arrive at a receiving barn and are sedated and anesthetized with gas before being transferred to an operating table. Farther on are two isolation stalls for horses with contagious diseases. The doc has fifteen stalls in total, and the overburdened groom waited by one. His horse was scheduled for an X-ray. I couldn't tell who looked more nervous, the groom or the horse. In another stall, a young vet had a gloved hand in the anus of a mare—a bowel complaint, I guessed, but no, she had suffered a rectal tear when a stallion mounted her.

Gowing keeps his modern equipment in a room close by. He was especially pleased with a new digital X-ray machine that permits him to see precisely what's going on inside a horse. He had used it the other day on a poor, shivery little creature, who stood quietly in a stall across the way. From a distance, I thought the creature was a donkey, or even a weird half-breed, but it was a Thoroughbred foal. Its air of misery and loneliness was so tangible I felt a tug at my heart. The doc probed a shaved area on the foal's ribcage, where he'd done some sector scanning. "He's pretty sick," Gowing said. "He was sick before he was sold. His owner got a raw deal. We'll save him if we can."

I rubbed the foal's nose. An equine vet's job didn't seem very different from a regular doctor's, really. At the lodge, there was the same blend of hope, despair, relief, and even prayer you find at any hospital. The sad groom could be any anxious relative eager for some good news. That anybody at all cared about the wretched foal was a minor miracle, and his owner must have known it, because the foal would never win a race if he did survive. The caring was an act of obligation, another example of the ancient, honorable covenant between horses and those who ride them, a welcome thing in a world where life of any kind is often cheap.

O'HERLIHY'S HAS MANY VIRTUES as a pub, not least its policy of elevating racing to a position above all other sports. In some places, you have to beg the barmen to show the jumps if a decent, or even halfway decent, soccer match is on, but at our local it isn't an issue, because Reilly controls the TV clicker by common agreement, flicking among the channels with the exquisite timing he's honed to a fine edge on his couch at home. The clicker means a lot to him, and he embraces it as he might a medal for valor he earned in some forgotten war.

On a Saturday in early January, Reilly sauntered into the pub ready to do justice to three big meetings in England at Ascot, Haydock, and Warwick, and I was waiting for him. His seriousness could be gauged by a handwritten sheet he dropped on the bar. It was his memory aid, a list of all the televised races arranged by channel and time. He had tips clipped from various tabloids, too, and a stack of blank betting slips from Boylesports to be filled out after a look at the horses. On his feet were new sneakers to facilitate his sprint to the shop. His goal was to complete the round-trip before a race started, and if he failed and got back a few seconds too late, he groaned and let his slip flutter to the floor. "Can't win now," he'd say. Silly, yes, but it always proved true.

We were both keyed up about the Peter Marsh Chase at Haydock, a three-mile race regarded as a superior Gold Cup trial. Four horses had come out of it to win the Gold Cup in recent years, so the presence of Kingscliff, still very much in the Festival frame, was auspicious. He was stepping up in class, but the experts predicted he would handle it. Woe be it to those who listened, because Kingscliff failed to run or jump with his normal verve, and Artic Jack defeated him soundly. The result threw a wet blanket on Robert Alner's ardor. The horse, he thought, must have a muscle pull.

"That's it," Reilly said in disgust. He had a large ante-post wager on Kingscliff. "Might as well give Henrietta the trophy now and save us all the bother."

He hit the clicker and switched over to Ascot, where the featured race was the Victor Chandler Chase, a two-mile prep for the Queen Mother. The eye-catcher was Azertyuiop, who looked intimidating, quite tall and graceful. Unbeaten as a novice chaser last season, Azertyuiop hadn't yet won a handicap for older horses, so Paul Nicholls and Ruby Walsh were hoping for a solid display after their gelding's failure in the Tingle Creek, even though he was the top weight by far.

Native Scout from Ireland held the lead until the furious pace found him out, after which the race was between Nicky Henderson's Isio and Azertyuiop, whose terrific jump at the second-last put him in front. Yet the gritty Isio fought back and held on to win by a neck. Still, Azertyuiop's performance was exceptional, given that he carried nineteen pounds more than the winner. Ruby Walsh had insisted his horse wasn't fit at Sandown when losing to Moscow Flyer, and the Victor Chandler seemed to confirm it and generated some fear and trembling in those of us who were already concerned about Moscow's ability to transcend the evil grip of the Pattern.

In the late afternoon, we had the Tote Classic Chase at Warwick, a marathon for stayers at three miles five furlongs, with twenty-two fences to be jumped. In general, I am more skeptical than Reilly, ever alert to the possibility that things aren't what they appear to be, but he surpassed me for once. He was sure the "villainous" Martin Pipe was about to broker a betting coup. After a close scrutiny of Pipe's three entries that required the assistance of dime-store reading glasses, he was convinced that Jurancon II, the least fancied of them, was the key to the plot. Tony McCoy, the stable jock, had picked the favorite

Akarus to ride, but that was part of the cover-up. How could I be so blind? Didn't I see that McCoy was in on the scam? Take Control, Pipe's third horse, was mere window dressing. Hadn't won a race in ages.

"Twenty each way," Reilly said, lacing up a sneaker. (An each-way bet covers a horse to both win and place.) True, he knew his stuff, but I refused his entreaties and asked him to put my ten bucks on Bindaree, a Grand National winner, who could do the distance in his sleep.

The Tote Classic was a gruesome spectacle. Fallers were everywhere, and some were good horses, too. Take Control fell at the sixth fence and had to be put down, while Behrajan fell at the second-last, broke his neck, and died. We didn't hear about the deaths until after the race, and when we did they cast a pall over Reilly's brilliant gamble. Though I doubted Pipe had planned it, Jurancon II was there at the end to slug it out with Southern Star, another prize pupil from Henrietta Knight's academy, who landed the heavier punches. Reilly's payoff for his bet was substantial, anyway, but we didn't have it in us to celebrate, not when so many horses had come to grief.

WINTER MARKS THE TRUE BEGINNING of Ireland's point-to-point season, so when Sunday dawned in a wash of radiant sunshine, Imelda and I decided to drive to County Wicklow for the Shillelagh & District Hunt's annual meeting at Tinahely, a first for both of us. Imelda packed her sketchpad, a camera, and a picnic lunch, and we left before noon and took a highway past Dun Laoghaire and Bray, tracing the coastline of the Irish Sea. We were your typical carefree lovers on an outing until we crossed over into Wicklow and encountered a profound change in the weather, with dark clouds massed on the horizon. A minute later, showery rain drummed against the windshield. "It'll probably blow over," I said, more a wish than a belief, but Imelda, being Irish, knew better.

In Tinahely, we saw a sign for the races, but no directions, so for help we dashed through the rain to Seavers Bar, almost colliding at the front door with a gent in tweed, who had his wife on his arm—a couple out for a drink before Sunday lunch, I thought, but they were racegoers, too, and just as lost. "Youse here for the pint-to-pint?" asked the barman, as if no other reason could account for strangers being in Seavers. Though we were only a mile away from Fairwood, the site of the course, I had to resist an impulse to stay warm and dry and go from one pint to the next, a suggestion the barman, with his country accent, had planted in my head.

Imelda wasn't having any. She meant to see those horses and have that picnic, the weather be damned, so we ran back to the car and drove until we came to another sign that could have been written in blood. EIGHT EUROS, it said in bright red ink, a caution to sundry farm lads with empty pockets that they wouldn't be able to sneak into the races for free. Two men from the hunt club were selling tickets, and they were wrapped in enough waterproof clothing to survive a monsoon. Only their hands and faces were visible as they waved us through a gate and into a soaked field, where our wheels sank into the ooze. I had a very disturbing premonition that I might be putting my shoulder to the car's rear end later on.

Then we got a break. A tiny hole appeared in the sky, revealing a patch of blue. That lifted my spirits. Maybe we'd have our sunny picnic, after all. A good crowd had already assembled, mostly in family groups, so the mood was upbeat. From a giggling red-haired girl, whose brother was making mudpies at her feet, we bought a race program filled with courtesy ads for local businesses. I expressed some curiosity about the Crocodile Lounge and Black Tom's Tavern, but Imelda took my hand, and we walked up a muddy path, propelled forward by the wind. Mud was everywhere, so our marching anthem became the *slurp-slurp* of boots and shoes being swallowed. The kids loved it, though, splashing in puddles and stomping through bogs.

What a scene at the crest of the hill! Here was a panorama worthy of Breughel, with activity at every corner of the frame. Teenage boys demonstrated wrestling holds on one another to impress the teenage girls; young mothers fed bottles to their nursing babies; nattily dressed country squires leaned on their walking sticks and packed their pipes with tobacco; and plump farmers with straw in their hair discussed the price of crops. They were all neighbors, too. A large tent for drinks was doing a brisk trade, as were a pair of chip shops on wheels that smelled of greasy cooking oil. The bookies were gathered in a soggy enclave and didn't look happy about it. This was just a notch above a dog track—or maybe not.

Spectators had convened at a fenced parade ring for the second race. They were ready for the horses, but the horses weren't ready for them. They turned up one by one, each on its own schedule, led right through the crowd by their grooms and narrowly avoiding infants in strollers and toddlers on the lam. Some of the horses wore blankets against the cold—that patch of blue had disappeared—with numbers pinned on them, frequently too small to read. Point-to-points are called the cradle of the jumps game, and though they've produced dozens of great chasers, including Best Mate, I had a strong inkling we wouldn't see a future star that afternoon.

The Shillelagh & District Hunt began preparing for its annual meeting in the early autumn, Mary Dagg, the club's honorary secretary, had told me before the races. When the leaves fall, the members cut the birch themselves and build the fences at night after work, a labor of love. Volunteers are the rule with most clubs, Mary said. Point-to-points occupy a significant place in the cultural life of rural Ireland, but they struggle to keep afloat because of escalating costs.

Mary's club pays almost ten thousand dollars a year for its insurance alone. Without the financial support that point-to-points receive from Horse Racing Ireland, they'd go the way of the draft horse.

HRI provides the support in order to give "not so good" horses, the country's overflow, a chance to compete. At Fairwood, owners shelled out an entry fee of fifty bucks against a winner's purse of about eight hundred dollars, although the feature race carried a purse of more than a thousand. Almost all the races (four of six were for maidens) had too many entries and needed to be run in divisions over a standard distance of about three miles, the minimum for pointers. The horses were certified hunters, meaning they'd hunted with a recognized club and had proved they could jump. In the two open events, their average age was twelve, and most had already failed disastrously at real tracks. The jockeys, all amateurs, held the status of qualified riders. Some aspired to be pros, but most were in it for—that word again—the *craic*, both the men and the women.

The horses continued to assemble for the first division of the second race. They were maiden geldings of five and six, and primarily first-time starters. If they'd run before, they'd fallen (F), were pulled up (P), unseated their rider (U), or were brought down (B)—made to fall by another horse, that is. Lost In The Snow's record was characteristic—BFPPUP, it read. It would take a courageous, or maybe self-destructive, jockey to ride Lost In The Snow, but the same was true for most of the field. The jockeys were already a mess, too, wet and covered with mud. You might expect young riders to get a kick out of this, but there were also leathery guys in their forties saddling up for more abuse.

Fairwood is one of the most testing point-to-point courses anywhere. It demands stamina in spades. It has five fences, and riders must negotiate a hilly route marked in spots by hay bales; they complete the circuit twice during a race. There isn't a grandstand, so we stood a few feet from a fence, near enough to hear the horses' bellies brush it when they didn't jump high enough. That sound, and the loud thump of their hooves on landing, captivated Imelda. She thought it was sublime to be so close to such tremendous energy and gave me a mini-lecture on Edmund Burke, who wrote that our astonishment at such moments, coupled with a degree of terror, suspended the soul's "motions," and caused our dependence on comforting concepts like order and clarity to slip.

The jockeys rounded a turn, bowled downhill, and vanished for a minute before they thundered back toward us on their second circuit. Only three horses finished the race, and Louisburgh, the winner, who was trained by Ted Walsh, had many lengths in hand—not that you'd know about Walsh from reading the program. It didn't give the names of any trainer or jockey. As for the lack of finishers, that was routine for a point-to-point. In Louisburgh's last race, where he fell, just five of seventeen horses had lasted the entire trip.

If the finish couldn't be described as thrilling, the loose horses certainly were. Two riderless geldings—they'd fallen, lost their jocks, and got up again—were on the rampage, galloping hellbent toward the chip shops on wheels. An old woman practically did a somersault to get out of the way. I had a vision of hot vats of oil being upended, while the french fries flew. Grooms and jockeys pursued the horses on foot, as did some hardy fans, while less intrepid folks hid behind a tree, as we did. The geldings were caught after a few minutes, and the crowd seemed disappointed. The chaos had delighted rather than threatened them. "There is a sympathy between the rush of the racing hunter and their own impetuous natures," as the *Dublin Saturday Magazine* once said.

Everyone regrouped for the race's second division. The Royal Dub won it in a Carberry family production, with Tommy the trainer and Nina Carberry, Paul's sister, the jockey. Those facts weren't in the program, either. I gleaned them at random, listening to the chatter. The

chief attraction of a point-to-point, I realized, was its glorious infor-
mality. If the sport became too organized (and less sublime), it might
lose its grassroots appeal. The program was only a document, no
more than a rough guide, and if you relied on it for information,
you exposed yourself as an outsider with no direct line to Farmer
Matthews, say, a dairyman from Carnew, whose speedy mare had a big
chance in the fifth race.

Yet long before the fifth race, there were problems. First came the
snow. That might have been fun and even romantic, but when the snow
turned to an icy, stinging sleet, we looked for shelter in the drinks tent,
but so many people had preceded us that even the tiniest, most under-
nourished jockey couldn't have squeezed inside. For some reason, this
got Imelda talking about the mass evictions of farmers during the
Potato Famine, their doors barred or padlocked and the roofs torn off
their cottages for good measure, with entire families tossed out into
just such a hostile environment, but I wasn't the best audience for a
history lesson since I was running for the car as fast as I could. There,
we cranked up the heat and ate our sad little picnic, scarcely able to
break off chunks of bread for the cheese because our fingers were so
numb.

THE VIRUS SCARE seemed to be passing at last. Horses were rising
from their sick beds with their health restored. In the *Post* I read
that Beef Or Salmon was already back in training, although Michael
Hourigan couldn't (or wouldn't) say when or where his horse would
run next. In England, an equine physiotherapist was treating Kingscliff
for muscle problems in his shoulders and withers, but Robert Alner
still had the Gold Cup as his target, while in France Guillaume
Macaire was readying Jair du Cochet for the Pillar Property Chase at
Cheltenham. If Jair du Cochet did okay, Macaire, too, would try for
the Gold Cup. Asked to explain the horse's abysmal performance in

the King George, Jacques Ricou replied sagely, "I don't understand why, and he isn't able to tell us."

In other news, the rabbits were wreaking havoc again at Down Royal. They ignored the sharp stones, burrowed under the chase course, and made it unsafe for racing. Paddy Power joked that the track should change its name to "Watership Down Royal," a quip that displeased the track's manager, who countered by saying, "I need this like a hole in the head." Elsewhere, the Irish Turf Club released the results of its random drug-testing program. The sixty-five urine samples donated by jockeys came back negative, even for alcohol, a balm to punters and bookies alike. Finally, Willie Mullins reported that Florida Pearl, perhaps the most popular chaser in Ireland, was ready to resume his illustrious career after a long absence.

If the National Hunt has a dynasty, it would have to be the Mullins family, who are even more entrenched than the Carberrys. Paddy Mullins, the revered patriarch, still trains horses at the age of eighty-five ("I'd like to *be* Paddy Mullins!" Hourigan once exclaimed, envying the longevity), and his four sons are also in the game, Willie and Tony as trainers and George as the operator of a horse transport business. George shares a farm with Willie and sells shredded newspapers for bedding as a sideline. (The paper generates less dust in a stall than straw does, so it's easier on a horse's breathing.) Tom, the youngest son, helps his father and will take over his yard when the time comes, all this despite Paddy's assertion that he discouraged his boys from joining the profession.

"I could not get them to do anything else," he complained to his biographer. "I wanted them to do something else. I thought there was not room in it for them all. When some of the boys were in school at Roscrea, I preached to them every chance I got. 'Go and do something else.' I might as well have been talking to the table."

As the most established trainer, Willie tends to attract the best stock, Florida Pearl being his treasure. Again Tom Costello had a hand in the magic. Willie first noticed and fell in love with the horse at Costello's yard, buying him as a four-year-old and later selling him to Violet and Archie O'Leary. "The size of him, the scope of him, it's tremendous," he enthused to me once. "He's a beautiful athlete!" The bay gelding, by Florida Sun out of Ice Pearl, proved it at the track, winning both the Champion Bumper and a big-money chase at the Cheltenham Festival, plus the Irish Hennessy three times, with only the Festival's Gold Cup eluding him, although he has placed in the race.

The current season had been dismal for Florida Pearl so far, though. Originally slated for the King George—he had won it over the young Best Mate in 2001—he suffered a sprain and had to be scratched. Almost twelve, he kept limping and failed to show his usual spark. That was a worry to Mullins, who had more than his share of anxieties, the chief one being a draining legal battle with the British Jockey Club over Be My Royal, a horse he trained. Be My Royal had won the English Hennessy at Newbury last winter, but the Jockey Club withheld the purse because of a positive test for morphine, later traced to a tainted batch of feed. A court battle loomed, during which Mullins would attempt to declare his innocence and reverse the decision before the club's disciplinary panel.

Frustrated with Florida Pearl's lack of progress, Willie had turned over the horse to Grainne Ni Chaba, an equine physiotherapist who has a practice on the Curragh and an intriguing résumé. She worked in Florida breaking yearlings; rode as an amateur jockey on the flat ("I didn't win any races") and on her own mares in bumpers; and cared for abused animals for the RSPCA before branching out. Because she doesn't have a trainer's pressures, she can concentrate all her skills on an individual horse. The intimacy can lead to unexpected results, as it did with Rebelline, a savage mare.

"I still have a scar on my bum from her," Grainne told me when we talked.

"How did that happen?" I imagined an explosive fall and a very hard landing.

"She bit me!"

From the start, Grainne liked Florida Pearl. "He was an ideal patient," she said. "He wanted to get better." She rode him every day, slowly and steadily, and got to know him, doing both dressage and pole work. By being on his back, she could isolate his problems and figure out how to fix them. He had a sore ligament in a near-side knee, for instance, and Grainne was dismayed about the way he looked from behind. He wasn't properly balanced and ran with his neck too high instead of down low, and that created a little hollow in his back and put extra pressure on the muscles. Though Florida Pearl had only fallen once in a race, Grainne believed the fall had thrown him out of kilter.

Her job was to rewire the horse completely. "It was like, okay, mister, time to sort yourself out," she said. She had to teach him to run correctly again—to relax and regain his confidence. She used balancing reins to strengthen his back and his hocks. For his minor pains, she gave him electrotherapy. He got some laser treatments for his sore knee and did plenty of stretching. To build up his cartilage, Grainne put him on Cortaflex, a dietary supplement. Soon he was involved in a regular routine that included an hour or so of dressage, a forty-minute massage, and thirty minutes of physio.

The program was a smashing success. Florida Pearl stayed with Grainne for more than two months, and when he returned to Mullins's yard, he was in super shape, transformed into a racehorse again. Grainne still missed him a bit. "He had a stall next to a horse called Chubaka, and they became wonderful pals. Chewie's the kind of horse who makes other horses happy. He's huge, too, at seventeen hands three, even bigger than Florida Pearl. They were mad about each other. They'd jump up and start playing the minute they met," she said. "You should have seen Florida Pearl! He had this great big bum on him. I meant to take some before-and-after photos, but I always forget."

Shortly after our conversation, I did see the rejuvenated Florida Pearl when Willie Mullins brought him to Fairyhouse for the Normans Grove Chase. The race was a trial balloon of sorts. If the Pearl did well after his 238-day layoff, he might go for his fourth Irish Hennessy in February. He was the classiest horse in the field by far, but the fans shied away from him because he'd been injured, letting the odds drift out to 8–1. Yet Richard Johnson had flown in from England to take the mount, and since Johnson rarely rides in Ireland, I assumed that Mullins wasn't fooling around.

The other five horses in the race (Rathgar Beau, Knife Edge, Rince Ri, Beachcomber Boy, and Arctic Copper) had knocked heads for months without any of them winning a race, so it seemed obvious that a fresh, classy, and healthy Florida Pearl could spring an upset. I felt smug about doping this out, another sign that my education was advancing nicely, but as I waded into the ring to bet, the earth must have wobbled, because I heard myself yell, "Twenty to win on Arctic Copper." Then I watched morosely as Florida Pearl dashed to the lead and garnered the prize with incredible ease.

CONFUSION HAS A HABIT of compounding itself. Once it sets in, you start to double-think every aspect of your life. Should I pour milk in my coffee, or drink it black? I hear the mermaids singing, et cetera. My hapless condition followed me from Fairyhouse to Gowran Park for the Thyestes Chase, a prestigious Cheltenham prep race for stayers. The Thyestes drew another record crowd of almost nine thousand, and the Irish gift for sociability was at its most expansive. Even I, the wandering American, met someone I knew—Tamso Doyle, a friend from HRI—and as we made a prerace promenade, passing the flat-capped bench sitters (only sixteen this time), she introduced me to people along the way.

First, we ran into Mary O'Grady, Edward's mother. Known as Grannie O'Grady, she was perky and chipper. "I've got my fingers crossed for Takagi," she confided. That was her son's horse. Next we crossed paths with Brian Gleeson, our moderator from the Dunraven Arms. He leaned toward us in a posture of utmost discretion, as the Irish do when they're about to whisper a tip, and said that Takagi had been *laid out perfectly* for the Thyestes. "His jockey used him very lightly in his last race at Leopardstown," Gleeson told us. "He'll have plenty of zip saved for today."

He spoke with such authority I began to waver about Willie Mullins's Rule Supreme, the horse I'd selected on the train to Kilkenny, but then Phil Rothwell put me right as we chatted by the parade ring. The son of a dairy farmer, Rothwell trains horses near Tinahely, and when I asked which horse he liked, he said, "Rule Supreme."

"That was my first choice, too." I was reeling a bit, actually. "But everybody's talking about Takagi."

"Always stick with your first choice," Rothwell cautioned me, with an oracular firmness that made me recall Allen Ginsberg's motto about writing and creativity, "First thought, best thought." In possession of such wisdom, I put fifty to win on Rule Supreme with Paddy Sharkey, violating a motto of my own that goes, "Never bet with a bookie whose name has a negative ring."

There's a wonderful relief in placing a bet. Like boarding an airplane or accepting a blind date, you're in the hands of fate. Freed of the obligation to decide, I walked to the stand Jessie Harrington prefers, but I couldn't find her in the swarm of fans, so I edged into the first available space and landed by chance next to Edward O'Grady. He was just back from a holiday in Barbados and still bore the traces of a tan, glowing like a beacon of good cheer in the midst of his pale-faced, sun-deprived countrymen. The moment was deeply unsettling for me—Grannie O'Grady, Brian Gleeson, and now the man himself. Why had I listened to Phil Rothwell? What did he know about the workings of the universe? The gods couldn't have been more direct. Takagi was destined to win.

It was too late to do anything, though. The horses were off, and I was stuck with Rothwell, Ginsberg, and Rule Supreme. With every glance at O'Grady, I sank a little lower. He looked serene and unflappable, a veteran trainer with impeccable bloodlines. His father had been a champion trainer, and when he died suddenly in the early 1970s, Edward, who was twenty-two, quit studying to be a vet and took over the yard. He had scored many triumphs since then and weathered many setbacks. In fact, he'd just been dealt another bad hand. Sacundai, revived at Leopardstown over Christmas, now had a bum leg that would scratch him from the Festival, reducing O'Grady's probables to just two, Pizarro and Back In Front.

O'Grady watched the race through binoculars. What he saw must have bothered him, but he didn't show it. He kept his cool, even though Takagi was struggling—no, worse, the horse could have been mired in a pot of molasses for all the headway he was making. Barry Geraghty was flat to the boards on him, to no avail. Takagi was trapped in that mire. After a mile or so, O'Grady muttered through clenched teeth, "Not today," and then, "Horse didn't run." He spoke not so much to me as to a spectral presence, his spirit companion. Takagi's lack of pace was a mystery to him, but Rule Supreme was still going a good gallop, although he jumped with more abandon than finesse.

One horse who did run was Hedgehunter, another of Willie Mullins's entries. A dedicated stayer, Hedgehunter had nearly won the Welsh National in December over almost four miles, so the three miles of the Thyestes didn't tax him. Substituting for Ruby Walsh, off toiling in England, David Casey let the horse go to the front rather than holding him up as Ruby did. Hedgehunter seemed delighted to be out there on his own. He had speed, pace, and style, and romped to an eight-length win, while Rule Supreme botched the last two fences and finished third. Why should it be any different? I hear the mermaids singing, et cetera.

Gowran Park is the Mullinses' hometown track, close to all their yards, so they raked in a number of pots that afternoon. Tony took the first race, while Willie later added a novice chase to his Thyestes haul. Noel Meade had a productive day, too, back on his feet again after the virus scourge. Meade's Rosaker hiked up his Cheltenham stock by winning the Galmoy Stayers Hurdle under Paul Carberry, who was nursing a bruised kidney from yet another spill, this one at Fairyhouse. That was the nature of the Festival beast, I realized. Fortunes rise, fortunes fall. Sacundai was out, and Rosaker was in, at least for the moment. Meade was overjoyed, anyhow. "Happy days are here again," he said, firing up a victory cigar.

THE TRIP TO GOWRAN PARK left me shakier than ever. Having committed the gambler's mortal sin of thinking too much, as worthless as reading tea leaves or probing the entrails of birds, I needed a break from handicapping and spent the next day strolling around Dublin in a Bloomish mood, casting a cold eye on the betting shops. To elevate my mind, I bought some books downtown and stopped for a noon pint at Davy Byrnes, the pub where snuffley Nosey Flynn, with dewdrops trickling from his nostrils, tried to pry a tip on the Ascot Gold Cup (due to be run that day, June 16, 1904) from the owner, who refused to cooperate. "I wouldn't do anything in that line," Byrnes scolded, his place being a moral one. "It ruined many a man the same horses."

"True for you," replied Flynn. "Unless you're in the know."

To be in the know! That was every real Dubliner's dream. Tips were circulating around the city with extraordinary brio as the Festival drew near, and I was blessed (or cursed) with one that morning when I bought *The Irish Times*—not, mind you, the *Post*. Brian Keighron, our newsagent, is a staunch racing fan, and privy to the steady stream of opinion that flows through his shop. With a discerning ear, he separates the conceivably useful information from the blatantly outrageous fantasies, Hasanpour being an example of the former. "I only got word of the horse the other day," he whispered, just as Gleeson had done, and tapped my forearm for emphasis.

Twice a winner on the flat in England, Hasanpour was purchased from a prominent British yard by an Irish buyer presumed to be the spendthrift J. P. McManus—or so Brian heard at first. But when Hasanpour was entered at Cork the Sunday just past, the owner was listed as Mrs. G. Smith. But Mrs. Smith could be related to McManus, couldn't she? Ah, whatever. Anyway, the rumor was that Charlie Swan, the horse's new trainer, called Hasanpour the best he'd ever sat on—and he'd ridden Istabraq! And Istabraq belonged to McManus! The chain of coincidences . . . well, that was all Brian needed. He backed the horse at Cork, and when Hasanpour shot to a twenty-length lead, he began reciting a traditional punter's prayer, "Jaysus, please don't fall!" Hasanpour didn't. The horse was the goods.

Tap, tap. "Hasanpour was 66–1 ante-post for the Festival," Brian said, his voice an octave lower. "You won't get him at that price now, but still . . ." So I put Hasanpour's name in my Cheltenham notebook, while I crossed off Nil Desperandum, who had knocked a piece of bone off a front-leg pastern and wouldn't be traveling to the Cotswolds. Hasanpour up, Nil Desperandum down.

Who would be the next pope? An article in the *Times* addressed that very question. The favorite was Dionigi Tettamanzi of Italy, according to Paddy Power Bookmakers (wrong, for once), whose PR chief, *the*

Paddy Power, expressed some wholly contrived shock that anyone in a Catholic country would be offended by a firm accepting bets on the papal succession. Yet everyone from ordinary churchgoers to the adepts of Padre Pio had taken offense, especially since the current pope was still "alive and strong," as the Right Reverend Thomas McMahon noted. In his own defense, Paddy said, "It is something people talk about in pubs, and because it is being discussed, I think it is something we should be betting on."

What a fine bit of logic! Fair play to you, Paddy, I thought, although I'd never discussed the next pope with anybody at O'Herlihy's. Had I been drinking at a heathen den? As a test, I asked the fellow next to me at Davy Byrnes if he liked Tettamanzi for pope. I cannot properly capture the blankness of his stare.

Around one o'clock, the lunch crowd began filtering in, so I packed up my little library and went over to McDaid's, where they don't serve food and a peaceful midday calm prevails. Down the bar, I saw the ghost of Patrick Kavanagh hunkered over the racing pages, irritable and hungover until the magical spirits lifted his own. Here, too, Paul Carberry was known to drop by of an evening. "You've been seen at McDaid's," I teased him once, and he smiled and said, "Yeah, sure, I've been seen at a lot of places in Dublin."

McDaid's is a properly bookish spot, quiet and conducive to study in the early hours of the afternoon, so I cracked open my new copy of Liam O'Flaherty's *A Tourist's Guide to Ireland*, first published in 1929. O'Flaherty didn't rate restaurants or hotels. Instead, in a witty, satirical style, he advised tourists how to deal with the "four pillars of Irish society"—the parish priest, the politician, the publican, and the peasant, whose influence could be ranked in that order. Maybe it was the talk about the pope, but I turned first to the section on parish priests, a dodgy bunch who were always soliciting donations, O'Flaherty remarked. He urged visitors to contribute only to a priest who is "fat and jovial and owns a good horse and wears riding breeches and goes around everywhere with a horsewhip," perhaps because the author was an obsessive gambler.

The parish priest is wary of outsiders, O'Flaherty wrote, and inclined to regard Ireland as the only ethical country, although his personal view of the Irish is "a very poor one." Such priests believe the English are immoral, and that the French are even worse. Americans are not to be trusted, because they allow divorce. Germany is acceptable on account of Catholic Bavaria, but the Russians are "beyond the pale of civilization," having overthrown the church. The Italians, Spaniards, and Belgians are "very nearly as pure as the Irish." As for the Chinese, they might still be saved through the efforts of the Irish mission to China, but the Mexicans are doomed, and it is the duty of every parish priest to lobby Ireland's leaders "to get the English to get the Americans to make war on Mexico."

DURING THE LONG, HARD YEARS when the church banned its clergy from going to the races, some priests didn't abide by the rules. They'd leave their collars and missals at home and travel to England, where they could go to the track incognito and return with their halos unblemished. I heard about this gambit from Father Sean Breen, who's known around Ireland as the Racing Priest and also, warmly, as the Breener. He takes great pride in being the only priest in the world with two racecourses in his parish, Naas and Punchestown, both in Kildare, and likes to say, "Isn't God good?" in praise of his bounty.

I had wanted to meet Father Breen ever since someone told me he dispenses tips on the Festival to his congregation. Though I'd been to both Naas and Punchestown, I got lost on the road to his parish, anyway, and when I phoned for directions, he asked, "So you're a lost soul, are you?" That gave me a moment's pause, but it was only an example of the gentle humor the Breener brings to bear on the complexities of being human. In his seventies, he has a sweet, boyish, untroubled face, and a talent for light banter and offering comfort that aging can confer. His house was next door to the Church of the Immaculate Conception, at a rural junction in Eadestown.

"You're very welcome," he greeted me, apologizing for the mess inside, as older people do, even though the mess didn't exist. "Come into my bachelor pad." He escorted me to the kitchen, his neatest room, and made a pot of tea.

Father Breen had held his current post for about nine years and served about four hundred families. (He has since moved to a new post in Ballymore Eustace, also in Kildare.) He grew up in a small town in farm country, but he didn't have any particular feeling for horses as a boy, once falling off a neighbor's pony when he tried to ride it, a deterrent to any further efforts in the saddle. Only later as a young priest in North County Dublin did he become fascinated by the races, largely through his friendships with such people as Jim Dreaper, Tom Dreaper's son, and Joanna Morgan, a trainer. (He owns a piece of two horses stabled at Morgan's yard in Meath.) On his initial trip to Cheltenham, he had the good luck to see Arkle win his first Gold Cup, and he has returned for every Festival since, barring illness.

Horses are integral to Irish culture, Father Breen thinks. In his parish not long ago, the priest still visited his parishioners on horseback.

"Racing is a marvelous social thing in Ireland," he said, his eyes twinkling. "So healthy out in the open air! You meet all strands of people, too. It isn't just the upper classes go racing here. Sure, there are those who overdo the drink and the gambling, but life is a temptation, after all. Anyway, I love it. I absolutely *love* it! It's so relaxing it takes me right out of my head. Nobody knows what goes on in our heads, thank God." Of all the Irish meetings, his favorite is Galway in July, a seven-day indulgence. "It's tremendous fun! Everybody's there. Even the politicians have caught on," he said drily. "The prime minister wouldn't dare miss it! The first three men I ran into one summer were the ministers for justice, finance, and agriculture."

The Breener was looking forward to his annual journey to Cheltenham. He'd be with his usual group, men who've bonded over the last twenty years or so, and he would say a Punters' Mass at his hotel on St. Patrick's Day, which always falls during the Festival and inflames the Irish crowd. He expected to have a good time, but there would also be some melancholy.

"A lot of people die," he said. "You don't see them there, and you say to yourself, 'He isn't at Cheltenham, he must be dead.' " When I mentioned that I was going for the first time, he assured me I'd be ecstatic about the quality of the races, although he had some reservations about how the Festival has changed and become less intimate since his earliest visits. "It's gotten very commercial. The corporate side ruins everything, doesn't it? The Tented Village, all those shops, they're a distraction." He didn't say this angrily, just in a resigned way, with a priestly tolerance for what others might prefer. "I'm just a purist, I guess. It's the racing that matters to me."

He poured more tea and passed the soda bread. Tacked to the kitchen door, I noticed a calendar from *The Irish Field.* On the table was a well-thumbed copy of the *Post.* Through a window over the sink, I could see a neatly kept back garden. The house was very still and peaceful, the kind of place where you can hear the tick of a clock and the drip of a faucet.

"The Irish used to ask me to bless their horses before a race at Cheltenham," Father Breen went on, "but I don't do it anymore. Do you know where the word *blessing* comes from? It means 'to speak well of.' I'll tell you an old joke, it's been around for ages. Seems this trainer had a horse he wanted blessed, so he got a priest to do it, and the horse won. A COI fella"—COI being shorthand for Church of Ireland—

"witnessed that, and the next time he saw the priest do a blessing, he bet on the horse, and the horse won again. That happened twice more, but the fourth time the horse finished last. The COI fella was upset because he'd lost all his money, so he cornered the priest and asked what went wrong. The priest gave him a disgusted look and said, 'Ah, you Prods can't tell the difference between a blessing and the last rites!' "

"Old but good," I laughed. "Are you a gambling man, Father? What are your Festival picks?"

The Breener does enjoy a bet, but he worries about getting carried away in the reckless carnival atmosphere at Cheltenham, so he puts down his bets in advance, three each morning with David Power, before he can be swayed. He was considering a treble on Moscow Flyer, Best Mate, and Rooster Booster, who won the Champion Hurdle last year and was favored once again, even though history and the statistics dictated against all three champs retaining their titles.

"Bookies love trebles," he said merrily. "Three chances for the punter to lose!" He already had an ante-post wager on Willie Mullins's Sadlers Wings and was pondering a plunge on Brave Inca, whose trainer Colm Murphy, a protégé of Aidan O'Brien's, was new to the game. "No young trainer would get his hands on a fine horse like that in the past," he told me. "The horse would have been sold right out from under him, gone from Ireland to England or France."

Soon Father Breen would become a "seven-day wonder," the subject of a media frenzy during the week before the Festival. He did interviews by phone with radio hosts. "They pick my brain," he said, joking again, "if I'm not being presumptuous about having a brain." His passion for the races was particularly striking to the English, and the BBC once pressed him to account for it. "What does your vicar do for entertainment?" he answered smartly. Alert to being manipulated, he refuses to play along with those who are fishing for stories about drink and debauchery. He relishes his brief burst of celebrity, but he surrenders it without a care.

As a good Christian, the Breener tired of talking about himself and asked me some questions, what type of books I had written and why I was in Ireland. "I met an Irish woman in London," I began . . .

"End of story!" he cried, interrupting me. "Best women in the world! And they're great mothers. They have to be." He halted for a second. "Why is that, I wonder?"

Certainly, Father Breen didn't fit O'Flaherty's satirical profile of a parish priest, being too good-humored and self-aware. It was a bad time for priests in Ireland and elsewhere, of course, and yet there were many decent, committed men like the Breener who accepted the foibles of their congregation and did what they could to meliorate them. His was a life lived in service, rich in the rewards of community. As I was leaving, I asked if he'd be going to the track anytime soon. "Oh, yes," he said emphatically. "If I didn't see a horse for a week, I'd be unwell."

THE NEXT TRAINER to watch a dream go up in smoke was Jessie Harrington, who brought Spirit Leader to Leopardstown for the AIG Europe Champion Hurdle. After Spirit Leader's second-place finish in the Bewley's over Christmas, the students of form were supporting her against Rooster Booster for the other Champion Hurdle, the one at the Festival. Gutsy and genuine, the mare thrives on a fast-paced fight, and Cheltenham's hilly racecourse would be another bonus for her. If she ran a good race in the AIG, the theory went, she might peak in the early spring, a trick Jessie had pulled off a time or two with other horses.

But Spirit Leader was hardly a banker at Leopardstown. In the AIG, a Grade One worth about one hundred thousand dollars, she faced a strong contingent of opponents. Golden Cross, the Bewley's winner, was in the mix, as was Noel Chance's Flame Creek, third in that same race. Willie Mullins had Davenport Milenium ready to go, too. His horse had come up against Spirit Leader once before, finishing second to her sixth in a race at Cheltenham in December while carrying a pound more. Today Spirit Leader had a five-pound advantage, as she did over two horses from the J. P. McManus stable, Fota Island and Foreman. German-bred, Foreman was the more feared of the pair. The horse had done well as a hurdler in France, prompting McManus to buy him for a handsome price.

The AIG was a strange contest, with an upside-down result. Fota Island made much of the running and wound up third, while Georges Girl, who'd only won a single handicap hurdle ever, was second. Under a confident ride from Thierry Doumen, his French jockey, Foreman picked up at the last and soon had the measure of the others, a dramatic spectacle on the big screen because Doumen's face was smeared with blood from a nosebleed he couldn't staunch while riding. He was overjoyed to win, doubly so because Foreman belonged to a string of horses he trained in Chantilly. All the favored horses failed to place, including Spirit Leader, whose name now had a big question mark next to it in my Cheltenham notebook.

IMMEDIATELY AFTER THE AIG, Willie Mullins put on a good suit and traveled to London, where on January 29 at Portman Square, the Jockey Club's disciplinary panel began its inquiry into Be My Royal's tainted win in the Hennessy Gold Cup at Newbury. A total of thirty-seven horses had tested positive for traces of morphine in Britain during the period under scrutiny—sixteen were winners—and the source in each case was the same—Connolly's Red Mills 14% Racehorse Cubes—so the outcome of the hearing would have a ripple effect on the other cases.

Morphine occurs naturally in feed, often in trace amounts. All the parties agreed on that. At issue was the definition of a threshold level, or how much morphine it takes to affect a horse's performance. On Mullins's behalf, scientists had submitted papers with evidence that trace amounts of the substance have no effect, positive or negative, and yet the Jockey Club was resolute about its "zero tolerance" policy. A horse was disqualified if any morphine at all turned up in a sample—a rule Mullins and his attorneys objected to as antiquated, considering the sort of technology available in the twenty-first century.

To get some background on the situation, I spoke with Noel Brennan of Connolly's Red Mills, whose headquarters are in Goresbridge, Kilkenny. The company is family owned, with no outside shareholders, and has been around since 1908, initially selling seeds and later diversifying into horse feed in 1963. "With this morphine business, some of us feel like we've been here since 1908," Brennan kidded, having a laugh at his own expense. The case sounded bad to the uninformed public, he admitted, a black mark on Connolly's proud history, because morphine carries a connotation of race-fixing and doped horses.

"Red Mills fed fifty-six percent of the winners in Ireland last year," Brennan said, doing some image-polishing. "We also fed thirty-three percent of the winners at the Cheltenham Festival." In truth, that's a noteworthy accomplishment since Red Mills has as many as fifteen competitors. The morphine incident was predictable, Brennan felt, a grenade waiting to explode. Everyone knew about the potential for feed to be contaminated, but no one was willing to do much about it. "The science is there, but the Irish Turf Club and the Jockey Club won't spend the money on testing," he said. "They say it doesn't occur often enough for them to bother."

As well as being a publicity nightmare for Red Mills, the disciplinary panel's hearing was expensive. Not wanting to lose a big customer like Mullins, the company had agreed to foot all the legal bills, and that would raise the cost of their insurance premiums—a waste, in

Brennan's opinion. Red Mills would much rather have tossed the money into a kitty to fund the research needed to rewrite the rulebook. He believed the Turf and Jockey Clubs were blinded by tradition, age-old bodies resistant to change.

The two-day inquiry did not go well for Mullins and Red Mills after their fourteen-month wait, despite the evidence compiled to support them. The Jockey Club stuck to its guns, upheld the disqualification, and ordered Mullins to reimburse the Club for its legal fees of about five thousand pounds. Mullins was aggrieved, as he should have been, since during the hearing Dr. Peter Webbon, the Jockey Club's chief veterinary officer, stated that any concentration of morphine up to fifty nanograms per milliliter couldn't possibly affect a horse's performance, and Be My Royal's level was far below the benchmark.

In light of that, Mullins suggested the samples be tested again to demonstrate the point. His offer was rejected, yet there was a single bright spot for him. The disciplinary panel also heard that the Jockey Club had instructed the Horseracing Forensic Laboratory to apply the fifty-nanograms-per-milliliter threshold level to all samples tested in the future. Mullins's solicitors grabbed at that as a hook on which to hang an appeal, but Willie was still bitterly disappointed, a scapegoat for a crime he didn't commit.

AFTER HIS SETBACK, Willie Mullins returned to a wet Saturday evening in Dublin. At our house, we had a coal fire burning against the inhospitable weather and a leg of lamb in the oven. I listened to the steady drip of rain on the roof, a pleasant sound if you're not at Thurles, while Imelda sat on the couch reading the paper. The boys were in their rooms doing whatever it was they did in their private realms—the older writing in his journal, maybe, while the younger blasted through the streets of Vice City, playing Grand Theft Auto. The heart of winter, the hearth for warmth, the afternoon's racing at

Fairyhouse over and the races at Punchestown due tomorrow, on the first Sunday in February.

I'd just come back from O'Herlihy's after a pint and a deep analytical discussion with Reilly, so the kitchen table was covered with my notebooks and old copies of the *Post*. I was charting the arc of the season to date, a record of the usual vagaries, of the mighty ascending and then brought crashing to earth. What had I learned in the past four months? Mainly how difficult it is for any trainer to keep a good horse fit when faced with a vast array of perils—viruses, injuries, and a random dagger of misfortune that could strike anywhere, at any time—all in hopes that the horse would be ready to shine, however briefly, at the Cheltenham Festival.

Best Mate and Moscow Flyer were idle now and wouldn't be seen in public for another six weeks. After Jair du Cochet's superior form in the Pillar Property Chase, Guillaume Macaire had signed on for the Gold Cup, after all. Michael Hourigan remained tight-lipped about whether or not Beef Or Salmon would run in the Irish Hennessy next Sunday, or be shelved until mid-March. The ante-post odds for the top horses, though they varied from bookie to bookie, made Best Mate the overwhelming favorite, as low as 4–7 in some shops, while Jair du Cochet was at 6–1 and Kingscliff and Beef Or Salmon at 14–1.

As I carved the lamb, fragrant with rosemary, I remembered Tom Costello and his five sons in their enigmatic kingdom in faraway Newmarket-on-Fergus. No doubt they felt an emotional attachment to Best Mate—Tom Jr. had broken the colt and helped to raise him—and would eagerly attend to his Gold Cup bid, but I was curious about whether the Costellos were already focused on a future champion. Were they a few steps ahead of the ordinary mortals again? Their horse-trading had acquired such an air of mystery I couldn't consider my education complete without a visit to their farm, although how many secrets they'd divulge to any outsider was an open question.

The Waiting Game

Along the River Barrow in Leighlinbridge, County Carlow, magpies were flitting about over a field, their colors flashing—black, white, iridescent greens and purples—against a drizzly sky. It was the sort of morning that makes you want to stay in bed with your book or your lover, or both, but I was meeting Willie Mullins to talk about the Jockey Club's ruling. He owns a hundred-acre farm near the river, where he lives with his wife and kids in an old stone barn he lovingly restored after his marriage. On the front lawn, I saw a sculpture of a horse and jockey fashioned from wire and hammered metal scaling a hedge, with some Christmas lights still threaded through the mesh.

I found Willie at his gallops. He has a pair of them, a newer one of about a mile and an older one of two and a half furlongs. He keeps about a hundred horses at the yard and stood by a sand ring, supervising ten or so as they warmed up. He gave me a formal handshake, more reserved than the other trainers I'd visited, concentrating intently on the movement of his stock and not inclined to chitchat. Whereas Michael Hourigan comes at the job with a boisterous energy, and Jessie Harrington with an equestrian's ardor, Mullins is conservative and business-like, meticulous by nature.

When the string had finished exercising, and the horses were cooling down, we left for his office in another converted barn to escape the rain. "Been here long?" I asked, making polite conversation.

"Not long. About eighteen years."

"Did you grow up around here?"

"No, the home place is about five miles away," he said, as if it belonged to a different archipelago in the great ocean of Carlow. The measures of time and distance were those of a country person, reflecting Mullins's deep-rooted sense of place.

His office was well organized, as you'd expect from a finicky man who cares about every detail. His assistant sat at one end, while Willie's desk was at the other, neatly stacked with faxes and mail, a laptop at the ready. The only farmer's touch was a fly strip dangling from the ceiling over Mullins's chair, dotted with dead flies. The shelves held rows of form books and stud books, and there were many trophies, plaques, and photos, including a montage of his four winners of the Champion Bumper at Cheltenham: Wither Or Which (1996), Florida Pearl (1997), Alexander Banquet (1998), and Joe Cullen (2000).

Mullins had won some of the trophies himself as a jockey. In early middle-age, he is still fit for the saddle. He has a long-jawed face, and his reddish hair is thinning and thatched with gray. In spite of his serious demeanor—his hands were folded, as if he were about to suffer through an exam—he's known to like a bit of fun. "You were a good rider," I said.

A half-smile. "Good enough."

He was being modest, a fitting trait for royalty. More than once, he'd been Ireland's amateur champion. Although Paddy Mullins had carried on about how he wanted his sons to choose a career that didn't involve horses, he was responsible for Willie riding in races. Arriving home from boarding school for a weekend visit in 1973, Willie learned that his dad had taken out a license for him. Not only that, he was booked to ride in a bumper at Fairyhouse on Sunday. He went on to win a big race at the Cheltenham Festival on Paddy's Hazy Dawn in 1982.

I'd heard similar stories countless times by now. So many Irish trainers shared a similar background, their lives joined to horses in childhood and linked to them forever after. Willie doubted he could do anything else, really. "I'd go bananas in a regular office," he said, although he doesn't find training easy. His season had been below par to date, I thought, with such horses as Hedgehunter and Florida Pearl just hitting their stride, but he disagreed. He believes a trainer is always going to be frustrated and must learn to cope with it or else. Some things just can't be fixed, no matter how skillful you are. Six of his horses had failed to scope clean that morning, for instance, and would miss their weekend races.

I glanced at the montage again. "Why do the Irish do so well in the bumper at Cheltenham?" I asked. The English have won it only twice in the past decade.

"We have a better program," Mullins informed me. "There's good prize money in bumpers here. If you've got a good horse in England, you don't bother with National Hunt races on the flat. You go off jumping right away."

Willie keeps a handful of flat horses himself, so he can race during the summer when the jumps game slows to a crawl. If a horse runs well, he might sell it, but he also turns some flat horses into hurdlers and even chasers on occasion. It's a question of establishing a horse's capabilities—of finding the right level, as Hourigan had said. Willie knows a Grade One type immediately, too, but he drops his novices and juveniles in wherever it seems appropriate. "Separates the wheat from the chaff."

"Lots of chaff," I said, recalling the Tattersalls sale, and he nodded.

When I changed the subject to Florida Pearl, Mullins brightened considerably. About Richard Johnson I was still curious. Why had

Johnson flown in to ride in the Normans Grove Chase? Was his presence part of a master plan to skin the bookies? "No, it was just that all the A-list Irish jockeys were unavailable, and Richard had been on the horse before," Willie said, and I felt strangely disappointed, robbed of the paranoia that has cost me so much money down the years. Was a belief in honesty and even justice the key to successful handicapping? If so, I'd go to my grave a loser.

Given the Pearl's age and his physical problems, Mullins was elated about his recovery and progress, all credit to Grainne Ni Chaba. On the Saturday just past, he had entered Florida Pearl in two important chases, one at Ascot and the other at Thurles, even though the horse would probably run next in the Irish Hennessy, but Willie likes to cover all the bases. Still, it seemed weird to me, and my paranoia, only half-dead, lurched back to life. "If you've got a horse that's good enough for Ascot," I asked, "why bother with Thurles?"

Another little smile. "In case the grandstand at Ascot had burned down."

You can't beat Willie Mullins when it comes to caution, I thought. In fact, he swears by multiple entries and plays a kind of poker at the Festival. He'll enter a horse in two or three races, each at a different distance, then wait till the last instant, when all the cards are on the table, before he declares himself. The strategy has its merits. Since 1994, Mullins has more Cheltenham winners than any Irish trainer, seven to Edward O'Grady's six.

"I've got about twenty-five entries this year," he reckoned, "but I may wind up with only four or five runners." His guess was way off— he wound up with seventeen. If an owner has a horse that's even remotely qualified for Cheltenham, you can be sure the horse will be on the ferry to Holyhead.

Yet the buy-in isn't cheap. Each Festival entry costs about two hundred dollars and has to be paid far in advance, often before a horse has proven itself. The policy, reasonably new, had upset some trainers, who saw it as a way for Racecourse Holdings Trust (RHT), Cheltenham's parent organization, to raise more prize money and increase the Festival's profile—a move, that is, toward a more corporate, commercial approach. Phillip Hobbs was the most vocal critic. He had forty entries at that point, but only two confirmed runners in Rooster Booster and Flagship Uberalles.

In response to the outcry, Edward Gillespie, Cheltenham's managing director, suggested the racecourse wanted to stimulate the ante-post market. When there are more entries, there are more choices and longer odds, leading gamblers who dream of cashing a monster, life-transforming bet to plunge more recklessly, but the idea that RHT would be so concerned about the bookies' welfare was a trifle far-fetched. RHT's decision to stretch the Festival to four days (and maybe pad it out with a few lesser races) also had many trainers scratching their heads. With his sense of history and tradition, Mullins was among them.

"I'm on the anti side," he said. "I prefer three days of top-class racing. If there are new races that ought to go in, I'd get rid of one or two of the handicaps to make room. I'm sure it will be financially rewarding for Cheltenham."

The rain was pounding on the roof now. Willie had some things to do, so he sent me back to the gallops, where Florida Pearl would soon appear. "I'll be there in five minutes," he shouted as I went out the door, but he was on farmer's time. With only a flimsy fold-up umbrella for protection, I waited twenty minutes before he joined me, and he'd had the nerve to change into a waterproof outfit. The riders going around, all wearing similar gear, were amused to see me there, a stranger drenched to the skin. How the stranger must adore horses! As at other yards, many of the riders were from abroad—Pakistan, India, Finland, Ukraine. The heavy winter ground made it tough for the

lighter ones. A jockey has to be strong to control a hor
and horses can be as contrary as us in nasty weather.

I threw away my umbrella after a while, its spokes c
wind, and resigned myself to a case of bronchitis. Floi
up from the stables in company with Alexander Banque
are pals and live in stalls next to each other. Every celebri
a sidekick, apparently, a Tonto for every Lone Ranger. D
always work together? "Not always," Willie said, as precis
"But often. They can both be lazy, and they like a bit of com
Alexander Banquet would do nothing on his own. Florida Pe
so bad."

The horses trotted through the mud, off to complete two one-mile
circuits of the newer B-shaped gallop. On Florida Pearl was Tracy
Gilmour, an American and his longtime lass, as alert to his psyche as
anyone could be. He *is* a beautiful athlete and seemed to know it, aware
of occupying a niche above the others, and when he swung into action,
he looked a proper consort for his trainer, all perfectly sculpted muscle and princely action. Alexander Banquet is a more rough-hewn type.
There's a hint of the barroom brawler about him, and he's able to take
a few knocks without coming unglued. He has stamina to spare, too.
A little Rottweiler named Sybil nipped at Florida Pearl's heels, and
Florida enjoyed the game and whinnied, but Alexander Banquet had
no use for the dog and scared it away.

As the horses began their first circuit, Willie and I discussed Ruby
Walsh, his jockey of choice, who rides out for Mullins up to three
times a week, although he's based mostly in England. Again I listened
to a litany of praise for Ruby, yet Willie also expressed an almost
paternal concern for him. Being away from Ireland for such long peri-
ods must be hard on Ruby's soul, Willie thought. "It's a difficult life,"
he commiserated. "On the motorways day after day."

Somewhere on the farm Be My Royal, now retired, was roaming.

Another irony of the morphine case was that the horse had suffered a career-ending injury in the Hennessy. I'd saved up until the last to ask Mullins about the scandal, imagining he might still be sensitive about the verdict, and he was. "Zero tolerance! That's an impossible standard to meet," he said heatedly. "Red Mills stated as much to the Jockey Club four years ago! Sure, we lost in court, but we got a jury of the people. It's all out in the open now. What do they call it? Natural justice."

Clearly, this was a matter of principle for him. Like Red Mills, he'd seen his good name suffer by innuendo. I detected an Irish home pride, too, along with a distaste for the English way of doing things, strictly by the rules, where the Irish are inclined toward sympathy and forgiveness.

"You're still pretty pissed off," I said.

He brushed aside the comment. "Ah, let the solicitors handle it."

Better to consider Florida Pearl's chances in the Hennessy, as we did when Willie walked me to my car. Could Florida win it a record fourth time? Mullins didn't see why not. He pointed toward the sculpture on his lawn. "Do you recognize that horse? That *is* Florida Pearl." He'd met Rupert Till, the sculptor, at an exhibition of Till's work. "We got to talking over a few beers, and I mentioned that I'd always wanted a horse sculpture, and Rupert just showed up with this one day." He patted the jockey. "It's supposed to be Ruby, but Ruby never won on Florida Pearl. Notice anything wrong?"

I checked the piece, touching it here and there, but it looked pretty accurate to me. The jockey was even wearing goggles. "Can't say that I do."

"Rupert took Ruby's measurements, but he also relied on a photo of Paul Carberry. Ruby doesn't have the same body type as Paul, or the same style of riding. So the jockey comes out in-between." There it was, that precision again. "Anyway, it's something different," Willie mused. He made a half-hearted attempt to remove the Christmas lights, but the strings kept catching in the wire mesh, so he did what most men would do under the circumstances and postponed the chore to go back to a job he knew he could handle. "See you racing!" he yelled as I departed.

IN THOSE EARLY DAYS of February, the Irish were under a black cloud, with nothing at all going right. The rain fell and then fell some more, flooding the courses at Fairyhouse and Clonmel, and canceling the races. Edward O'Grady, his Cheltenham squad already whittled to the bone, faced another potential loss when Back In Front developed an irregular heartbeat. After working ineffectively, the horse was shipped to the Veterinary Hospital in Dublin for more tests.

In Limerick, Michael Hourigan came clean about Beef Or Salmon's iffy season. The horse had a sore muscle in a rear hindquarter, he said, probably as a result of his tumble in the Gold Cup last year. His jumping hadn't been the same since then, so he was receiving some physiotherapy, and though he was ninety-five percent right, he would skip the Hennessy and go straight to Cheltenham.

In Kilkenny, Connolly's Red Mills threw in the towel and mailed checks for any forfeited prize money to the connections of all forty-six horses in England and Ireland who'd tested positive for morphine. The payout amounted to almost a million dollars when legal and specialist fees were included. The company accused the Jockey Club of being inflexible and insisting on a technical interpretation of its rules at the expense of fairness.

Only Paddy Power Bookmakers were unaffected by the tides of misfortune. If a customer brought his wife or his girlfriend into any shop on Valentine's Day, she would be given a free box of Butler's chocolates and a chance to win a trip for two to Paris with no strings attached.

THE HENNESSY GOLD CUP, held at Leopardstown, drew nearly as large a crowd as the Ericsson Chase with Best Mate. Anticipating a juicy handle, the bookies were more active than usual, humming and whistling at the prospect of all those euros landing in their laps. Among them was Francis Hyland, who heads up the Irish National Bookmakers Association. If anyone doesn't fit the raffish image of a turf accountant, it's Hyland. Formerly a dealer on the London Stock Exchange, he was dressed as if for a bullish round of trading in a top-coat, a tie, and a pinstripe suit. Only his worn-looking shoes, scuffed and muddy from tramping from course to course, hinted at his profession.

Though I was not unfamiliar with the bookmaker's art by now, having met the Old Bookie, talked with the weather-beaten gents on the Thurles train, and lost money to the likes of Paddy Sharkey, I hadn't yet filled out the big picture, and Hyland was the ideal person to help me, since he takes a scholarly approach to his work. An authority on Irish racing, he has written histories of both the Irish Derby and the Grand National. He began by showing me the essentials of his trade, known collectively as "a joint." Bookies have been using them for centuries, with no need to change a thing.

"A joint is designed to be cheap and portable," he lectured, "so you can set up anywhere they're racing, in a field or on a farm." The kit included a long, hollow, telescopic pole that Francis extended to its full length and tied to a fence with some twine. Next, he attached a cash tray for coins up top, then the slate on which he chalks his odds, and finally a holder for his umbrella. The single modern touch was a laptop that Francis's only employee uses to record bets and issue receipts for them.

Hyland's leap from being a broker to a bookie sounded dramatic, but he told me racing had always intrigued him. When the stock market hit a slump in 1974, he took a year off to write his history of the Derby and also have a fling at making book. He did well enough ("Meaning I survived," he said) to go at it full-time. His experience as a dealer gave him a slight edge, since he'd sharpened his math skills under pressure. "There isn't any finish at the stock exchange," he laughed, "and the betting is all 'in-running.' " (An in-running bet occurs during a race; bookies will offer odds, say, on whether the horse in front will win or lose.) Yet he didn't want to create an impression that his job was simple. "The punters in Ireland aren't mugs," he claimed. "They're very well informed. This is the only business where insider trading is legal."

By insider trading, he was referring to tips. "But tips . . . ," I said, my voice trailing off as I recalled the worthless ones I'd heeded.

Hyland addressed the ambiguities. Real inside information does exist, he believes, and he guards against it by being a shrewd student of faces. "In this game, faces are very, very important," he explained, and I could feel him inspecting mine for nervous tics of a devious nature. If he finds somebody regularly winning on horses of Noel Meade's, for example, he assumes the bettor has a line to Meade's yard. He'll memorize the person's face and decline any bets in the future. But it's equally true that the Irish tend to accept any tip as valid, a grave mistake since most trainers are wary and seldom tout a horse to win, because if the horse loses they'll never hear the last of it. "Do you know what the English bookmaker William Hill once said?" Francis asked cheekily. "People with inside information have made a rich man out of me."

I was enjoying Hyland's sprightliness. His pitch is about two hundred yards from the rails, a preferred and central position. A rails bookie straddles the divide between the reserved enclosure, where the tickets are more expensive, and the ordinary one, and he can take bets from either side, thereby increasing the pool of possible suckers.

"A pitch on the rails here might cost about three hundred thousand dollars," Hyland said, and maybe a little more for an absolutely premium spot, but the price drops drastically as you move away, because lazy punters won't do any walking. For a pitch just five yards beyond Hyland's, a bookie might pay ten grand less, and so on to the outer reaches of the betting ring, a region as isolated as the Skellig Islands off the Kerry coast. On an average day, the bookies at Leopardstown handle about six hundred thousand dollars, Francis estimated, with about eighty percent of the total going to those on the rails.

To compensate for his distance from the hot spot, Hyland delivers service. "It's what I sell," he said, with a theatrical flair. "I'm their bank, I'm their cloakroom attendant. They leave their coats and bags with me. They ask to use my mobile phone. I cash checks for them, and if they argue about the odds, I'll adjust them ever so slightly. In essence, I am their servant." Some customers have credit with him and can bet "on the nod," but he doesn't like to grant the privilege. It goes to people's heads, and they wager too much and often get into financial trouble. Bad debts are bad for business, so Francis keeps his patrons afloat rather than letting them drown.

Thinking about Nosey Flynn and T. P. Reilly, I wondered if English racing truly was more honest than the Irish version. Hyland gave me a withering stare, as though he couldn't believe how innocent I was. "All racing is bent!" he shouted. "Everyone knows that! Racing's bent, football's bent, *darts* is bent, any sport with betting is bent!" He wasn't alluding to fixed races so much as to the shifty ways a trainer can manipulate the handicap system and still stay within the rules.

"How often have you seen it?" he asked. "A trainer has a horse who loses time after time. The horse runs in races he's not good enough for—or at the wrong distance, or at a racecourse that doesn't suit his style—with J. T. Unknown riding. And after every loss, the handicapper [he's employed by the Irish Turf Club] who assigns the weights takes pity and deducts a few more pounds. Pretty soon, the horse is at the bottom of the weights, carrying ten or even fifteen pounds less than he ought to be. And then, surprise! J. T. Unknown has been fired, Ruby Walsh is the new jockey, and the horse goes on to win."

"Do jockeys really matter that much?" I was playing devil's advocate.

"Ruby is a stone [fourteen pounds] better than an average professional jockey, I can tell you that," Francis said. "Ruby, and also Carberry and Geraghty. And in a bumper, a top amateur rider is worth three stone more than the average amateur."

In the past, before bookmaking was tightly regulated, high-street bookies paid jockeys to throw a race when they were on the favorite. A jockey's life could be miserable back then. Heavy drinking was the norm, and a rider often died broke. Sometimes a poor Irish family sent off a small, skinny boy to be an apprentice, just so they'd have one less mouth to feed. Though race fixing isn't so blatant anymore, and doesn't exist at the highest levels, the stable staff at any yard can supposedly inhibit a horse's performance. They can deny the horse any water the day before a race, for instance, then bring it to the track and allow it to drink its fill, or they can let a horse gorge on hay the morning of a run. According to a recent magazine article I'd read, they can also dose a horse with ACP, an animal tranquilizer hard to detect in a urine sample.

When Francis began checking the card for the first race, I was astonished at how little time he spent. He didn't even consult a *Post*, merely a list of entries torn from a newspaper. In a minute or two, he had the competition reduced to three horses. That wasn't an exceptional talent, he felt. He just searches for the good jockeys and trainers, and there aren't very many. The quality of Irish racing has declined in recent years, he said, except at the top of the game.

"We used to have about three thousand horses in training, and five hundred were okay, five hundred were moderate, and the rest couldn't keep themselves warm. Now we have almost six thousand in training, and five hundred are okay." Besides, as he pointed out, a bookie isn't looking for the form horse. All that concerns him is the public's choice. If he doesn't get the odds right on the favorite, he'll blow his margins completely.

My session with Hyland had been very productive. I'd gained the straightest picture yet of what an on-course bookie needs—a decent head for numbers, some psychological insight into his clientele, ample operating capital, the balls to take a risk, and the smarts to know when to take it. But what makes for a successful gambler? When I put the question to Francis, he reiterated a key factor from J. P. McManus's bible—impulse control. A gambler has to be patient enough to recognize good value.

"Show me someone who only bets three or four times a year," he said, "and I'll guarantee that person will be a winner. The more you play, the harder it is to come out ahead. In effect, you pay me a commission on every bet." Most of us are doomed, though, and lose control in stressful situations, particularly on the last race—pure gravy for a bookie. If we're ahead, we try to double the money, and if we're in the hole, we dig down deeper in a fruitless attempt to break even.

How well I knew the syndrome! As the races began, I looked at the crowd milling about and saw it the way Francis might, as a horde of impulses barely held in check, fish about to be fried, and I vowed to avoid my usual mistakes (reading tea leaves, probing bird entrails, and so on) and sit tight until the Hennessy, when I planned to jump off the bridge and bet big-time on Florida Pearl. At a pleasant remove, I watched Brave Inca win a Grade One hurdle, and Pizarro (whose poor sire was called Broken Hearted) squeak out a victory in a Grade One chase, both stamping their Cheltenham credentials. Up next was a handicap with nineteen runners—a surefire invitation to confusion—so I confined myself to the Jodami Bar for a pint.

The choice was appropriate, really. Jodami had won the Irish Hennessy three times between 1993 and 1995, a feat Florida Pearl would soon try to surpass. With Beef Or Salmon on the shelf, I was invested in the Pearl. The opposition looked weak. Cloudy Bays and Be My Belle were stepping up in class, and Rince Ri was an aging graybeard. Harbour Pilot hadn't tackled fences since the Festival last year, while McManus's Le Coudray was wildly overvalued because he'd been second to Best Mate in the Ericsson—but by how many lengths? No, Florida Pearl was my only option, and a very appealing one at 5–1, so I descended into the ring and placed my wager, although not with Francis Hyland, who is too intelligent for his own good.

Sometimes after a bet I want to go back a minute later and beg the bookie for a refund, as people do when they send a nasty or unguarded e-mail, but at others I'm enveloped in a profound aura of well-being and entirely regret-free, as if the result of the race were preordained, and that was how I felt about the Hennessy. When Cloudy Bays took the early lead, I smiled because I knew he'd fade, as he did at the fourth-last fence, yielding to Florida Pearl and Harbour Pilot. Had I underestimated the Pilot? The notion didn't cross my mind.

Richard Johnson was on Florida Pearl again, while Paul Carberry rode Harbour Pilot. As a Leopardstown veteran, Carberry knew every twist and turn of the track and had an advantage, but I still remained steadfast, convinced the fates would intervene—and they did at the second-last when Harbour Pilot, who'd been jumping well, lost his bearings, barged into the fence, and sent Carberry bouncing to the ground. The race wasn't over yet, though, because the riderless Harbour Pilot, an unpredictable free radical, veered toward Florida Pearl at the last fence. For a moment, it looked as if they'd smash into each other and go down in a heap, but the Pearl scraped by and denied the fast-closing Le Coudray by three lengths.

Afterward, Richard Johnson said that the loose horse had helped rather than hindered his mount. It forced Florida Pearl to focus instead of slack off as he often does with an easy lead. For Willie Mullins, the race was emotional. "I'm over the moon," he said. "I would have cried if he'd been caught in the stretch." Now Florida Pearl was back with the big boys and might even go to Cheltenham for another crack at the Gold Cup. I was fairly emotional myself as I darted through the crowd to collect my cash. My hundred bucks had blossomed fivefold, so I stopped at the Jodami again, this time for a glass of champagne.

HOWEVER DISAPPOINTED J. P. McManus might have been about Le Coudray's near miss, he didn't have time to dwell on it. He had a more serious controversy on another front, one that involved the 25.49 percent share of Manchester United he owned with John Magnier. The football club's most rabid fans had distributed a leaflet, *Just Say Neigh*, to a capacity crowd during a home-field game at Old Trafford that same weekend, urging everyone to disrupt the pair's racing interests in any way they could. The leaflet was a gesture of support for Sir Alex Ferguson, United's beloved manager, who had engaged McManus and Magnier in a world-class pissing match.

At the heart of the dispute was Rock of Gibraltar, a very special racehorse. As a three-year-old, the colt had reeled off a string of five straight Group One wins on the flat, making his value at stud enormous—a classic example of Coolmore's strategy for nurturing and developing stallions. Sir Alex owned a piece of Rock of Gibraltar, at least in theory, since Magnier had presented him with a half-share as a gift, and he felt entitled to a share in the stud fees, too. But Magnier reportedly argued that the stallion rights were separate—they were Coolmore's property. The absence of any paperwork added to the mix-up, so Fergie had filed a lawsuit.

Magnier and McManus, every bit as belligerent, put the club and

Ferguson under the microscope. They ordered its board of directors to answer ninety-nine questions about United's finances, business affairs, and player trades. That was too much for the Manchester U. loyalists, whose leaflet supplied Coolmore's phone numbers and e-mail addresses. The nerve of those effin' Irishmen! Some lout had already tagged a wall at Magnier's home in Fermoy, scrawling "Fuck you, Magnier" in red letters four feet high. Moreover, the loyalists had dared to stage a protest at Hereford during the races, marching onto the track with banners that read QUIT THE HORSEPLAY, COOLMORE! and UNITED NOT FOR SALE!, delaying the action for a full twelve minutes.

Bad enough, you might say, but now the zealots known as United4Action were threatening to infiltrate the Cheltenham Festival on Gold Cup Day. Heresy! Sacrilege! The outrage of the jumps fraternity cycled off the charts. Though the threat beggared belief, the zanies had to be taken seriously. They were buying up tickets as fast as they could and claimed to hold eighty-eight for the Tattersalls enclosure alone. (Cheltenham has three enclosures, with Tattersalls the midprice one.) The group's messages to the media were becoming more volatile, too, military in their ardor. They spoke of "cells" being activated and dispatched on a mission to cause "immense embarrassment" to McManus.

Somewhere in deepest, darkest Manchester, the spirit of Ho Chi Minh must be alive and well, I thought, although desperately perverted. There was a way out for the Cheltenham officials, of course. They just had to permit United4Action to hold a peaceful demonstration on Gold Cup Day. If that smacked of blackmail, so be it. I sympathized with Edward Gillespie and his staff, who already had a pile of contingencies on their plate. In all the planning for the Festival, the computer models and the preparations for incidental disasters—a pregnant woman going into labor, say, or a dustup between patrons—

nobody in his right mind would be gearing up for a possible attack by . . . *football guerrillas!*

TOM COSTELLO, the legendary horse trader, has such a reputation for being reclusive that I thought I might have to fast-talk my way past his gate, maybe even posing as a buyer, but Tom Jr., his next in command, had no objection to a visit. On the phone we worked out a time for me to see his father, and soon I was driving by the farms of the midlands, around Lough Derg, and along the Shannon River near Limerick, sensing that I was about to enter a part of Ireland where tourists seldom go, and the local traditions and rituals are still intact—tranquil, isolated, misty country ideal for Costello's cloaked style of doing business.

Horse country, too, it has always been. Not far from Newmarket-on-Fergus lies Turret Hill, across from Dromoland Castle. The turret dates from the 1740s, built so that Sir Edward O'Brien could watch his horses gallop. Sir Edward also gambled on them and fell into such dire straits that his son, a Dublin attorney, tried to curtail his spending. In a furious letter of reply, Sir Edward stated that "I neither play cards or dice, keep neither whores or hounds . . . and I should have been in my grave long since, choked with fat and eaten up with infirmities and disorders, had it not been for the exercise and amusement my horses afforded me."

Tiny Newmarket-on-Fergus was drowsy, still asleep centuries after Sir Edward had departed from this earth. The only souls about were some workmen banging around in a gutted structure adjacent to the Hunters Lodge. I saw nowhere else in town to stay for the night, but the lodge's front door was locked, and the desk in the lobby was vacant. Fortunately, the owner was one of the workers, pitching in to renovate his restaurant, and he was delighted to rent me a room, although he warned I'd be his only guest. How could he be so sure? Strange, I thought. Even a bit creepy. Alone inside, I felt the musty staleness of a place long unoccupied, sure that Sir Edward's ghost was afoot.

After bolting my door against the spirit world, I called Tom Jr. to confirm my appointment. He had suggested I meet with his father in the late afternoon, but he gave me directions to his own home rather than to the famous Fenloe House I'd seen photos of in Henrietta Knight's book. That made me slightly uneasy because of Costello's distrust of outsiders, particularly writers. "No, I don't let the press in," he once told Michael Clower of the *Post*, conveniently ignoring the fact that Clower *was* the press. "I'm only a small farmer and lead a quiet life," Costello insisted, raising the Irish art of self-deprecation to a masterly high.

Still, I'd been able to find out a fair bit about Costello before the trip by consulting the public record. His story was again typical of the rural Irish. As a boy, he rode and raced ponies, a common pastime for a lad "on the other side of Ennis." In those days, every farmer had a mare he mated to a local stallion, selling the foal for whatever price and glad for the extra income. Costello's father dealt in half-breeds in large quantities, so horse-trading was in Tom's blood from early childhood, as familiar to him as breathing the air.

As a young man in the late 1940s, when racing was banned in Ireland because of the war, he "flapped" horses in the north—flapping was a bush league form of the sport that the authorities ignored—where lots of American soldiers were stationed and waiting for their orders. With little else to spend their money on, the GIs gambled like crazy—craps, poker, horses, anything. Often Costello left for Ulster in May and didn't return until August. The prize money was excellent up there, too, and though the racing did have handicappers, the scene was very scrappy. A horse might compete under one name this week and a new one the next, moving from town to town. Later, Costello held a proper trainer's license in the Republic. His strike rate was high, and he even won the Irish Grand National with Tartan Ace in 1973. His ability to lay out a horse for a race and score a betting coup was supposedly unrivaled.

Yet he seems always to have been more attracted to the speculative aspects of the game, to the buying and selling of stock. He has no interest in breeding horses, because a breeder gets stuck with what nature delivers. Instead, he thrives on the liberty of swapping and the thrill of discovering a special foal or yearling and snapping it up, a most inexact science. It's said that he pays more attention to the look of a horse than to its pedigree, and that he owns about twelve hundred acres in Newmarket-on-Fergus, most of it on good limestone, where his 120 horses have plenty of space to roam.

Tom Jr.'s place was a big yellow house on a high hill with a stable and a pretty expanse of land around it. Like his four brothers, he has an operation similar to his father's, although on a smaller scale. The other boys wanted to be horse traders since they were kids, he said, but he inched into it a toe at a time, considering his options until he took the dive. There was nothing of the cowboy about him. He was gracious, clean-cut, and softspoken, and could easily have passed for an accountant. For a while, we stood outside and made small talk in the mist. I kept expecting Tom to invite me to Fenloe House, but I realized as the minutes ticked by that I wouldn't be meeting the Old Lion as arranged.

I was disappointed after the long drive, of course, and Tom was apologetic and offered a plausible excuse. His father, now seventy-two, had been suffering from kidney problems, and after a period on dialysis, he'd just undergone a transplant. He was still in charge of the empire—no change there—but he hadn't fully recovered from his surgery yet, and his energy flagged at times, as it had that afternoon.

Although Ted Walsh had alluded to Costello's poor health, I couldn't shake a feeling the Old Lion was being true to form in dodging a writer and protecting his seclusion.

Tom Jr. was an adequate stand-in, though. He works closely with his dad and knows all the angles. He told me the business isn't as ragged as Walsh had portrayed it, not anymore. That satchel full of cash was history. "Farmers want the money wired to their banks now," he laughed. But his father does still stoke the rumor mill before he runs a horse for sale in a point-to-point, and he's also adept at playing down the merits of a horse somebody covets to kite the price. Ancient tricks, I thought, that were practiced at bazaars and flea markets around the world.

Tom Jr. described the rigorous Costello training program for me. His father buys up to thirty foals and a few yearlings annually in private deals and turns them into racehorses as quickly as possible, before they become set in their ways. The males are gelded when their testicles are small and their sexuality is undeveloped. As two-year-olds, the colts and fillies are broken and learn to jump over low poles without a rider on their back. They do this in a big indoor arena that resembles a circus tent, completing twenty rounds and forty jumps on an average day. The routine makes jumping fun and second nature to them, while it also burns off fat and builds muscle.

In the spring, as three-year-olds, the horses are very quietly ridden, cantering for six to eight weeks. Costello has a school of fences, three all-weather gallops, and grass gallops everywhere, each presenting a different option for his sons, who do the training. At four, the graduates of the program are ready to be shown off and sold unless they're lemons. The point-to-point season around Clare divides in two with a short autumn season from October to November, and a longer one from January until June. The British trainers who are repeat customers (Paul Nicholls, Martin Pipe, Robert Alner, Henrietta Knight) concentrate on the second season, because the form book says more winners come out of it.

As I'd heard, the Costellos won't sell to just anybody. Their name stands for quality, and they cherish that, but turnover matters to them, too, so they never hang on to a horse for long, regardless of how tempting it might be. "If there's a good horse here, he's for sale," Tom said. The part of the job he likes best is scouting for foals. It's a treasure hunt, really. There are no guarantees, so even a clever buyer can get stung. "Gambling runs deep in the Irish," he suggested. "I have a feeling we might die without a bet, even when we're losing."

Tom confirmed that the Old Lion has a gift for spotting a racehorse in the rough, and he tries to copy it. He couldn't explain the process in detail, as if to put it into words would rob it of its mystery, but when he shops for a foal, he might take in twenty different aspects of its being, although not consciously. He'll check the conformation, say, and watch how it moves, and notice whether or not it has a bold outlook. It sounded to me like a meditative state, almost a trance, that facilitates the exchange of information between species—an act of surrender any poet courting the muse would understand.

In the gathering dusk, I recalled Tom's history with Best Mate. "Will he win the Gold Cup again?" I asked.

"He should. Cheltenham brings out the best in him. It's a unique course with those big fences, so jumping is very important—and Best Mate has always been a beautiful jumper. You pay for every mistake, though. A horse has to put in a flawless round to win."

Tom walked me to his stables and introduced me to Bannow Strand, the current talk of Ireland, who was reported to be as good as (if not better than) Best Mate at the same stage. The horse was a very creature of myth at seventeen-plus hands high, so broad and solid he looked able to carry twelve stone, or 168 pounds—the standard weight in a point-to-point—along with three or four jockeys. He had an intimidating aura of strength, superiority, and dominion. Only a four-year-old, he had trounced a maiden field of pointers at Tallow on his debut, registering the day's fastest time, and became the subject of intense transatlantic bidding before David Johnson, a prominent British owner associated with Martin Pipe, bought him. For how much? My question went unanswered.

We had some tea in Tom's kitchen. When I took mine black, he teased me. "Jockeys' drink," he said. No milk or sugar, hence no calories. He was such a friendly, accommodating man, and yet I was sure I'd seen only the tip of the operation, but that was okay. I'd decided the Old Lion's secrets probably weren't all that secret, anyway. I knew how the Irish treat their horses, with love and respect, and assumed those qualities were just raised to a higher power in Costello. There is a poetic side to searching out a special foal—the ability to make an imaginative leap that even those who've never read Yeats or Kavanagh would comprehend—and Costello has it to an extraordinary degree. When you couple that with a caring, sensitive environment, the chances are that any foal will develop into the best possible version of itself.

ON VALENTINE'S DAY, I stopped at our neighborhood Paddy Power shop to enter the drawing for the free trip to Paris. It didn't fall my way, but I couldn't complain since Imelda and I had been to Paris not long after we met, holed up in a borrowed flat in the Marais and seldom leaving it, except to dart across the street to a row of shops for more provisions, stocking up on cheese, bread, sausage, and wine. On those sweet spring nights, with our picnic (dry and warm unlike Tinahely) spread out on the sheets, we talked for hours, listened to music, swapped stories, and had no need for any world beyond our own.

One evening, feeling guilty about not exploring the city, we finally roused ourselves from bed. We ventured out for dinner, only to be caught in a massive downpour without an umbrella, so we ducked into the first bistro we passed. Through a steamy window, it looked to be a perfect spot for lovers, small and intimately lit with candles, but once we were inside, it was as if we'd stumbled into an inn somewhere in the Black Forest. A wrinkled old woman with the air of a neglected servant seated us at a plank table, ordering us to share it with a robust glutton who was well into his second (or maybe third) bottle of Côtes-du-Rhône. He held the last of his steak in his hands and chewed the meat off the bone, simultaneously picking at the *pommes frites* scattered around his plate. His napkin was stuffed into the neck of his shirt. Once white, it now suggested an improvised work of Abstract Expressionism.

He gave us a wave and mumbled a few words, maybe a greeting but more likely a curse. We waved back and took in the décor. The walls were covered with crayon drawings, the work of someone's grandchildren. Toward the rear of the room was the pièce de résistance, a big brick oven where the proprietor (and probably the grandfather), daringly dressed in a lime-green shirt open almost to his navel, cooked meat over a blazing wood fire. Resting on a butcher block by his side was a haunch of raw beef, and he carved it up as necessary when the orders came in, slicing off T-bones and entrecôtes. The scraps of fat and gristle he tossed on the floor, where the dog—there would be a dog—made a meal of them.

We had a marvelous time, of course, and drank only one bottle of Côtes-du-Rhône, but in the morning, Imelda had to return to Dublin. Her Ryanair bus to the airport left from the James Joyce Pub, where copies of Joyce's books, and not even first editions, were kept in a locked case to block anyone from reading them, an irony the author would have enjoyed. The bus departed in a plume of exhaust fumes, and all at once I was alone and looking at another week in Paris before I flew home to California (and that hermit's cabin) on the round-trip ticket I'd bought at the start of my wandering.

In an instant, the city lost its appeal, so I turned to the horses for solace. At Longchamp, I cashed three of my first four bets, but I still had the blues, unable to think about anything but Imelda. Now I was just another lonely American guy in a sea of hand-holding couples, pitiful somehow and an item of gossip at the neighborhood pâtisserie, where the young woman behind the counter, who used to greet me with a conspiratorial wink, frowned when she saw me. The clerk at the wine shop, also formerly chatty, regarded me with pity, as if I were drinking too much of his product, and that was true. As I moped around the flat with the lights out, I listened to "our" music and poured glass after glass of red, every inch the forlorn romantic.

I flew home as intended, but I stayed only two weeks. Instead, I raided my storage locker, where the artifacts of my life are still filed (fifty cartons of books, five hundred albums on vinyl, and some truly grotesque furniture and kitchenware I couldn't imagine unpacking if I ever did settle in California again), fished out a few essentials, and booked a one-way flight to Dublin. I had no idea what to expect and trusted only the depth of my emotions, believing that even if I fell flat on my face, I'd suffer a harmless embarrassment no worse than any other I'd visited on myself. It was a gambler's play, and I got lucky. Such were my thoughts on Valentine's Day.

FOR BARRY GERAGHTY, the approach of the Festival meant even more work than usual. As last year's Miracle Man, he had to hustle at double-time to meet the demands of everyone who wanted his services. When I pulled up at his family's farm near Batterstown, in Meath, to hear about his riding arrangements for Cheltenham, he was out doing an errand in his Jeep, so his mother, Bea, showed me into a bright living room where Barry's younger sisters, just home from school, were curled up by the fire watching a teen sitcom on TV.

"You can talk to those two while you're waiting," Bea joked. That didn't seem like a bad idea at all, really. The girls might have an insight or two into what made their brother tick, but I didn't want to commit the colossal adult error of interrupting their viewing pleasure, so I waited for the credits to roll before I said a word.

"Barry's doing well, isn't he?" I asked Holly, breaking the ice. Holly is fourteen and was still in her school uniform, maroon-colored.

"He's flying!" she replied, her voice soaring appropriately. She was at Leopardstown for the Hennessy and saw Barry win on Pizarro, only to finish second to Florida Pearl in the big race. "I wish he could have got a little more out of Le Coudray, though."

The talk drifted to Macs Joy from Jessie Harrington's yard, who had lost a good purse that same day, disqualified for interfering with Timmy Murphy on Kilbeggan Lad down the stretch. The unfortunate Andrew Leigh was the jockey at fault, and he was later suspended for careless riding. Did Andrew deserve it? Holly shook her head. She didn't think so. Neither did Jessie, who'd lodged an appeal.

Then Barry swept in, his car keys jingling in his hand. He's a restless sort, the type who has trouble sitting still and taps a foot on the floor in frustration. When I repeated Holly's praise to him, he shrugged and said, "They're not always so nice. They criticize me, too." For a little privacy, we moved to the dining room, where some of Barry's trophies were stacked on a sideboard. There were trophies all around the house, crystal bowls from Waterford and sterling silver cups, enough to stock a small museum.

The Macs Joy incident was still on my mind, so I asked Barry's opinion. "Well, you know how it is with the stewards," he said. "Andrew's never been to court before, has he?" Timmy Murphy, an old pro, had done a much better job of pleading his case, he implied.

Bea brought me some coffee and wondered if Barry would like a Coke, but he declined. "I might eat something later," he told her, a sentence he's uttered countless times. The calories had him at their mercy. He used to be able to drop eight or ten pounds in a single day without any fuss, but the best he can do now is six pounds, and that requires effort. In fact, I noticed a world-weary quality in his eyes at times, even a trace of sadness, as if he'd seen too much too soon, but then the weariness would vanish, and he was engaged and enthusiastic again. I recalled Michael Hourigan's formula for what a jockey needs, an old head on a young body.

Geraghty left school at fifteen and began riding shortly after that. Too tall and heavy for the flat, he signed on with Noel Meade as an apprentice and had his first winner in January 1997, making such steady progress that he had sixteen wins by the end of May. There was nothing magical about it, he felt. He put it down to hard, hard work. He rode out in miserable weather, mastered the game's political intrigues, and learned how to keep his trainers happy, so he was mildly offended whenever someone suggested he was an "overnight success" because of his five winners at the Festival last year. Yet he also conceded that he'd been lucky lately. He's blessed with a strong constitution and hasn't been seriously hurt for a while, but that hasn't always been the case.

"I once broke my back twice in twelve months," he said with a smirk, as if in the presence of the blackly comic. He had to wear a full body cast for ten weeks the first time and twelve the second. The situation would've been much hairier if the surgeon, who'd once patched up a knee for him, hadn't designed the cast with a zipper, so he could bathe. He never truly believes it when he's injured and has even ridden with crushed vertebrae, denying the pain. If a bone or a bruise does feel wrong after a fall, he tells himself it's nothing, postponing a visit to the doctor until it becomes inevitable. He doesn't dwell on the damage, nor does he like to think about getting older. "I'll always be the kid," he said, but he knew better.

When the Hennessy came up in our conversation, I carried on about how terrific Florida Pearl had looked, forgetting that Barry had been on Le Coudray. His affable manner changed in a flash as he reacted to the slight. His eyes grew cold, and I saw the steely resolve that separates a great jockey from an ordinary one.

"You want to win them all, don't you?"

"Yeah, I do," he admitted. But he was aware that talent and hustle alone weren't enough to do the trick. "Do you remember Richard Pitman, the jockey? He wrote a book called *Good Horses Make Good Jockeys.* And that's the truth, too. If you don't have the horse beneath you, it doesn't matter how good you are. You have to be lucky."

Barry seemed obsessed with luck. When I kidded him about it, he was adamant. "But so much of it *is* luck!" As an example, he cited a steeplechase he'd lost at Leopardstown on Tom Taaffe's Kicking King, a celebrated gelding. "A sixty-five grand race, right?" he said, sounding wounded. "Taaffe had Kicking King at the top of game, better on the day than he's been since then, and the horse just clipped the very edge of a fence and fell—not even a bad mistake, just an inexperienced one!" In a second or two, his gloom lifted. "Ah, well, you can't live in the past. There'd be no *craic* if things went right the whole time, would there?"

Speaking of luck, Geraghty was hoping for another blast of it at the Festival. His agent had four solid rides lined up in Kicking King, Pizarro, Back In Front, and Moscow Flyer, but two key mounts had dropped into his lap unexpectedly last year, and he'd be delighted if that happened again.

"Moscow's the ace in my pack," he confided. That was music to my ears. Maybe I should forget all the nonsense about the Pattern and quit being a superstitious throwback to the caveman era. "He's the best I've ever ridden." But Barry also touted Pizarro's chances after the horse's run on Hennessy Day. Though Pizarro had won, his tremendous stamina didn't come into play as it would at Cheltenham. "That uphill finish is very tough," he said. "If you stand there and take a look, you wouldn't want to walk up it. It's an honest test."

"What about Back In Front?" I hadn't heard anything since the horse's trip to the Dublin Veterinary Hospital.

"The vibes are good. He's much better. He's had the heart problem before."

A jockey has to be a skilled diplomat to secure a place as the primary rider for such expert trainers as Harrington, O'Grady, and Taaffe, performing a balancing act as he chooses among their horses without causing offense, and Geraghty brings it off admirably. He's mature beyond his years, but his boyish side popped out again when he spoke of a pub in Kells, where he's a part-owner. We were thinking about going there for a drink, but it was getting too late.

"Maybe you could put a photo of the pub in your book?" he asked, as any ambitious young man might. I doubted I could do that, I said, but I did promise to mention the Arches Bar, where Barry sometimes can be found pulling pints on a Saturday night.

Though Geraghty knows his stuff, he was wrong about Back In Front. The vibes were not so good, alas. Shortly after the scare with his heart, the horse turned up lame in his near-foreleg. Vets, physios, chiropractors, and even a farrier had examined him, but nobody could fix him, so he wouldn't be going to Cheltenham. Edward O'Grady described himself as "hugely disappointed." He might have seventeen Festival victories, but he'd never won the Champion Hurdle, Back In Front's intended race. With all the twists of fortune O'Grady had gone through, you'd need somebody other than a Pierce Brosnan smoothie to play him in a movie, I thought. You'd have to cast an actor with a spooky, shell-shocked look, such as Christopher Walken.

SNOW WAS ON THE WICKLOW MOUNTAINS when I traveled to Moone for a last visit to Jessie Harrington's farm before the Festival. I could feel the tension in the air and almost hear a whispered prayer that trouble would stay outside the door. Jessie had already lost Imazulutoo and would soon lose Spirit Leader, too, who lacked her ordinary sparkle and was only ninety percent right. Her Cheltenham squad had been whittled down to four: Green Belt Flyer, Colca Canyon, Macs Joy, and Moscow Flyer.

Horses were on the move as usual, with the morning's second lot headed for the gallops. In an open field down below, where four sturdy birch fences were set up, Jessie and Eamonn, both on horseback, were supervising a schooling session. As I watched, a pair of horses approached the first fence at a fair clip. This was just for practice, so I was unprepared for an accident, but one horse clobbered the fence and unseated his jockey, poor Andrew Leigh, who left the saddle upside-down, a foot caught in a stirrup. The horse shook him off after dragging him along for a few yards, and he hit the ground with a thump and smashed his left wrist against it.

I had seen dozens of falls by now, but they still terrified me. Andrew appeared to be okay, though, grinning as he brushed the grass and dirt from his clothes. It was a sheepish grin, to be sure, but he carried it off with grace and pretended his wrist, purple and swollen, belonged to another person. After Eamonn conducted an inspection, he sent the lad to Jessie's house to pack the wrist in ice prior to a trip to Naas for an X-ray. Meanwhile, riders were chasing the loose horse around the yard, joined by a bunch of grooms on foot. It looked like a roundup in Texas.

Eamonn isn't a man to sigh in public, but I guessed he must be sighing inwardly as parents do. When the schooling session ended, I walked to Jessie's house with him to see how Andrew was feeling. Two men I'd never met before were hanging around the kitchen. They were shy and tentative, as if they'd arrived by chance and were waiting for instructions on what to do next. Pat Abbey and Brian Willis turned out to be part-owners of a horse, new to the role and still wet behind the ears. They were members of a twenty-person syndicate, all employed at a pharmaceuticals company in Kildare. Their horse—La Dearg, or Red Dawn—was a four-year-old gelding who hadn't raced yet.

"We interviewed other trainers, but Mrs. Harrington's one of the best," Abbey said, in his sober way. He was the more talkative guy and the most infected with racing fever. He'd even had a fling at being a jockey, but he quit to take a job at a meat factory, as he called it, and later switched over to pharmaceuticals. Willis kept quiet, mostly, and looked a bit puzzled, as people do when they decide to try something unique and different and can't tell whether or not they like it yet. But he was definitely a fan and had been at Leopardstown when the stewards screwed Andrew Leigh over his ride on Macs Joy—or such was the spin he and Abbey put on the incident.

"Ah, Andrew wasn't cheeky enough in the stewards' room." Eamonn agreed with Geraghty's take on the inquiry. "He needs to fight his corner better."

"It's your man Timmy Murphy," Abbey said suspiciously. "He's been around for centuries. An old pro like Murphy, how could you trust him? He'd lie and tell the stewards what they want to hear."

Andrew walked in just then, still acting sheepish. He had a damp towel wrapped around his battered wrist and a slash of blood across the bridge of his nose. I assumed he must be upset and maybe a little embarrassed, so I tried to cheer him. "You're having a pretty good season for an apprentice, aren't you?" I said.

"A pretty good season?" he asked, laughing. "At times!" His memory of every fall and suspension was vivid, but he had no intention of giving up. He'd be riding at Limerick later that week for the trainer Gerald Cully, he told us. It's a cliché to say that racing is about dreams, but I did feel surrounded by dreamers in the kitchen, each with his own vision of transcendence.

We snapped to attention when Jessie came in, like schoolboys caught fooling around by the teacher. The new owners were desperate for a word about their horse, *any* word, but Jessie didn't know enough about La Dearg yet to advise them, so she suggested we go up to the gallops for a look at him. He was in the third lot of the morning. While the horses circled in a sand ring, Abbey grabbed a spot by a fence, and Willis fetched his infant son, Gary, snuggled in cute winter clothing, from a car seat. Babysitting was probably the price he had to pay for investing in a horse, such forfeits being common in most marriages.

Abbey and Willis were chomping at the bit, stymied as they tried to pick out La Dearg from the crowd. "Is that him?" Abbey asked, pointing. "I think that's him."

"They all look the same," Willis protested. He had his hands full with Gary, who was wriggling like a bug. "At least four or five of them do."

The rider on La Dearg caught on to their plight and signaled to them. "He's a nice one!" she shouted, patting a robust chestnut with a white blaze. The owners waved at her appreciatively. They were beaming. There he was—their horse!

The string left the sand ring for the gallops, where Jessie waited. She was on horseback again and resembled a general posing for an equestrian statue. She was riding Moscow Court, a hurdler with two wins and four places to his name. "He'll make a grand chaser next year," she predicted. She noticed Gary for the first time and smiled. "How old is the little fella?"

"Nine months," his dad replied, chucking him under the chin.

"I became a grandmother for the second time nine days ago," Jessie said, turning her horse to join the string.

I didn't stay for La Dearg's workout. Instead, I went over to Moscow Flyer's paddock, where he stood calmly watching the traffic. He'd have a last gallop at the Curragh to sharpen him, Eamonn had said, and then it was off to Cheltenham. What was going on in that eccentric brain of his? Tom Costello might know, but I didn't. I tried to communicate with him, anyway, and asked if I should ignore the Pattern and bet on him in the Queen Mother, and I think he answered, "It's up to you." After that, I was left to ponder all the dreams afloat in the world, my own included, wondering if someday in the distant future Gary Willis would sit down with some friends over a pint at Punchestown, or even Thurles, and remember the time Jessie Harrington had smiled down on him from a very great height on a cold winter day.

ANDREW LEIGH did not fare well at Limerick. His horse Batang, an import from Germany, was a long shot in a two-mile maiden hurdle. Early in the race, at the crest of a hill, Batang began to gurgle as if he had a virus, so Andrew eased up on him. That was the proper thing to do, but when the horse quit gurgling seconds later, Andrew went back to work and drove him to a decent sixth-place finish behind Rabble Run, who was ridden by Timmy Murphy, his old nemesis. Would Murphy always pop into the picture whenever a problem arose? The notion might have crossed young Andrew's mind.

Batang's stop-and-go dance led to an inquiry. Gerald Cully told the stewards his horse often gurgled on soft ground, and that Leigh could have been closer to the pace halfway through, but otherwise Cully was satisfied with the ride. Yet the Turf Club vet couldn't find anything wrong with Batang, so the stewards judged the trainer and jockey to be in violation of Rule 212, which states that "every horse shall run on its merits, and the rider shall take all reasonable measures to ensure his mount is given every opportunity." Cully was fined a thousand bucks, Batang was banned from racing for forty-two days, and Andrew received another suspension, this for ten days, one more bump on the rocky road to experience.

ON THE LAST SUNDAY of the month, there was a spectacular show after the races at Leopardstown. Standing by the rail at twilight, I watched about fifty horses bound for Cheltenham being put through their paces. As befuddled as Abbey and Willis, I couldn't identify any of them in the near dark, except for Mouse Morris's ghostly Rostropovich, all white from head-to-toe. The track failed to offer a commentary, but I knew from the banter that Florida Pearl was out there, and so were Solerina, Hardy Eustace, Hasanpour, and Sadlers Wings.

Willie Mullins had the most horses working, around fifteen, many of them prospects for the Champion Bumper, his specialty. Rule Supreme, still an iffy jumper, was being schooled over fences, and again he crashed into one and banished Ruby Walsh from the saddle. Timmy Murphy, David Casey, Jim Culloty, and every other jockey on the course were focused on the Festival, sampling horses and experimenting with rides before they and their agents made a final commitment. Cheltenham was gradually taking over the available space in everybody's head.

My own Festival plans were fixed at last, after I'd consulted a travel agent in Kildare about package tours. The hotels in town were already full and frighteningly expensive, so I was left to decide between two inns in Stratford-upon-Avon, about twenty-eight miles from Cheltenham, and the Twigworth Hotel, billed as "popular with our clients" and under new management, not necessarily a recommendation in my view. But beggars can't be choosers, so despite my affection for the Bard and Stratford's literary cachet, I settled on the Twigworth at a cost of about nine hundred dollars for three nights, including breakfast, dinner, and airfare. My tickets to the races were extra, and I was down more than a grand before I ever reached the Promised Land.

Festival

So my long winter's education was coming to an end. The many
miles I'd clocked around Ireland by road and rail amounted to a
diploma of sorts and qualified me as a graduate of the jumps academy,
hardly an authority but still entitled to attend the Festival and offer an
opinion freely, whether or not anybody listened. I had paid my dues, as
they say, cold and wet for days at a time, had won and lost money—I
was ahead by the paltry sum of $183—and had drunk pints in pubs
both quaint and unruly, and that, I believed, stood as my own peculiar
badge of honor, on a par with Andrew Leigh's bruised wrist and
bloodstained nose.

With a week to go, my thoughts were all of Cheltenham, and I was
not alone. The Irish, more than five thousand strong, were preparing
for their annual pilgrimage, one that started in earnest after World
War II. The catalyst was Vincent O'Brien, arguably the finest trainer
of racehorses ever, whose assault on the English and their big prizes
enlisted an army of followers. In those lean times of postwar shortages
in England, O'Brien's countrymen did not depart for the Festival
empty-handed. They packed the fixings of a full Irish breakfast—
bacon, eggs, and the mealy blood sausages known as puddings, black
and white—as well as bottles of whiskey and even jugs of bootleg
poteen, Ireland's moonshine, to fortify themselves at crucial moments.

Even before I opened a biography of O'Brien, I could have guessed at the story of his childhood, so familiar were its elements. Born in Churchtown, County Cork, in 1917, he learned to ride as a boy, and later schooled point-to-pointers and hunted with the Dashing Duhallows, the oldest club in the country. He had no interest in formal education and dropped out at fifteen to work at Leopardstown. His father, Dan, held a permit to train his own horses, loved a game of cards, and feared ginger-haired women because they brought bad luck. Vincent became his amateur jockey and assistant, taking over the yard when Dan died in 1943.

The yard operated on a shoestring. The prize money in Ireland was still ridiculously low, so most trainers supplemented their income, or tried to, by gambling. In contrast, the purses at Cheltenham were worth a fortune, plus the stakes in the betting ring were high. England was awash in black-market currency after the war, and a bookmaker's check was one way to launder it. Those incentives weren't lost on O'Brien, who was anonymous and secluded in rural Cork, where his privacy could be guaranteed. Beyond the scope of rumors and far from prying eyes, he set in motion a plan to sting the bookies with antepost wagers on his little-known horses, the only means to survive.

He conducted his first foray in 1948 with Cottage Rake, delivered to him three years earlier as a six-year-old. O'Brien was always patient with his stock, never hurrying the horses along. Cottage Rake jumped well, and had some class in his pedigree and enough speed to have won good races on the flat, and that allowed him to beat Happy Home in the Gold Cup—an astonishing feat for a young Irish trainer on his first trip to the Cotswolds, and a huge gamble landed in the bargain. (O'Brien had even put down some money for his parish priest.) Barrels of stout lined the streets of Churchtown on his return, fuel for an all-night party where the bonfires blazed.

The next year, as an experiment, O'Brien sent his horses to the Festival by plane. Trainers usually relied on the ferry, as they do today, although the route went from Rosslare to Fishguard then. For the flight from Shannon to Bristol, O'Brien requisitioned a converted bomber for Castledermot, Hatton's Grace, and Cottage Rake, who was a feisty traveler even over land and kept his handlers occupied by almost fainting. However ill at ease in transit, the Rake won the Gold Cup again, and once more in 1950, while Castledermot triumphed, too, but it was Hatton's Grace, a horse with a big heart, who was the major surprise.

Small and furry, with a pronounced dislike for cold weather, Hatton's Grace had bounced from yard to yard until O'Brien took him in when he was eight in 1948—too old for a Festival bid over hurdles, most trainers would agree. In fact, he had run at Cheltenham that spring and hadn't placed, another strike against him. As patient as ever, O'Brien coaxed Hatton's Grace out of his doldrums and entered him in the Champion Hurdle two years later. The horse won at odds of 100–7, but O'Brien had the foresight to back him at ante-post odds as high as 33–1 and made another killing.

Twice more Hatton's Grace would collect the Champion Hurdle trophy, while Knock Hard won another Gold Cup for O'Brien in 1953. Through the decade that ended in 1959, he had twenty-three Festival winners, a record without parallel, and he tossed in three Grand Nationals for good measure. It was probably inevitable that he'd switch to the more lucrative field of flat racing, where again he set new benchmarks—six Epsom Derbys, four 2000 Guineas, three St. Legers, and so on—with such great horses as Nijinsky, Roberto, and The Minstrel. Ultimately, he transferred his operation from Cork to Tipperary, where he still lives on the Ballydoyle compound, well into his eighty-eighth year.

Others helped to forge a link between the Irish and Cheltenham, of course, with Tom Dreaper and Arkle vitally important. Dreaper tallied twenty-six Festival winners, a total yet to be matched—his success began when Prince Regent won the Gold Cup in 1946—but it was the flair and bravado of Vincent O'Brien that captured Ireland's fancy, invoked its sense of pride, and demonstrated a home truth that might have been written into the constitution: the Irish will travel many a mile to watch one of their own get a leg up on the English.

THE CASUALTY LIST for the Festival continued to grow, with Florida Pearl the most recent addition. He was observed walking oddly around Willie Mullins's yard, as if he weren't sound, and a vet diagnosed a ligament injury and prescribed some rest as the cure. Grainne Ni Chaba had checked on her old friend with Tracy Gilmour, and she assured me the Pearl was in good spirits. "He doesn't know he's hurt," Grainne said. "He isn't in any pain." She wished his owners would retire him, though, before he came to a bad end like Dorans Pride, and the O'Learys soon complied. Florida Pearl went on parade at the Galway Festival in July, looking very satisfied, indeed.

As for Best Mate, he'd yet to hit a snag. He kept sailing along at Henrietta Knight's yard near Oxford, but the tension was taking its toll on his trainer. An intruder had wandered onto her property not long ago, just a drunk sleeping it off in a stall, but the incident was scary enough for her to hire some security guards. Her superstitions were also reeling out of control. To placate any malign forces, she ordered a load of hay, not straw, for delivery on Gold Cup day, and put bets on all Best Mate's rivals. Late into the night, she sat up writing replies to Matey's fan mail, and that caused her husband, Biddlecombe, to grumble and urge her to come to bed.

Meanwhile, organizations all over Ireland were holding Cheltenham preview evenings where, for the price of a ticket, the fans could hear trainers, jockeys, and pundits of varying stripes and worth analyze the races. I boycotted those in Dublin because I had no use for hot tips or inside information anymore, particularly when they were bandied about in public and devalued at the source. Instead, I invited Noel O'Brien, the country's senior National Hunt handicapper, to lunch at the Stand House Hotel to see if I could pick his brain. He's no relation to Vincent or Aidan O'Brien, and was such an indifferent rider as a boy in rural Kildare he never shared the common Irish dream of becoming a jockey.

"Talking is not a problem with me," Noel said, when he breezed in. He does leap right into a conversation with both feet. Spirited and witty, he has the elfin, red-haired look that naïve tourists expect of the Emerald Isle. He's always loved racing, if not riding, and could remember when Kildare kids were let out of school every April to attend the Punchestown Festival. He was so enthralled with the National Hunt that he invented a game to simulate the races, cutting out paper horses and "jumping" them over obstacles like his shoes. Some horses were better than others, so Noel designed a staggered start as a handicap, an early indicator of his future career.

Even before he finished high school, O'Brien had landed a job in the accounts department at the Turf Club. Only seventeen, he was starstruck at first, in awe of the notable racetrack people he met. Four years later, he applied for a new post as an assistant National Hunt handicapper, although not with any confidence because he was so young. "I was still riding my bike to the office, and the other candidates drove up in cars," he said. "One fella owned a Mercedes!" During his interview, he developed a case of stage fright and could only speak in monosyllables. He thought he was sunk, but he got lucky—luck again!—when a board member asked what he knew about Adirondack, a horse of trainer Dermot Weld's. Strictly by chance, he knew everything and recited it chapter and verse, and that led the board to take him seriously.

As much as he coveted the position, it had a single drawback. He couldn't gamble anymore, because it was against Turf Club rules—not that he was a dedicated plunger, but he still felt deprived and said to himself, "Oh, God, this is going to be awful!" At the Stand House he gripped his head between his hands and made an agonized face to demonstrate the extent of his pain, but he later discovered that being a handicapper generated the same rush as betting, since it involved the same element of comparison. Tutored by Captain Louis Magee, his boss, he was taught to rate a horse on its best form—on what the horse beats, and not on what beats it—and soon realized the job was wholly subjective.

"Logic goes out the window," he said in a chipper way, as if the absence of logic increased his fun. "Too many anomalies. It's always a judgment call, regardless of the data."

For Noel, the challenge is to make each handicap as evenly balanced as possible. He works at home, where he has a huge bank of statistics in his computer. He also depends on videos of past races from the Turf Club's file. In theory, a 20–1 long shot should have the same chance of winning as a 2–1 favorite, but that's easier said than done. When a 2–1 favorite wins by ten lengths, Noel has to figure out what went wrong and adjust the weights as necessary. The result always displeases some trainers, so he's usually unpopular in one quarter or another for piling on too many pounds, or too few. It's all about fairness and balance, though, and he believes that Irish handicaps are more competitive because of it. In general, Irish racing is better than ever, he feels, for reasons I'd heard before—better prize money, good horses staying at home rather than sold abroad, and superior jockeys. "Ruby Walsh, Barry Geraghty, and Paul Carberry, it's a golden age," O'Brien said.

As tactfully as possible, I nudged our conversation toward Cheltenham. Did O'Brien have any special favorites among the Irish runners? Yes, he did. His two top choices were Sadlers Wings and Kicking

King. I wrote down the names, but the pen trembled in my hand when he said next, "I doubt Moscow Flyer is a shoo-in." Could he be referring to the Pattern? No, it was just that Azertyuiop was honestly to be respected, a noble adversary with every opportunity to steal Moscow's fire. He praised the Queen Mother as the most exciting race on the card, being the best test of both speed and stamina, and reminded me that the Festival always uncorks a number of shockers.

"It's often an unfancied horse who wins," Noel said. Some horses collapse under the pressure, while others, touched by the heroic, soar to unimagined heights.

Our lunch failed to have the desired effect. Why did O'Brien have to plug Azertyuiop? It bugged me through the night. Among the coterie of self-styled experts plying their trade, Noel was a real one, somebody who actually earned a living at it. I might be ahead for the season, but was I up to the complications of Cheltenham? Insofar as I had a method, it was to drink my mystical Guinness, cross out the inferior horses as Francis Hyland did, focus on the best trainers and jockeys, and take a shot. That was all right for the majority of Irish races, but at the Festival I'd be hard-pressed to find a single horse to discard and felt the way a lazy student does when he hasn't cracked the books before an exam.

So off to O'Herlihy's I went for a cram session with Reilly. He was in rare form, envious that I was going to the Festival, while at the same time taunting me about being a swell. "Must be nice to have that kind of money," he said, as if he hadn't gone himself two years ago. He brought a mountain of study materials with him—the results of key races clipped from the *Post* (like past performance charts), his special notes and comments, and some feature articles culled from tabloids and magazines. Knowing that Tony McCoy ate Jaffa Cakes with his tea lacked significance for me, but Reilly embraced every factoid, no matter how trivial, as a tile in the grand mosaic.

What Imelda made of this frenzy I can't say for certain. Wisely, she let it swirl around her, no more than a minor distraction. She knew better than to judge me by my obsessive behavior, aware that it wouldn't last. Not a critical word did she say about the papers scattered over the dining room table, nor did she tune out completely when I discussed my betting strategy with her, even faking some interest. I would imitate Father Breen, I told her, and confine myself to three bets a day rather than spread myself thin over the entire card, although that didn't happen, of course.

The worst of it was the trilby episode. I'd noticed the hats in a window at Coyles on Aungier Street, fanned out in a display marked with a sign that said CHELTENHAM, but they'd vanished by the time I decided I had to have one—snapped up by other pilgrims, I assumed. Inside the shop, amid the bare and dusty shelves, the aged proprietor was huddled by a gas fire, and he wearily recounted how his next shipment of trilbys was stranded on the Naas Road. "I could have sold six this week alone!" he groaned, as if that might equal a record. I had to settle for a waterproof hat that resembled a trilby. How this would affect my luck I couldn't guess.

As for luck, Guillaume Macaire had none. Only hours before the Festival, Jair du Cochet fractured a cannon bone while doing a final piece of work in France. The fracture couldn't be repaired, so the horse was put down, and the Gold Cup lost some more of its allure. Macaire sounded inconsolable. "He was like a member of my family," he said, perhaps regretting the harsh words he'd spoken earlier about Jair du Cochet. "Before the end of the gallop, I was dreaming of Cheltenham. A few seconds later, I was looking at a horse on three legs." If the fates truly had a darling, Best Mate appeared to be it.

ON THE MONDAY of Festival week, I joined a host of Irish fans on a charter flight to Birmingham, stunned to be on a plane where almost every passenger carried a *Racing Post*. The paper might have been issued with our tickets, then assigned as essential reading, so many noses were buried in it. That was fine with us, though. Nobody wanted to talk about politics or current events, only about horses. Strangers fell easily into conversations, sure they'd be neither intrusive nor boring if they stuck to topic A.

A bus was waiting for our tour group on arrival, and as we rode through the Cotswolds, dreary looking at the tattered end of winter, my heart sank as we progressed toward Twigworth. In my fantasies, I'd pictured a jolly English village with some shops and pubs, where large-bellied gents with faces like Toby mugs played darts and poured from flagons, but our hotel *was* Twigworth, an island unto itself in the midst of farm country, with only a gas station nearby to keep it company.

The hotel was plain but acceptable, at least, rather like an American motel, clean and neat, with a friendly staff. The management understood the needs of its guests quite well. In my room, I found a complimentary packet from William Hill, the bookie, with a free pen, some betting slips, and a booklet instructing an innocent person, should any exist in the vicinity, how to place a bet. (Hill's flagship shop in Cheltenham opened at eight every morning, so that the disadvantaged people with steady jobs could wager on the way to work.) The inescapable *Post* was outside my door before breakfast, and the morning-line odds were chalked on a board in the lobby. We were as isolated as shepherds on the Isle of Man, and as distant from the world's concerns.

That evening, I joined the gang at the bar after dinner, my choices for entertainment in Twigworth being severely limited. They were a lively bunch of lads, with a few wives and girlfriends in the mix. The lads were so versed in the sport's history and fine points they outdid T. P. Reilly, something I would have thought impossible. I was glad I'd studied up on Vincent O'Brien and could contribute an anecdote or two, but again the talk was primarily of horses—Istabraq and Dawn Run, Desert Orchid and Arkle. Even those who were too young to have seen Arkle run, except on film or video, could recite his life story and the tale of his rivalry with Mill House, an English giant of seventeen hands.

The two met first in November 1963 at the English Hennessy, I learned, after Mill House had won his only Gold Cup at Cheltenham that spring. It wasn't Arkle's day at Newbury. Despite a five-pound advantage, he slipped after jumping the last open ditch and finished third, beaten by eight lengths. Little wonder, then, that Mill House was favored to win a second Gold Cup the following year, but the Irish horse was foot-perfect this time and reversed the decision by five lengths, while shaving four seconds off the track record—sobering news for Mill House, who had turned in a career-best performance himself and still lost.

In their next engagement, the 1964 Hennessy at Newbury, Arkle conceded three pounds to his opponent. Under Willie Robinson, Mill House dashed to the lead as he'd done before, but Pat Taaffe on Arkle was soon with him, the pair locked together until the fourth-last, when Arkle picked up and flew home ten lengths to the good, a margin he extended to twenty lengths in the 1965 Gold Cup. With Mill House injured in 1966, Arkle won his third Gold Cup by thirty lengths, a shamrock threaded through his bridle, but he hit a fence and almost fell. He had no competition, so he didn't concentrate—shades of Moscow Flyer.

Arkle ran just two more races (and won just one) before his legs began to hurt. Tom Dreaper reported that his horse was lame, but some vets disagreed, saying Arkle was only "pottery," or shaky. As with Back In Front, nobody could pinpoint the source of his problem. He improved during a summer at his owner's farm in Bryanstown and received 160 cards on his birthday, but when autumn came he was stiff in his hindquarters. Diagnosed with arthritis, he was retired in October 1968.

Yet Arkle responded fairly well to treatment, and he was healthy enough to go to England for Wembly's Horse of the Year Show, where he was the star attraction. He paraded twice daily, let himself be petted, and ate whatever he pleased—a bouquet of hydrangeas and all the apples and pears off a vendor's cart. His theme song, selected by the Duchess of Westminster, was "There'll Never Be Another You," but his reprieve did not last long. Once he was home again, his arthritis grew more severe. Often he lay idly in his stall and had trouble standing up. Crippled and failing, he was put down in May 1970 and buried in a field at the Bryanstown farm, where his gravestone bears only a single word—Arkle—as if to consecrate his uniqueness.

TILL PAST MIDNIGHT I listened to Arkle's story, more dramatic with each new pint, and woke at gray dawn to realize I'd gone to bed without a glance at Tuesday's card, so I sat at my Twigworth minidesk to make amends. I had allotted myself a budget of five hundred dollars for the Festival, a pittance by Cheltenham standards (although not by mine), and I intended not to lose it—no, more, I wanted to go home a winner, bragging all the way to Dublin and loaded with gifts for the family. I was so hopped up I couldn't wait for the tour bus to leave for the track and ordered a gypsy cab. It had no meter, and the driver gouged me for twice the normal fare.

Well, it's the way of the world, I counseled myself. Everybody gets screwed at the Kentucky Derby and the Breeders' Cup, too. Anyway, I was delighted to be at Cheltenham ahead of the crunch. The traffic was already snarled on the main road, and race-goers were risking life and limb to dart across it. In the ceaseless stream of cars, I saw some fancy horse vans, the expensive air-conditioned kind, and also some humble one- and two-horse trailers from smaller yards, pulled along behind a trainer's SUV. Familiar names were painted in big letters on the sleekest, flashiest vans—Martin Pipe, Jonjo O'Neill, Paul Nicholls, and Phillip Hobbs, the elite of British-based jump racing.

With a mild flourish, the attendants threw open the gates at ten-thirty. The press of flesh was immediate and substantial, a reflection of pent-up desire. I squeezed through a door and was carried unwillingly into the Centaur, new since my last visit—a noisy, overbright, Vegas-style room with six bars, food stands, bookies, and slot machines for the terminally addicted. On stage beneath a gigantic screen for show-ing the races, a lounge lizard band was churning out the sort of brassy, pseudo-jazz you don't really want to hear in the morning, if ever. The Centaur was a universe apart, and some fans occupied it as cozily as a couch in front of the TV, avoiding the fresh air and the sight of a horse all day.

Though the Centaur's bars were already busy, I chose not to com-pound last night's folly and instead went to an HRI press conference, held in a suite in the Tented Village. On the panel were Jessie Harring-ton, who looked tired, Noel Meade (relaxed), Edward O'Grady (amused), Barry Geraghty (intense), and Noel O'Brien (elfin). The atmosphere was more formal than in Ireland, and it had a distancing effect. The intimacy I so cherished on the Irish circuit—that sensation of being inside rather than outside the races—was gone, replaced by the contradictions of the major leagues, with all the usual hoopla.

The session opened with a question for O'Grady. Did he have many commitments? "A lot," he replied, his wit still sharp, "but not many runners." How would his horse John Oliver do in the Supreme Novices' Hurdle, the day's first race? "He's like the little girl with a curl in the middle of her forehead," O'Grady said. "When he's good, he's very, very good, but when he's bad . . ." A reporter ostensibly interested in gender issues addressed himself to Jessie. "We're always hearing about Henrietta Knight's feelings. You must have feelings, too?" he blurted out.

Jessie dodged the bullet. Her feelings were probably the last thing she cared to reveal, so she spoke about the Queen Mother and how much simpler it was to bring Moscow Flyer back this year, a cheerful note I liked. She swore there was less agonizing, as well, although I didn't buy it, not after seeing how difficult it is to get an Irish horse to the Festival in one piece, much less win a race in England after hard travel and before a hometown crowd. Since the 1998–99 season, Noel Meade had had just one winner from forty-two runners—and he kissed the ground after that race—Willie Mullins was two for forty-two, and O'Grady was two for twenty. Only Jessie was an exception with four winners from nine entries, the best percentage by far.

Around noon, with the races two hours away, I sat by the parade ring and watched a master of ceremonies conduct interviews with such luminaries as Pipe and John P. McManus, who was as cool as ever in spite of the stakes. He had five horses entered that afternoon, three in the Champion Hurdle, yet he radiated serenity. When a groom led Istabraq into the ring, shipped to Cheltenham from McManus's farm in Limerick, the fans applauded mightily, and Istabraq responded with a powerful buck, as a man might tip his hat to an admiring crowd. It was a lovely moment and all about the horse, as Ted Walsh would say.

In an hour or so, that lovely moment had fled, and my nerves were frazzled. As impatient as I was for the Festival to begin, I dreaded the mental challenge ahead. If I hoped to achieve my goal of going home a winner, I had to kill off my partiality toward the Irish, block any sentimental wagers, and stick to my three-bet plan with the icy calm of a hired gun. During my belated study period at the Twigworth, I'd only had time to comb through the first two races, though. My picks were Brave Inca in the Supreme Novices and Pipe's Well Chief in the Arkle

Chase. For a third horse, I chose Chicuelo, also trained by Pipe, in the William Hill Handicap Chase, but that was just a stab in the dark.

Ireland had seven runners in the Supreme Novices, among them Willie Mullins's Arch Stanton and Euro Leader. Ruby Walsh had won on both, but as Paul Nicholls's stable jock, he was obligated to ride Albuhera. As for Barry Geraghty, he'd made a late switch from Garde Champetre to O'Grady's John Oliver. What had gone down at that press conference? Had they cooked up something? I was curious, but a hired gun can't be swayed by such trifles, so I put twenty to win on Brave Inca. At first, I thought I'd kissed the money good-bye, because Arch Stanton looked invincible, but he fizzled and let Conor O'Dwyer on War Of Attrition storm to the lead. Yet Barry Cash on Brave Inca was right there, too, casting a long shadow, and he wore down O'Dwyer's horse as they battled up the hill.

All at once, the fabled Irish victory cry rose around me, a bellow of sheer unadulterated joy that had in it the roar of the ancient high kings, of Finn McCool and Brian Boru, and a touch of Molly Malone's melodious pitch for cockles and mussels, and most definitely the echo of well-oiled voices bouncing off the cobbled streets of old Dublin through an eternity of late-night exits from a thousand different pubs. Men were hugging one another, holding up fistfuls of bills, raising cups of beer, and singing, of course, off-key at times and yet unashamedly, with force and vigor. When Brave Inca passed down the chute on his return trip, the fans ran along the rail to accompany him, waving and reaching out, a couple of them in tears, and Barry Cash smiled and thanked them with a salute of his whip, a very god on horseback.

Young Colm Murphy was waiting for Brave Inca in the winner's enclosure. "That's the nearest I've ever been to a heart attack," he said with a shiver.

THE IRISH WERE off to a brilliant start. They might have been dosed with helium, so giddily were they behaving. Their momentum was building, too, since they held some aces in the Arkle Chase— Central House, Colca Canyon, and Kicking King. As often as certain people (Geraghty, Noel O'Brien) had touted Kicking King to me, I stuck to the plan and bet twenty to win on Well Chief. Tony McCoy, who was Pipe's principal rider, preferred him to Puntal, another from the Pipe yard. Jockeys don't always choose correctly, but I had a hunch about McCoy—a vibe, let's call it. I believed *he* believed Well Chief was special, even though the horse had just one chase (and one win) to his name.

Had any jockey ever looked as grim and determined in the paddock as McCoy? I doubted it. Nearly thirty, with a face so starved of fat it was skeletal, the cheek and jaw bones in stark definition, he seemed in a state of perpetual misery. "Yes, and I'll stay miserable," he once threatened, "and I'll keep winning." As Britain's leading jump jockey every season for the past eight years, McCoy had a strike rate of twenty-six percent and at least fifty more wins than his nearest challenger. He was fitter this season, too, after a disciplined routine of gym workouts, and also riding better than ever, down low in the saddle for a tighter grip on his horse.

Cocky, aggressive, and strong, those were McCoy's trademarks. In the Arkle, he kept Well Chief out of trouble at the back, while Geraghty pushed Kicking King up with the pace. Thisthatandtother, the favorite, came to grief at the second fence, and five other horses fell or unseated their riders in a very sloppy race. With so many gone, McCoy saw a clear path on the inside and zipped along it. Well Chief was just too much for Kicking King, who had to settle for the second spot, as he'd done in the Supreme Novices last year. A momentary silence descended on the Irish, but my own feet were a few inches off the ground.

There was a story behind Well Chief's success, I later learned. Pipe, the master manipulator, had pulled off another stroke, or betting coup, laying out his horse for the Arkle over the past two weeks. Every day Well Chief had been schooled over thirty fences to counteract his lack of experience in chases—a fact that didn't turn up in the *Post* or travel far beyond the confines of Pipe's yard. Serious punters steered clear of Well Chief because he was lightly raced over the birch, so David Johnson, his owner, was able to back him at 33–1 ante-post, while small fry like me, who were out of the loop, were thrilled to get him at 9–1 on the day.

My betting book was a thing of beauty. I was two-for-two and had earned a profit of almost three hundred dollars. Now all I had to do was to sit back and enjoy the scenery until the William Hill, but I fell into a familiar trap. Infatuated with my own intelligence, and convinced I was in harmony with the universal flow, I ditched the three-bet plan and dropped fifty to win on Rigmarole, certain he could upset Rooster Booster in the Champion Hurdle, the afternoon's centerpiece with the fattest pot.

Rooster Booster looked eminently beatable on paper. The stats were dead against him. He was ten, and only three ten-year-olds had won the Champion Hurdle in seventy-four years. Also, the Rooster had run poorly in his races this season, because he failed to get the fast pace he requires—or such was Phillip Hobbs's excuse. His one magnificent outing at Newbury in February, where he gave away seventeen pounds to Geos and only lost by a stride, had cost him some energy, plus three horses in the field had already beaten him at level weights, including Rigmarole. The fans supported him, though, and sent him off as the favorite, with Richard Johnson riding.

The race set up ideally for the champ. Hardy Eustace, one of four Irish entries (and dismissed by the punters at 33–1) took the lead at a good gallop, so Hobbs and Johnson got the pace they needed. Like Rooster Booster, Hardy Eustace had fared badly this season, losing all four starts and bothered by sore shins, but he seemed to have revived. In first-time blinkers, he ran loose and free and rebuffed every thrust until Johnson came at him. Rooster Booster was electrifying as he slashed through the field from far back, but Hardy Eustace refused to buckle, and the big gray horse's surge fell short by five lengths.

Again that monumental cry engulfed us. What an amazing afternoon for Ireland! Exactly as described in the anecdotal literature, I got carried away. So I'd just lost fifty smackers—so what? The heady atmosphere had me in a whirl. Hired killer, my eye. I couldn't control a single impulse and launched myself on a string of sorry wagers. In the William Hill, I forgot about Chicuelo, who lost, and backed Marlborough, another loser, and next the loser Jasmin D'Oudairies in the Challenge Cup. Trying to get even on the last race ("pure gravy for the bookies"), I lost on Keepatem, who was trounced by Creon, a 50–1 shot. J. P. McManus owned both horses, and no doubt he'd backed both, too. That did little to heal my troubled psyche.

Later that night, I lay in my lonely Twigworth bed and licked my wounds. Having closed down my accounts, I was still up $120—not too shabby, really, given the error of my ways. Down the hallway at intervals came guests retreating from the bar, their voices hoarse from the drink, smoke, chatter, and cheers. They were busy inventing a narrative that would become the myth of this particular festival, each player's tale of woe or glory a strand in the overarching brocade. Still ahead were the myth's core events, the Queen Mother and the Gold Cup, after which the story would be over and ripe for countless retellings. Such were the lofty thoughts of a tired punter on the edge of sleep.

ON WEDNESDAY—St. Patrick's Day—Moscow Flyer had a walk over the course in the early morning mist. "He's himself," Eamonn Leigh told the TV folks, a gnomic remark I interpreted as positive. Moscow figured prominently in my approach to the afternoon. I'd talked myself out of that silly, superstitious nonsense about the Pattern, replaying Barry Geraghty's words in my mind. "He's the ace in my pack," Barry had said, and I trusted him. Why shouldn't I? Moscow had already destroyed Azertyuiop once, so the horse was my banker—the key element in the three-bet strategy I'd stick to (definitely, absolutely) this time.

Then, too, I had virtue on my side. Rather than swap lies at the bar, I did my homework, retired early, and slept well, and that gave me a buoyant sensation of clarity that faded almost the second I got to the track. There were distractions everywhere, among them a pair of short chubby guys in leprechaun costumes who were hamming it up for the crowd, their faces painted green and their bloodshot eyes brimful of booze. I was in the midst of a Lorca rhapsody, caught in a swirl of green shirts and ties, green scarves and socks, green dresses and beer, and probably green underwear. Hawkers were even selling garlands of shamrocks by the gates and had the nerve to guarantee they'd bring good luck.

Arkle, Mill House, Cottage Rake, and Istabraq, they all had bars named in their honor, and the green hordes had already taken command of them with the authority of invading troops. No glass or bottle would go untipped today, not when there was a patron saint to be celebrated. The shepherd boy who imported Christianity to Ireland and banished every snake would be toasted repeatedly with a fierce, partisan energy, so I sought refuge from the bedlam in the Head on Stand, where for an extra thirty dollars, I could buy a seat to call my own, not insignificant when fifty thousand or so fans are aching for a place to rest.

Fundamentalist, Pizarro, and Moscow Flyer. Someday they, too, might have their own bars, but they were only my picks in the first three races at present. Fundamentalist had impressed me in a race at Haydock in February, plus Nigel Twiston-Davies, his trainer, had a yard near Cheltenham and did well at the track, so I chose the horse for the Royal and Sun Alliance Novices Hurdle, even though he was up against Inglis Drever, the best British novice in ages. Under Carl Llewellyn, Fundamentalist dawdled at the rear of the field, then burst to the front three hurdles out, trailed by Inglis Drever, who was in an ideal spot until he crashed into the second-last. There would be no catching Fundamentalist row, I believed, and I was already tallying the return on my bet when the horse grazed the last hurdle and lost a few strides. The race was on again with Inglis Drever closing rapidly, only to fall short by a half-length.

I let go of the breath I'd been holding. I had forty to win on Fundamentalist at 9–1, and that increased my profit to almost five hundred dollars. It was as if yesterday's stupidity had never occurred. I was on top again, where I belonged. As ever, I saw my bulging wallet as a mere prelude to the riches yet to come and imagined how I'd spend the windfall, maybe on a trout-fishing trip to California. More important, though, was a gift for Imelda, so I did some window shopping at the Tented Village. How about some expensive boots from Dubarry of Ireland? Or a pashmina woven from the fleece of a Tibetan Capra Hircus goat? Exotic, yes, but I was leaning toward a simple gold bracelet when I had to leave for the Royal and Sun Alliance Chase.

Fifty to win on Pizarro, that was my wager, and I hesitated only a little. Our Vic, another horse from Tom Costello's impeccable nursery, and one he had praised to the sky, looked to be a monster. He'd won three straight hurdles for Martin Pipe, then switched to fences and demolished a Grade Two field at Ascot. His odds stood at 11–8—too short, really, when you had such talented contenders as Mossy Green and Royal Emperor. As if to prove my point, Our Vic banged into the very first fence and jumped sketchily throughout, while Royal Emperor committed blunder after blunder and shook up Dominic Elsworth, his jockey, so badly Elsworth dropped his whip.

Yet both horses survived and stayed close to Mossy Green, the pacesetter. On the second circuit, Pizarro threw in an awkward jump over the water. He might have been spooked, because Irish courses don't have water jumps. At the fourth-last, the race got very untidy. Calling Brave, who'd been error-free, clobbered the fence and lost his rider. Pizarro had recovered and traveled decently through the scramble, but Mossy Green misjudged the second-last, interfered with Pizarro, and brought my horse down. David Casey on Rule Supreme swung wide of the fallers and gained some ground. Our Vic was quitting, and Elsworth lacked a whip for the drive, so Rule Supreme held on to become the third Irish winner, and the only one from Willie Mullins's seventeen entries.

THE IRISH WERE STILL gaily waving their flags when the horses entered the paddock for the Queen Mother Champion Chase. I'd placed my bet early, two hundred to win on Moscow Flyer at 10–11, and pressed my way into the front ranks to watch the Harrington team get him ready. The yard at Moone, the beech and lime trees, the Wicklow Mountains, and even Ireland itself seemed a galaxy away, and I saw Moscow as a stouthearted country horse up against the city slickers. Not that he looked like a bumpkin—no, he looked splendid, a tribute to all the work and care Jessie, Eamonn, and the others had lavished on him. I only hoped he would concentrate, *really* concentrate, and do the job for which they'd so thoroughly prepared him.

Azertyuiop did not look as good. He was washy, dripping sweat. "Excellent," I muttered to myself. "May buckets of the stuff pour out of him." Ruby Walsh's bad-luck streak was another benefit for our side, I thought. Ruby had ridden five losers on Tuesday and two this afternoon, plus he'd just taken a fall on Mossy Green, but Barry Geraghty wasn't doing much better, really. He hadn't been on a winner yet, either, and had hit the deck with Pizarro, so egos were bruised all around. That made both jockeys hungrier than ever. The opposing colors of their silks reflected the tension. No costume designer could have done it any better. Walsh was as bold as a crocus in bright yellow, with a red star from the Mao era on his chest, while Geraghty wore black-and-white chevrons such as an escaped convict might sport, a thief out to steal the race. They were the only two in it, and they knew it.

The horses who contested the early lead, Cenkos, Ei Ei, and Eskleybrook, were destined to burn out. Meanwhile, Ruby played a waiting game on Azertyuiop, coasting along in mid-division behind Moscow Flyer. To keep from sweating myself, I remembered my talk with Jessie back in October and how she had explained why the Queen Mother suited Moscow. "The competition is so intense, he has to pay attention," she'd said, whereas his mind wandered during Irish races because they unfold more slowly, only turning into a sprint at the end. And Moscow did seem attentive and very smooth until he reached the water jump—the same one that rattled Pizarro—and fouled up.

Some horses hate the water and can become phobic about it, although I doubted that was the case with Moscow. But I could see that the slight hitch had broken his rhythm, and rhythm is all in a fast-paced chase. Even Geraghty, an expert at restoring a horse's balance, couldn't get him right. Before my eyes, as if on a scrim, I saw the Pattern in enormous numbers and letters, *111* and then *FUB*. Navan, Sandown, and Leopardstown, that added up to three wins in a row, and I knew something awful was about to happen. Sure enough, Moscow jumped tentatively at the next fence, and at the one after that—an open ditch, the fourth-last—he lost his timing completely and paddled through it. Geraghty couldn't hang on and landed on the ground.

The collective groan that greeted Geraghty's flop was a melancholy counterpoint to that Irish victory cry. Heaps of cash had slipped into the bookies' pockets, my own two hundred included. I could almost hear the howls in faraway Dublin. Incredibly, Moscow Flyer had done it again. What a quirky animal he was! Had he watched too much traffic in Moone and scrambled his brain waves, as kids do with computer games? There wasn't any answer. Moscow would be a mystery forever to us human beings, even to Geraghty, his intimate companion, who was at a loss to account for the accident. "Stunned about sums it up," he said.

For Jessie and Eamonn, it was a bitter defeat, their months of dedicated work smashed to bits in a few seconds. With his adversary gone, Azertyuiop mowed down the other horses, streaking clear by nine lengths. It was a win, all right, but not a definitive one. Instead, it recalled Moscow's contests with Istabraq, those races decided by phantom blows. But for Ruby Walsh, who'd been adamant all along that Azertyuiop was too fresh in the Tingle Creek, not yet himself, the Queen Mother provided a welcome corrective, and he could ignore his recent spill, stand tall in the saddle, and shout, "Jaysus, what a relief!"

The rest of the afternoon dragged by for me. I was depressed, as if I'd taken a fall myself. I still had some of the house's money, but it seemed like chump change after my elaborate fantasies—no fishing trip to California, that had vanished. I ignored the next two races and hoisted a Guinness at the bar where the leprechauns, ever less merry, were drowning their sorrows, then violated my three-bet plan again by throwing away fifty bucks on Fondmort (also again) in a handicap chase. That left only the Champion Bumper, where almost half of the twenty-four entries were from Ireland.

I settled on Martinstown, yet another McManus horse, who had won his only two starts in Ireland and been saved for this race since November. Martinstown couldn't keep himself warm. He finished fourteenth and cost me another fifty. Total Enjoyment, a five-year-old mare, stole the show. Her trainer Tom Cooper, a part-timer from Tralee in County Kerry, had a winner on his first trip to the Festival, a regular Vincent O'Brien. Cooper seemed to have alerted all of Kerry to the mare's promise, too, so the bookies lost more than a million dollars. Jim Culloty, a Kerryman, was in the irons, and the horse's owners—the It Will Never Last Syndicate, composed mostly of Kerrymen—were so pumped up (and newly wealthy) they carried Cooper around on their shoulders, while they serenaded him with "The Rose of Tralee."

AHEAD LOOMED another lonely, studious evening at the Twigworth, a prospect I couldn't abide, so I boarded a shuttle bus for the city center, determined to do St. Patrick's Day in style. I sat next to a mailman from Coventry, who looked the way I felt, half-elated and half-wrecked, a function of violent mood swings. When I mentioned the Gold Cup, he frowned. He wouldn't be coming back on Thursday. "Too exhausting," he said. I understood his dismay. I'd lost touch with ordinary life, too. In town, I was astonished to see people doing normal things—they were buying shoes! They had an existence apart from horses and racing, and I envied them, almost.

On both sides of the Promenade in Cheltenham, race-goers in little groups, some dazed and some chirpy, were being drawn as if by pan pipes to the Queens Hotel, a grand old structure with columns out front and a pair of bouncers possibly on loan from the World Wrestling Federation guarding the door. In the lobby, an overtaxed gent dozed in an armchair, with a wilted shamrock curled in his lapel. Surely he intended to go to the track, but the undertow of alcohol was too strong. He was the only victim so far. The night was young, after all, and a band was just setting up in a ballroom, but I heard Irish tunes playing on tape at a small bar off the lobby, where I found a vacant table, my first good break since Fundamentalist.

Here I held court for a while. I had two empty chairs and could have rented them by the hour, so intense was the demand. First to join me were Harold and Ginger, locals as evidenced by their tweeds. They'd never been to the Festival before and were exhilarated to have lived through it. Gambling, drinking, and so on. This stop at the Queens would cap and certify their racecourse experience (never to be repeated), although Ginger seemed tempted. She had three paying guests at her house, gentlemen from Ireland, and thought they were "interesting." Harold knocked back his beer so fast I offered another round, but that was a bridge too far for him, so he grabbed Ginger and split.

Next came a captain of industry, an Irishman in exile forced to earn his fortune outside London, which he'd done. The smell of money was all over him. He marched in whistling along to "McNamara's Band" and asked to borrow my *Racing Post*, so he could check why all his bets had been losers. That should have endeared him to me, but it didn't. He was a bully. The Queens had been his base forever, so he felt privy to its secrets and entitled to do as he pleased. He was in no rush to finish his drink. Instead, he'd pace himself—instinct control!—and change to vintage wine with dinner, before moving on to brandy and a cigar. Bastard!

The captain's wife was more friendly. She loved racing and had traveled the world in pursuit of it. She'd been to Australia, New York, Kentucky, and even Hong Kong, she said—I drifted, thinking of the stickers on old luggage trunks—but I was also glaring at the captain as he read the *Post* and whistled "The Wild Colonial Boy." Why did I have an urge to strangle him? It was a low thing to feel, but I couldn't stand the guy, so I surrendered my table and joined the crush at the bar, where a giant from Kerry was holding forth. He offered a toast to Total Enjoyment, Tom Cooper, and Kerry itself, and though I had a pint in hand, he bought me another. "God's country," he mumbled, listing toward me like a building about to collapse. I bought him a pint, and he bought me a pint, and I bought him a pint, and he tried to buy me a pint, but I escaped.

The bar was jammed now. I saw two working girls among the customers, one a busty redhead in a miniskirt. Hookers had fared poorly with the Irish at Cheltenham in the old days. "They're only interested in cards and horses," ran the apocryphal quote. It's even money the redhead will flash her knickers tonight, I said to myself, my brain in Paddy Power mode. The drink was getting to me, and I was still fuming about the captain, who lorded it over the room. He'd invite a chum to rest for a few minutes in a precious chair (my chair!), then dismiss him and summon the next jester. His losing bets were my only solace. "May they haunt you forever, captain," I said, hoping he'd hear me.

In search of some breathing room, I struggled to the lobby. The band was so loud the hotel had the feel of a deafening echo chamber, but nobody seemed to mind—quite the opposite, in fact. All the noise, palaver, and marginal behavior were part of a more general release the Festival encouraged, a chance to forget ordinary cares and sink them in a sea of booze. At the Queens, judges and CEOs clinked glasses with farmers, burglars, and dope dealers. There were no class distinctions, no banal conversations about mortgages or orthodontia, and especially no imperative to better yourself. Here you could let it all hang out. For many of the revelers, this was as good as it got.

Hunger spared me from total ruin. On the brink of being excessively tipsy, I excused myself (though nobody noticed), located an Italian café nearby, and ordered some pasta. I was desperate, though, because I had nothing to read. The menu was no help, either, being short on digestible prose. The captain had my *Post*, damn it, and I imagined it had gone that way for him since birth, every momentary desire satisfied. A kindly waitress, registering my distress, brought me a wrinkled, sauce-stained paper. The sports pages were missing—they're always missing, everywhere on earth—but in the news section I found a feature on Best Mate, who would soon have his "appointment with destiny," as the overwrought reporter put it.

A LIGHT RAIN SPATTERED against my window on Gold Cup morning. The guests were sleeping in at the Twigworth. On most doorknobs, I saw signs that read HANGOVER RECOVERY IN PROGRESS, the hotel's semi-clever version of DO NOT DISTURB. The breakfast room was quiet, the staff subdued. On the bus ride to the track, our mood was somber, even respectful. We had a sense of occasion, I suppose, knowing we were part of something unique. If the day went well and Best Mate won again, we'd be telling our grandchildren about it in years to come, and if we didn't have any grandchildren, we'd rent some to bend their ears.

The coach dropped us at the gates around noon. I stepped over some puddles as deep as little ponds. Though it was dry and cool now, the rain had done its work and softened the ground considerably. The official going was "good (good to soft in places)," an advantage for the Irish horses, although also for Best Mate. Despite the dull weather, the fans came in droves—57,463 people, a new Cheltenham record. I looked around for the Manchester United guerrillas, but a mild scolding from Sir Alex had nipped their rebellion in the bud.

We arrived early enough that I could beat the crowd to the Arkle Bar. I ordered a much-needed coffee, wistfully recalling when I was so far ahead of the game, but I'd returned most of my profit to the bookies on Wednesday. I was almost even now, an unacceptably wishy-washy state, the province of pinched souls who store pennies in jars and never cross a street against the light. Better to win or lose big than go home untouched or even unscarred by the experience, I thought, but once more I'd neglected to study the form, having lingered too long at the Queens. Always an excuse, as my teachers used to say.

The JCB Hurdle, the afternoon's opener, was a devilish affair for twenty-three lightly raced four-year-old novices. So much depended on racing luck I was going to stay away from the JCB until I saw Hasanpour's name on the card—Hasanpour, my newsagent's tip, an enticing echo from Dublin! Charlie Swan told the *Post* he liked his horse's chances, too, and explained that a virus had affected his last outing, a pitiful one. I had to grip my left wrist with my right hand to block access to my wallet, but it worked, and I was glad, because Hasanpour was pulled up. The first five finishers were all long shots, with Phillip Hobbs's Made In Japan the winner at 20–1.

The Stayers' Hurdle was another race to avoid, although for a different reason—the presence of Baracouda, already a champion twice at the Festival. French-bred, out of Peche Aubar by Alesso, a U.S. stallion, Baracouda was among J. P. McManus's most prized possessions. McManus had purchased the gelding and also First Gold from the Marquesa de Moratalla after meeting her at a London dinner party in 2001, according to a report in the *Times* of London. The Marquesa recognized a kindred soul who'd treat her horses humanely, it was said, but the estimated six-figure price tag must have had some influence on her willingness to sell.

Finding a flaw in Baracouda's armor was a thankless task. His overall record was formidable, with sixteen wins and four seconds from twenty-one starts. Only two things counted against him, a tendency to stall when he was in front and his age. In the past eleven years, sixty-four eight-year-olds had tried the race, but only three had won, and Baracouda was nine. The competition would come from Iris's Gift, a close second to him last year, losing by just three-quarters of a length, but Iris's Gift had question marks, too. Niggling problems had affected him all winter, so the horse's preparation had been less than ideal. He'd had only one run before the Festival.

Statistics and form aside, it would be another factor that affected the race—the wiliness of the Irish, Barry Geraghty in particular. He'd ridden Iris's Gift in the last Stayers' Hurdle and had learned that Baracouda thrived on a fast pace, letting the other horses burn out before firing, so he warned Gary Hutchinson on Solerina—a speedy front-runner—to take it easy, or he'd be handing the race to Baracouda. Since Hutchinson was already doubtful about Solerina's ability to last for three miles, he agreed to conserve the mare (if he could) for a late sprint. By keeping a tight hold, he slowed the pace and left Geraghty with plenty of horse. When Iris's Gift skipped past Solerina two hurdles out, Thierry Doumen on Baracouda released the brake. Baracouda closed with a predatory swoop, as if on the scent of blood, but Geraghty's intrigue paid a dividend, and his horse drew clear over the last fifty yards.

EVERY FESTIVAL DEVELOPS its own thread of meaning, a strand of occurrences that ultimately define it, and ours might well be called the Graveyard of Champions with Rooster Booster, Baracouda, and Moscow Flyer all defeated. Only Best Mate still held his title, and we'd know soon if Matey would be the exception to the rule. No horse could have been nurtured toward his goal with more care or patience, each in infinite supply thanks to Henrietta Knight and her devoted crew, who had fine-tuned Best Mate so minutely he might have been an instrument for detecting tiny disturbances in the atmosphere.

The Gold Cup in 2002 came seventy-eight days after Matey's last race, for instance. The spread was seventy-seven days in 2003, and this year it was eighty-one days, an extraordinary degree of precision. Again the horse had just three prep races, the same as last year, with the Ericsson substituted for the King George. A skilled squad of specialists saw to his every need, as well. He had a physiotherapist to massage his back muscles, and a dentist to repair his teeth. Jackie Jenner was almost saintly in her devotions. As if that weren't enough, Best Mate had the public's support. Admirers had sent him more than eight hundred cards, often with sprigs of heather or clover enclosed, to wish him good luck.

For Knight, the detail work didn't stop with her horse. Every human movement had to be plotted, too, and made as identical as possible to other Gold Cup days. She wore the same blue suit as before—the same blouse and hat, of course, and her lucky pearls—while Terry Biddlecombe retrieved his lucky hat, a bashed-in trilby, from the cupboard where it gathered dust between its annual appearances. Their houseguest, Andrew Coonan, head of the Irish Jockeys' Association, had gone home to Kildare on Wednesday, just as he'd done in the past, and Knight would watch the race on TV (if she could bear to) in a press tent behind the weighing room, where she had watched it last year.

Whatever you thought about Knight's precautions (and who dared to judge her, after the infuriated fates had capsized Moscow Flyer?), Best Mate deserved his spot at the head of the market. He did look like a lion in the paddock, possessed of a vital nobility. Where was the threat, I wondered? Beef Or Salmon was too green, while Harbour Pilot was too risky. A high-strung type, he had lost some weight on the ferry, plus Beef Or Salmon had beaten him twice. What about First Gold? In my opinion, he was over the hill. First Gold had won only a single race in England, the King George VI in 2000, prompting McManus to buy him, and had run just once this season, again in the King George, where he trailed in third.

Keen Leader, Barry Geraghty's mount, had attracted some money. The horse had class, but his record was too in-and-out for my taste. As for Truckers Tavern, second in 2003, he'd blown every race since then.

No, the only two outsiders who appealed to me were Therealbandit and Sir Rembrandt. With Therealbandit, Martin Pipe was rolling the dice. His horse liked Cheltenham, having won two novice chases there, and would have an easier trip among veteran horses than he would have had among the sloppy novices in the Royal and Sun Alliance Chase. Yet only one novice had ever won the Gold Cup, and that was Captain Christy in 1974.

The punters liked Therealbandit, though, and made him second favorite to the odds-on Best Mate—wishful thinking, maybe. But as I studied Sir Rembrandt, I became convinced he had an outside chance. True, you'd doubt it on his recent form, since his last good run was in the Welsh National in December. After that, he'd been pulled up in the Pillar Property Chase and had weakened disastrously in the race after that. Robert Alner couldn't account for his decline, but Sir Rembrandt had put it behind him, at least by the look of him. He, too, had an animal vigor, along with a magnificent aura of well-being, so I tossed a fast fifty on him to win.

For the Gold Cup I had an invitation to the HRI box, high up among the corporate and members' boxes in the privileged precincts of the grandstand. I could see the full panorama of the racecourse without battling the crowd, and I felt a very potentate to be hobnobbing with such dignitaries as Paddy Mullins and Father Breen. As I helped myself to some lunch from a buffet, a young waiter tapped me on the shoulder. He was still a teenager and bore the normal burdens of adolescence. He had braces on his teeth, blotches on his face, and a crop of unruly hair that spiked up in weird cowlicks. On a crumpled napkin, he'd written, "First Gold, Two Pounds." Would I place the bet for him? Servers couldn't gamble while on duty, he explained.

Of course, I agreed. Why not facilitate the dreams of a fellow dreamer? But I was curious why he chose me from so many eligibles. I attributed it first to my gentle nature, only to realize a second later that he took me for the only fall guy in the room. Whatever the reason, I did his bidding and put ten dollars on First Gold myself, because the napkin had to be an omen—even though First Gold was eleven, and no horse older than ten had won the Gold Cup since 1969. What pits of deception can swallow us! Anyway, I took it on the chin, topped up my wineglass, and gave the kid his ticket. Good luck, kid, you'll need it.

We moved onto a balcony for the race. The sky provided an operatic backdrop, thundery purple above the deep-green grass of the course. The air, too, had a stinging bite, as sharp as a wake-up call. A team of red-coated huntsmen led the field onto the track, and the horses acquired a shimmery grace in the fine mist. Utterly beautiful, they must have been aware of a heightened moment. They'd recognize it from the intensity of the crowd, I thought, and from a sound most of them had never heard before, the slightly altered breathing of nearly sixty thousand human beings in a rapturous state of suspense, on the cusp of every mystery.

All the hype, all the boozing and carousing, even the slot-machine frenzy of the Centaur, they were swept aside by a cosmic broom, and we were delivered to the heart of the matter and understood our purpose again. It went that way at every major sporting event, be it the Super Bowl or the World Cup final, because the event itself was often buried under so many layers of commerce that its essence was obscured. But there always came a revelatory moment such as this, when everyone remembered the why of it and snapped to attention, ready to witness the impossible forward pass, the amazing penalty kick, or the making—or unmaking—of a champion.

For the jockeys, it was all business. They said as much themselves. Any anxiety they might feel about the importance of the Gold Cup, or the big payday involved, vanished once the race was on. They were caught in a rush of synapses that obliterated any individual details, except those that pertained to winning. They could have been at

Thurles, so little did the externals concern them. Their only injunction was to ride the best race they were capable of, according to plan. For Jim Culloty, who'd walked the course with Terry Biddlecombe, that meant clinging to the inside rail where the ground was slightly better—although that was dangerous because a horse can get pinned on the rail. For Paul Carberry, the assignment was to "sit and suffer," as Noel Meade put it. Harbour Pilot could be finicky and frustrated when asked for a jump or a run, so Paul's instructions were to let the horse dictate.

From the start, First Gold took the lead. He set a good pace, too, tracked by Harbour Pilot. Beef Or Salmon and Therealbandit were held up, while Sir Rembrandt, to my distress, was slow away. Best Mate stayed inside as intended, a few lengths back of the pacesetter. What a joy it was to see him jump! His sloppy performance in the Peterborough was a distant memory, eclipsed by his return to form. He jumped each fence in the same measured way, hitting it dead right, with the middle of his body poised over it. It was a classic display of prowess. Sleek and streamlined, he never wasted any energy, nor did Culloty have to whisper a single word to encourage him. Matey was a natural—a true "lepper," as the Irish say.

Truckers Tavern, Alexander Banquet, and Irish Hussar were the first to drop from contention. Therealbandit jumped like a novice—no surprise there—and never got into the race, another gamble lost. The speedy pace ate up Keen Leader, and when he blundered four fences from home, he was done for. First Gold also blew that fence, but he hung on to the lead, although his tail was dragging. Best Mate, on his heels, began to quicken. As the horses galloped toward the third-last, it looked as if Matey would break free again in his patented, headlong rush, but instead the unimaginable happened. Paul Carberry rose up on Harbour Pilot and boxed in Culloty and Best Mate behind the leg-weary First Gold, trapping them on the rail.

This was a smart, aggressive bit of riding. Carberry had called Culloty's bluff. If you think you deserve special treatment, he was saying, you've got another think coming. You cheeky bugger, Jimbo! Any jockey worth his salt would have done the same—and Culloty knew it—but Matey's public disapproved. They wanted to see history made and viewed the move as vaguely sinister, a mean trick only a blackguard Irishman would pull, so they cheered for Best Mate, except in our group, where the chant was, "C'mon, Paul!" Culloty had to act quickly. He checked his horse for a split second and swung wide to get around First Gold and Harbour Pilot for an unobstructed run. That was aggressive, too. It cost Best Mate a step or two, but I hardly noticed because Sir Rembrandt was storming up the hill.

Could Sir Rembrandt actually win? It was too far-fetched, wasn't it? I couldn't invest in the fantasy, afraid I'd jinx the horse. As First Gold's legs began to quit, Best Mate and Harbour Pilot jumped the second-last together, but Sir Rembrandt committed a minor error, and that, I figured, would be that. But no, Sir Rembrandt was all heart and picked up again, a force still to be reckoned with—the wild card in the deck. The script called for Best Mate to accelerate as usual now and assert his right to join the pantheon of Gold Cup immortals, but Carberry hadn't read it. For once, Matey was in a serious battle—a real bare-knuckles bout. Harbour Pilot wouldn't roll over, and Sir Rembrandt kept gaining ground, but Best Mate found some more, labored on, and beat my horse by a half-length.

The crowd went wild. Here was the happy ending they craved, a fulfillment of every expectation and desire. Henrietta Knight burst from the press tent to hug her teary-eyed husband, while the Irish gathered around Carberry to congratulate him on the superb ride. The debate over whether or not Best Mate was better than Arkle, or vice-versa, raged on in all the bars long into the night. I glanced at the teenage waiter, who stared disconsolately at his ticket, as though it forecast his future. His dream of riches was in tatters, and so was mine—by a measly half-length! Since Sir Rembrandt was a 33–1 shot, why hadn't I backed him each way? Another riddle for the ages, as unanswerable as those Moscow Flyer posed. Evidently, there were still gaps in my education that needed to be closed.

The Irish had no more winners at the Festival. Ted Walsh came close with Never Compromise in the Christie's Foxhunter Steeplechase, second to the ancient Earthmover, as did Charlie Swan in the Grand Annual with Ground Ball, who made St. Pirran work for the victory. No horses from Ireland ran in the Cathcart Challenge Cup, and the five entered in the Vincent O'Brien County Hurdle failed to place. Ruby Walsh, deputizing for the injured Robert Thornton, took the County Hurdle, the Festival's conclusion, on Sporazene and earned the top jockey award despite his abysmal start with three wins from fifteen rides.

I cashed one of my four bets—the one on St. Pirran—and shut my betting book. Sad to say, I never surmounted my losses and finished in the red, down about $250. It could have been much worse if I hadn't controlled my impulses (finally) and decided against going for broke on the County Hurdle. That lesson, at least, had sunk in. I felt strange after the last race, though, and I suspect others did, too, because our little utopian bubble had abruptly burst. It shouldn't have come as a shock that the Festival was over, and yet it did. Sheep still grazed on Cleve Hill, but the horses had gone away. Our real lives were out there waiting for us, dimly glimpsed but beckoning, and as the shock began to wear off, I was eager to reclaim my own.

THEN I WAS HURTLING through the night on a bus bound for Birmingham Airport, a Festival veteran who'd been at Cheltenham on the day Best Mate won his third straight Gold Cup. Already I was polishing up my version of the race to brighten the narrative effect. The story would stand me in good stead at O'Herlihy's when I was an aged yarn-spinner surrounded by callow youths hungry for such tales. They'd take me for an authentic and reliable source of historical information, and I'd try not to disappoint them, although I had a strong feeling I'd lie about my bet on Sir Rembrandt and say I played the horse each way. Would I admit to coming home a loser? That's an interesting question, I thought, tapping a box in my jacket pocket that held a gold bracelet. It depends on how you look at it.

Away

On a fine May morning in Dublin, just after Giacomo won the 2005 Kentucky Derby and I'd donated twenty bucks to Paddy Power on behalf of Afleet Alex, I walked out to the garden shed where I work. The first shoots of lettuce had sprouted in our vegetable patch, a welcome hint that summer, never a sure thing in Ireland, might actually arrive. No birds were at the feeder nearby. The sparrows who outnumber and outmaneuver the blue tits were gone for the moment, flying over the city on an errand known only to themselves. I remembered Gautier's white pigeons, those poor hirelings of the bookies. In a dreamy mood, I was subject to idle fancies in the way of Moscow Flyer.

So much had happened during the past year. Whenever I thought about Moscow, I recalled Jerome Kern's "Pick Yourself Up." It could have served as his theme song. He'd done a terrific job of starting over. Only two weeks after the disastrous Queen Mother, Moscow dusted himself off and won a big steeplechase at Aintree, then went to Punchestown in April and won another good race before being turned out for his holiday on the grass. When he came back to the track in October for the Fortria at Navan again, he looked splendid, and Jessie said she'd send him to Sandown next for a rematch with Azertyuiop in the Tingle Creek in December—his fourth race after three wins.

It was almost too much to bear. If Moscow had another accident,

I'd be forced to admit the world operates on principles that only Henrietta Knight understands. She'd been consumed with Best Mate since the Festival, because her horse was an industry now. He had his own line of clothing (for human beings), and the Courage Enclosure at Cheltenham had been named after him—better than a bar, even. His season would start at Exeter in November, in a race created especially for him. Jim Culloty had a broken thumb, so who'd be Matey's jockey? Knight pushed for Timmy Murphy, while Jim Lewis wanted Tony McCoy. Old feuds die hard, and Murphy got the nod.

If Best Mate really was a wonder horse, his third Gold Cup didn't prove it. According to the form book, he beat a weak field by historical standards. The comparisons to Arkle seemed ever more far-fetched. His outing at Exeter, deemed so important to the nation that the BBC broadcast it live on a weekday, did little to change that impression. Only three opponents took him on, including Sir Rembrandt (another losing bet for yours truly), but he barely squeaked by Martin Pipe's Seebald, who had just a four-pound advantage. The champ was vulnerable, and that was heartening news for Michael Hourigan, who still believed in Beef Or Salmon.

Reilly and I watched the Tingle Creek at O'Herlihy's, where I was finally accepted as a full-fledged regular and entitled to be cranky if I found someone sitting in my chosen spot—a table close to a gas fire I insisted I deserved, being a Californian not yet entirely accustomed to Irish winters. On the other hand, so many aspects of Irish life were old familiars to me now, and I liked that feeling of belonging, of being a link in the chain of community, liked coming home from the pub to see Imelda's sons turning into young men, even as I got older and ever-so-slightly wiser.

On a living room wall, we'd hung a new painting of Imelda's. Working from photos, she had pictured herself as a college girl in Amsterdam and me as a budding hippie circa 1969—long hair, cool shades, I was bound for San Francisco, man. The images flowed seamlessly together, as if that were destiny's desire as well as our own. O mystical lady! Often I stood before the painting and thought about the thousands of miles I'd traveled, blindly at times, to be where I was, and I'd bow to the great unknown that haunts us all. The falls I'd taken, the missteps and false starts—no wonder I identified with the jumpers.

I had backed Moscow Flyer in the Tingle Creek, and not for peanuts, so I was panicky before the race and had to order a medicinal Jameson to calm my nerves. Superstitions are mere phantoms and ought to be ignored—I knew that—but when Moscow put in a messy jump at the ninth fence, I almost keeled over. Was he as doomed as a character in a Greek tragedy? For a couple of seconds, I imitated Henrietta Knight and hid my eyes, but when I looked again, Moscow had recovered his stride and briskly disposed of Azertyuiop to reclaim his title as the best two-mile chaser around, at least for the time being. The Queen Mother and the challenge of Pipe's Well Chief lay ahead.

So the Pattern was put to rest, along with sundry demons. The world was an enlightened place where reason, not phantoms, ruled. It followed, then, that Best Mate would improve after the Exeter race and demonstrate his superiority in the Lexus (formerly Ericsson) Chase at Leopardstown, but Beef Or Salmon wasn't a gawky adolescent anymore. He had a new steadiness. With Timmy Murphy suspended, Paul Carberry snatched up the ride and never had it so good. While Matey puffed and labored, Beef Or Salmon was so keen to run that Carberry couldn't hold him up, so he relaxed and let the horse jump its way to an easy, seven-length victory.

Passing the finish, Carberry's high spirits got the best of him. He stood up in his stirrups, glanced back at Jim Culloty, and gestured with a cupped hand, as if to say, "C'mon, Jimmy boy, catch me if you can!" There were echoes of Cheltenham in the gesture, traces of the last time the two had locked horns, so this was sweet revenge. For his antics, Carberry got a mild slap on the wrist from the stewards, while Michael Hourigan flew off to Lanzarote to celebrate with his wife.

The ground at Leopardstown displeased Best Mate, Knight said later. But she also said a more telling thing: great horses win on any ground, so Matey might only be very good. Still, she swore the champ would be ready to defend his crown at the Festival, but here, too, she was stymied. Only a week before the big meeting, Best Mate burst a blood vessel and had to withdraw, leaving the door wide open for Beef Or Salmon—or so I thought. Sadly, though, the Beefster reverted to type at Cheltenham, half-awake and dragging his feet, and Carberry had to pull him up. He didn't even complete the race.

Kicking King was our new hero. Now seven, he'd been advancing his Gold Cup case for months. He won the Durkan at Punchestown and the King George VI, and Tom Taaffe had him primed for the Cotswolds when the horse fell ill in early March. Taaffe was sick at heart himself and nearly gave up on the trip, but Kicking King conquered the bug and miraculously regained his momentum. Stronger than ever, he took charge under Barry Geraghty at the fourth-last fence, and from three out there was no doubt he'd be the first Irish-trained winner in many years. That was soothing for Geraghty, because Moscow Flyer had failed in the Queen Mother, defeated by Well Chief.

All is flux, Heraclitus said. Now the horses were gorging on grass in lush pastures, but soon they'd be in training, and the cycle would begin once more. I wondered if I'd ever attend the Festival again, balancing the potential fun against the abominable expense, another toss-up. As I sat daydreaming, I saw a solitary blue tit land on the bird feeder, its little eyes flicking about, on the lookout for that bossy gang of sparrows as it pecked hastily at the seeds and gulped them down in a hurry. Then the sparrows descended with a noisy flurry of wings, back from their mysterious errand, and the blue tit disappeared. Where did it go? Into the slipstream of eternal questions, maybe, where people ask: Has anybody seen my hat? What's for dinner? Who'll win the Gold Cup?

Acknowledgments

I am most grateful to Tamso Doyle of *Horse Racing Ireland*, who provided the introductions, racing know-how, and general good cheer that made the writing of this book so much more pleasant than it might have been. The *Racing Post* was an indispensable tool, particularly the dispatches of Michael Clower and Tony O'Hehir, its chief Irish correspondents, as were the richly informative pages of *The Irish Field*. Of the writers listed in the bibliography, I am most indebted to Raymond Smith, a fine racing journalist, whose books were a helpful source on both John P. McManus and Vincent O'Brien. T. P. Reilly is a pseudonym, as is O'Herlihy's, an essential precaution to protect my table by the gas fire. Wherever necessary, I have translated euros and pounds sterling into dollars, but the figures should be taken as rough estimates only.

My heartfelt thanks, of course, to the trainers, jockeys, and bookies who gave so generously of their time, poured tea into me when I was cold, and answered my sometimes bone-headed questions with grace. Without their kind assistance, there'd be no book at all.

Bibliography

Bowen, Elizabeth. *The Shelbourne.* London: Vintage Classics, 2001.

Broderick, Jacqui. *The Shane Broderick Story.* Dublin: Merlin Publishing, 1999.

Fitzgeorge-Parker, Tim. *Vincent O'Brien: A Long Way from Tipperary.* London: Pelham Books, 1975.

Herbert, Ivor. *Arkle: The Classic Story of a Champion.* London: Aurum Press, 2003.

Holmes, Richard. *Sidetracks.* London: HarperCollins UK, 2000.

Kavanagh, Patrick. *The Green Fool.* London: Penguin Books, 1975.

Knight, Henrietta. *Best Mate: Chasing Gold.* Newbury: Highdown Books, 2004.

Lyons, Larry. *The Gay Future Affair.* Dublin: Mercier Publishers, 1983.

McCoy, A. P., with Steve Taylor. *The Autobiography.* London: Michael Joseph, 2002.

O'Flaherty, Liam. *A Tourist's Guide to Ireland.* Dublin: Wolfhound Press, 1998.

Oh Ogain, Daithi. *Myth, Legend, and Romance.* London: Ryan Publishing, 1991.

O'Neill, Peter, and Sean Boyce. *Paddy Mullins: The Master of Doninga.* Edinburgh: Mainstream Publishing, 1995.

Pipe, Martin, with Richard Pitman. *The Champion Trainer's Story.* London: Headline Books, 1992.

Reynolds, James. *A World of Horses.* New York: Creative Age Press, 1979.

Sheedy, Kieran. *The Horse in County Clare.* Dublin: Colour Books, 2001.

Smith, Brian. *The Horse in Ireland.* Dublin: Wolfhound Press, 1991.

Smith, Raymond. *High Rollers of the Turf.* Dublin: Sporting Books, 1992.

——. *The Master of Ballydoyle.* London: Virgin Books, 1990.

Wilde, Lady. *Ancient Legends, Mystic Charms, and Superstitions of Ireland.* London: Chatto & Windus, 1975.

A NOTE ABOUT THE TYPE

The text of this book was set in Centaur, the only typeface designed by Bruce Rogers (1870–1957), the well-known American book designer. A celebrated penman, Rogers based his design on the roman face cut by Nicolas Jenson in 1470 for his Eusebius. Jenson's roman surpassed all of its forerunners and even today, in modern recuttings, remains one of the most popular and attractive of all typefaces.

The italic used to accompany Centaur is Arrighi, designed by another American, Frederic Warde, and based on the chancery face used by Lodovico degli Arrighi in 1524.

Composed by North Market Street Graphics, Lancaster, Pennsylvania
Printed and bound by R. R. Donnelley & Sons, Harrisonburg, Virginia
Designed by Wesley Gott